GLOBAL DISASTER
MANAGEMENT

GLOBAL DISASTER MANAGEMENT

by

Arun Kumar

2008

SBS Publishers & Distributors Pvt. Ltd.
New Delhi

ISBN 10 : 81-89741-60-8
ISBN 13 : 978-81-89741-60-0

Indian Price -INR 895.00
Foreign Price -USD 45.00

First Published in India in 2008

Published by:
SBS PUBLISHERS & DISTRIBUTORS PVT. LTD.
2/9, Ground Floor, Ansari Road, Darya Ganj,
New Delhi - 110002, INDIA
Tel: 23289119, 41563911
Email: mail@sbspublishers.com
www.sbspublishers.com

Printed in India by SALASAR IMAGING SYSTEMS.

Preface

Disasters are events, which disrupt the lives of people and cause large-scale social or economic damage, such as floods, oil spills or major fires. Disaster management refers to the process of managing disasters, including the development of systems to mitigate against and prevent disasters; responding to disasters when they occur; providing relief to communities affected by disasters; and assisting in the rehabilitation of communities affected by disasters. Disaster management initiatives cover mainly the body of policy and administrative decisions and operational activities, which pertain to the various stages of a disaster at all levels. For instance, at a Governmental level, recently Japan has launched a satellite-based alert system to speed up evacuations if earthquakes, tsunamis or missiles hit the country. Authorities, who earlier relied on low-tech ways to spread alerts, will now be able to send instant warnings via sirens of imminent tsunamis, volcano eruptions or other disasters. The new system, known as J-Alert, will soon be expanded to warn residents of approaching missiles and earthquakes, which Japanese meteorologists can predict seconds before they occur. The J-Alert's trial launch took place, with some hiccups, in the western city of Kobe, which suffered a giant earthquake in 1995 that killed almost 6,500 people. In the drill, disaster authorities relayed news of a medium-size quake to Kobe's Ichikawacho area. On the second try, radio speakers installed in public places sounded a hypothetical alert to leave. Today, 4 cities and 10 of Japan's 47 prefectures will initially receive the satellite alert system, which will be expanded to 80 percent of the country by March 2009. Similarly, at an inter-governmental institutional level, an important part of the World Bank mission is providing assistance to prepare for and recover from natural or man-made disasters that can result in great human and economic losses. Indeed, developing countries suffer the greatest costs when a disaster hits - more than 95 percent of all deaths caused by disasters occur in developing countries; and losses due to natural disasters are 20 times greater (as a percentage of GDP) in developing countries than in industrialized countries. Poorly planned development can turn a recurring natural phenomenon into a human and economic disaster. Allowing dense populations on a floodplain or permitting poor or unenforced building codes in earthquake zones is as likely as a natural event to cause casualties and losses. Similarly, allowing the degradation of natural resources increases the risk of a disaster. In this connection, the World Bank's Hazard Risk Management team aims to reduce human suffering and economic losses caused by natural and technological disasters. They do this by helping the World Bank provide a more strategic and rapid response to disasters and promoting the integration of disaster prevention and mitigation efforts into the range of development activities. In consultation with different stakeholders, the World Bank Board has approved a new partnership, the Global Facility for Disaster Reduction and Recovery (GFDRR), based on three key guiding principles:

- The new United Nations International Strategy for Disaster Reduction (ISDR) system provides coherent and coordinated approach among all global stakeholders for disaster reduction and recovery.
- The ongoing ISDR processes, particularly joint work programs, strengthen global advocacy, knowledge sharing, and partnerships in disaster reduction.
- The focus of the Facility is on building capacities at the local and national levels to disaster proof the MDGs.

The Global Facility has three-track operations to achieve its development objectives at the global, regional and country levels. These include the key deliverables under each track, in order of increasing financial importance. Under Track 1, global and regional deliverables, it will support ISDR's global and regional processes to enable leveraging country resources for ex-ante investment in prevention, mitigation and preparedness activities, particularly in low and middle-income countries. The key deliverables are:

- ❑ Enhancing global and regional advocacy, partnerships and knowledge management facilitated through the ISDR secretariat for mainstreaming disaster risk reduction (DRR) in low and middle income countries at risk (e.g., strengthening ISDR platform and its outreach in different regions; regional and sub-regional initiatives in benchmarking of risks and resilience; regional/ sub-regional plan of action for DRR; regional/ sub-regional early warning strategies; global/regional/ sub-regional catastrophic risk financing initiatives; promoting/ strengthening partnerships in disaster risk reduction particularly with universities, scientific and technical institutions, private sector, research organizations and professional bodies etc; establishing a virtual clearinghouse for disaster risk reduction);
- ❑ Standardizing hazard risk management tools, methodologies and practices (e.g., reporting on national good practices in disaster reduction and recovery; developing country-driven and country-owned risk assessment methodologies, country-based damage and needs assessment techniques, environmentally sustainable disaster reduction and recovery practices; promoting and supporting global disaster reduction research forum to highlight ongoing national research in DRR and gaps;)

Under Track 2, country level deliverables, it will provide technical assistance to assist low and middle income countries to mainstream disaster risk reduction in strategic planning, particularly the Poverty Reduction Strategies (PRSs) and various sectoral development policies. The key deliverables are:

- ❑ Ex-ante risk management strategy and institutional development including early warning systems and emergency preparedness in low and middle income countries (e.g. National Strategies for Risk Reduction,

Institutional framework for risk management, including policy, legal, and organizational elements, national plans for multi-hazard early warning systems, national incident management system for emergency response, etc.)

- ❑ Supporting innovative projects to demonstrate cost-effective hazard mitigation to reduce risks associated with critical infrastructure (e.g., strengthening education and health infrastructure in hazard prone areas through community-based initiatives in hazard-prone areas, promoting use of traditional construction techniques for disaster-resilient housing etc.)
- ❑ Learning, research, and knowledge management for current and future risks (e.g., documenting lessons from national experiences in disaster recovery and dissemination; research in management of current and emerging risks; documenting traditional coping mechanism; scientific research in climate change management and adaptation; managing the risks due to sea level rise etc.)
- ❑ Developing frameworks to catalyze investment in hazard prevention, mitigation and preparedness.
- ❑ Ex-ante disaster recovery financing mechanism established in middle income countries (e.g., insurance and reinsurance, catastrophe bonds, weather derivatives, Contingent credit, reserve fund etc.

Under Track 3, accelerated disaster recovery in low income countries (in pipeline), popularly known as the standby recovery financing track, proposed to be operated through a mechanism linked to IDA, support will be given to disaster-stricken countries' immediate recovery needs before medium and long term recovery programs are formulated and launched. However a low-income country would be eligible for this only if pre-disaster preparedness and mitigation instruments (Track 2) have been institutionalized in the country, measured in terms of investments in risk reduction as a percentage of GDP or such other measures agreed by the partners of the Global Facility. This is being developed in close collaboration with World Bank's

IDA team and a position paper on this will be available soon for wider consultation.

The objective of this book entitled "Global Disaster Management: Initiatives & Programmes" is to provide readers / students with an integrated understanding of various kinds of initiatives and programmes required to tackle major disasters, hazards and crises and their control, mitigation / prevention and reduction with special reference to possible management solutions. This book will be devoted mainly to the practical management aspects of disaster mitigation, risk assessment, hazard minimization and vulnerability analysis. In addition to what is being done with respect to disaster management at the global and Indian levels in spatial context, this book will also attempt to cover the training dimensions of disaster management. The legal and policy initiatives, the action plans and strategies, the best-practices guidelines and code of conduct at various levels of disaster management has been also touched upon in detail as these are vital subject areas of disaster reduction and control. This book will also deal with the various elements of disaster management process; including the required disaster management plans for specific kinds of disasters. Focus will be on awareness, capacity building and training, so that enough manpower could be developed to tackle the situations, including psychological support in disaster response and managing human behavior. The role of NGOs, CBOs, international bodies, inter-governmental organizations, regional agencies and respective government institutions in the whole process has been discussed. This book is user friendly and comes with select acronym, glossary, bibliography and index.

Author

Contents

Glossary of Terms

Armed Conflict

A gontested incompatibility that concerns government and/or territory where the use of armed force between two parties, of which at least one is the government of a state, results in at least 25 battle related deaths.

Civil Society

A realm of political action lying between the household and the state but excluding for profit private sector organisations. Civil society organisations are commonly exemplified by non-governmental and community-based developmental organisations, but also include a wide range of other groups including sports clubs, interest groups, trade unions etc.

Complex Emergencies

Complex Emergencies are forms of human-made emergency in which the cause of the emergency as well as the assistance to the afflicted are bound by intense levels of political considerations. This sort of emergency is normally associated with the problems of displaced people during times of civil conflict or with people in need caught in areas of conflict.

Complex Emergency

The definition that the IASC officialised for use by its member organisations is "a humanitarian crisis in a country, region or society where there is total or considerable breakdown of authority resulting from internal or external conflict and which requires an international response that goes beyond the mandate or capacity of any single agency and/or the ongoing United Nations country programme." Such "complex emergencies" are typically characterised by:

- Extensive violence and loss of life; massive displacements of people; widespread damage to societies and economies.
- The need for large-scale, multi-faceted humanitarian assistance.
- The hindrance or prevention of humanitarian assistance by political and military constraints
- Significant security risks for humanitarian relief workers in some areas.

Coping Capacity

The manner in which people and organisations use existing resources to achieve various beneficial ends during unusual, abnormal and adverse conditions of a disaster phenomenon or process.

Disaster Management

A collective term encompassing all aspects of planning for and responding to disasters, including both pre- and post-disaster activities. It refers to the management of both the risks and consequences of disasters.

Disaster Management

It is the body of policy and administrative decisions and operational activities which pertain to the various stages of a disaster at all levels.

Disaster Risk Management

The systematic management of administrative decisions, organisation, operational skills and abilities to implement policies, strategies and coping capacities of the society or individuals to lessen the impacts of natural and related environmental and technological hazards.

Disaster Risk Reduction

The systematic development and application of policies, strategies and practices to minimise vulnerabilities, hazards and the unfolding of disaster impacts throughout a society, in the broad context of sustainable development.

Disaster

A disaster is a catastrophic occurrence, a sudden or major misfortune that disrupts the basic fabric and normal functioning of a whole society or a community within it. It is an event or series of events which gives rise to casualties, damage to or loss of property, infrastructure, essential services or means of livelihood on a scale which is beyond the normal capacity of the affected communities to cope with unaided.

Sudden-Onset or Sudden Natural Disasters: Sudden calamities triggered by natural phenomena such as earthquakes, floods, tropical storms, and volcanic eruptions. They strike with little or no warning and have an immediate adverse impact on human populations, activities, or economic systems.

Slow-Onset or Creeping Disasters: Situations in which the ability of people to acquire food and other necessities of life slowly declines to a point where survival is ultimately jeopardised. Such situations are typically brought on or precipitated by drought, crop failure' pest diseases, or other forms of "ecological" disaster or neglect

Early Warning

Early Warning is the process of monitoring situations in communities or areas known to be vulnerable to slow onset hazards. For example, famine early warning may be reflected in such indicators as drought, livestock sales, or changes in economic conditions. The purpose of early warning is to enable remedial measures to be initiated and to provide more timely and effective relief including through disaster preparedness actions.

The emergency phase is the period during which extraordinary measures have to be taken. Special emergency procedures and authorities may be applied to support human needs, sustain livelihoods, and protect property to avoid the onset of disaster. This phase can encompass pre-disaster, disaster alert, disaster relief and recovery periods. An emergency phase may be quite extensive, as in a slow onset disaster such as a famine. It can also be relatively short-lived, as after an earthquake.

Emergency

An extraordinary situation in which people are temporarily unable to meet their basic survival needs, or there are serious and immediate threats to human life and well-being or when a disaster threatens and emergency measures must be taken to prevent or at least limit the effects of the eventual impact.

Empowerment

A process in which individuals learn by their own actions to become fully engaged in shaping their development potential. The process is necessarily self-led, but benefits from facilitation by supporting actors.

Governance

Governance is the exercise of economic, political and administrative authority to manage a country's affairs at all levels. It comprises the mechanisms, processes and institutions, through which citizens and groups articulate their interests, exercise their legal rights, meet their obligations and mediate their differences.

Human Vulnerability

A human condition or process resulting from physical, social, economic and environmental factors, which determine the likelihood and scale of damage from the impact of a given hazard.

Human-made Disasters

These are disasters or emergency situations where the principal, direct cause(s) are identifiable human actions, deliberate or otherwise. Apart from "technological" and "ecological" disasters, this mainly involves situations in which civilian populations suffer casualties, losses of property, basic services and means of livelihood as a result of war or civil strife, for example. Human-made disasters/emergencies can be of the rapid or slow onset types, and in the case of internal conflict, can lead to "complex emergencies" as well.

An even broader definition of human-made disaster acknowledges that all disasters are caused by humans because they have chosen, for whatever reason, to be where natural phenomena occurs that result in adverse impacts on people.

Risk is the expected losses (lives lost, persons injured, damage to property and disruption of economic activity) due to a particular hazard. Risk is the product of hazard and vulnerability.

Income Poverty

A status whereby a lack of financial resources limits the ability of an individual or household to meet basic needs. What is included in basic needs is culturally determined so that different levels of financial status may be described as conveying relative forms of income poverty.

Livelihood

The means by which an individual or household obtains assets for survival and self development. Livelihood assets are the tools (skills, objects, rights, knowledge, and social capital) applied to enacting the livelihood.

Mitigation

Migration is the collective term used to encompass all actions taken prior to the occurrence of a disaster (pre-disaster measures) including preparedness and long-term risk reduction measures. (Mitigation has been used by some institutions or authors in a narrower sense, excluding preparedness.)

Natural Disaster, Rapid Onset

A disaster that is triggered by an instantaneous shock. The

impact of this disaster may unfold over the medium or long-term. An earthquake is a prime example.

Natural Disaster, Slow Onset

A disaster event that unfolds alongside and within development processes. The hazard can be felt as an ongoing stress for many days, months or even years. Drought is a prime example.

Natural Disaster

A serious disruption triggered by a natural hazard causing human, material, economic or environmental losses, which exceed the ability of those affected to cope.

Natural Hazards

Natural processes or phenomena occurring in the biosphere that may constitute a damaging event.

Physical Exposure

Elements at risk, an inventory of those people or artifacts that are exposed to a hazard.

Population Displacements

These are usually associated with crisis-induced mass migration in which large numbers of people are forced to leave their homes to seek alternative means of survival. Such mass movements normally result from the effects of conflict, severe food shortages or collapse of economic support systems.

Preparedness

Preparedness consists of activities designed to minimize loss of life and damage, organize the temporary removal of people and property from a threatened location, and facilitate timely and effective rescue, relief and rehabilitation.

Rapid Onset disasters

The definitions below correspond to the time sequence following the occurrence of a rapid onset disaster.

Reconstruction

It is the actions taken to reestablish a community after a period of rehabilitation subsequent to a disaster. Actions would include construction of permanent housing, full restoration of all services, and complete resumption of the pre-disaster state.

Rehabilitation

It is the operations and decisions taken after a disaster with a view to restoring a stricken community to its former living conditions, while encouraging and facilitating the necessary adjustments to the changes caused by the disaster.

Resilience

The capacity of a system, community or society to resist or to change in order that it may obtain an acceptable level in functioning and structure. This is determined by the degree to which the social system is capable of organising itself, and the ability to increase its capacity for learning and adaptation, including the capacity to recover from a disaster.

Risk

The probability of harmful consequences, or expected loss of lives, people injured, property, livelihoods, economic activity disrupted (or environment damaged) resulting from interactions between natural or human induced hazards and vulnerable conditions. Risk is conventionally expressed by the equation: Risk = Hazard × Vulnerability

Slow Onset Disasters

The sequence of a disaster continuum for slow onset disasters is similar in framework but has important distinctions.

Social Capital

A shorthand term used to describe a combination of social norms (such as trust), relationships (such as reciprocity) and ties (such as hierarchical clientalism or horizontal group bonds) held by an individual or predominant within a social arena.

Sustainable Development

Development that meets the needs of the present without compromising the ability of future generations to meet their own needs. It contains within it two key concepts: the concept of 'needs', in particular the essential needs of the world's poor, to which overriding priority should be given; and the idea of limitations imposed by the state of technology and social organisation on the environment's ability to meet present and future needs.

Technological Disasters

Situations in which large numbers of people, property, infrastructure or economic activity are directly and adversely affected by major industrial accidents, severe pollution incidents, nuclear accidents, air crashes, major, fires or explosions.

The Relief Phase

It is the period immediately following the occurrence of a sudden disaster (or the late discovery of a neglected/ deteriorated slow-onset situation) when exceptional measures have to be taken to search and find the survivors as well as meet their basic needs for shelter, water, food and medical care.

Vulnerability

Vulnerability is the degree of loss (for example, from 0 to 100 percent) resulting from a potentially damaging phenomenon.

Acronyms/Abbreviations

ADB: Asian Development Bank
ADPC: Asian Disaster Preparedness Center
ADPC: Asian Disaster Preparedness Centre, Bangkok
ADRC: Asian Disaster Reduction Center
AFDB: African Development Bank
AGREMP: Percentage of labour force in agricultural sector
ALIT: Augmented Intervention Team
AOML: Atlantic Oceanographic and Meteorological Laboratory
APDMC: Asia Pacific Disaster Management Center
AUDMP: Asian Urban Disaster Mitigation Programme
BCC: Baroda Citizens Council
BCPR: Bureau for Crisis Prevention and Recovery
BCPR: Bureau for Crisis Prevention and Recovery (UNDP)
CAP: Consolidated Appeals Process
CCA: Common Country Assessment
CCEP: Canadian Centre for Emergency Preparedness
CDB: Caribbean Development Bank
CDC: Centers for Disease Control and Prevention
CDC: Centre for Disease Control and Prevention
CDERA: Caribbean Disaster Emergency Response Agency
CDIAC: Carbon Dioxide Information Analysis Center

CDMC: Cranfield Disaster Management Centre
CDMP: Caribbean Disaster Mitigation Project
CDMS: Comprehensive Disaster Management Strategy
CEPREDENAC: Coordination Center for the Prevention of Natural Disasters in Central America
CERF: Central Emergency Revolving Fund
CGIAR: Consultative Group on International Agricultural Research
CHAP: Common Humanitarian Action Plan
CICITE: China International Centre for Economic and Technical Exchanges
CIESIN: Center for International Earth Science Information Network
CMA: Cape Town Metropolitan Area
CMAP: CPC Merged Analysis of Precipitation
CNSS: Council of the National Seismic System
COE-DMHA: Centre of Excellence in Disaster Management and Humanitarian Assistance
COPECO: National Commission for Contingencies
CPC: Climate Prediction Center
CPI: Corruption Perceptions Index
CRC: Convention of the Rights of the Child
CRED: Centre for Research on the Epidemiology of Disasters
DAC: Development Assistance Committee
DFID: Department for International Development of the United Kingdom
DiMP: Disaster Mitigation for Sustainable Livelihoods Programme of the University of Cape Town
DMC: The Disaster Management Center, University of Wisconsin/Madison
DMFC: Disaster Mitigation Facility for the Caribbean
DMSIA: Disaster Management Institute of South Africa

DMTP: United Nations Disaster Management Training Programme
DPA: Department of Political Affairs
DPC: Direction de la Protection Civil.
DPKO: Department of Peace-keeping Operations
DRB: (OCHA) Disaster Response Branch
DRC: Disaster Research Centre
DRI: Disaster Risk Index
DROC: Disaster Response and operations Co-ordination Division
DRRC: Disaster Reduction and Recovery Cluster
ECHA: Executive Committee on Humanitarian Affairs
ECHO: European Community Humanitarian Office
ECHO: European Community Humanitarian Office
ECLAC: Economic Commission for Latin America and the Caribbean
EEC: European Economic Community
EMA: Emergency Management Australia
EM-DAT EM-DAT: The OFDA/CRED International Disaster Database
EMOPS UNICEF's: Office of Emergency Programmes
EMPRES: Emergency Prevention System for Trans-boundary animal and Plant Pests and Diseases
ENRA: Environmental Emergency Notification/ Request for International Assistance
ENSO: El Niño/Southern Oscillation
EPC: Emergency Post Conflict Division
EPF: Emergency Programme Fund
EPIX: Emergency Preparedness Information Exchange
ERC: Emergency Relief Co-ordinator
FAO: Food and Agriculture Organisation
FAO: Food and Agriculture Organisation of the United Nations

FAO: Food and Agriculture Organization
FCSU (OCHA): Field Co-ordination Support Unit
FEMA: Federal Emergency Management Agency
GDP: Gross Domestic Product
GDPAGR: Percentage of agriculture's dependency for GDP
GDPCAP: Gross Domestic Product per capita
GEO: Global Environment Outlook
GEOHAZ.ORG: Geohazards International
GIEWS (FAO): Global Information and Early Warning System
GIS: Geographical Information System
GLASOD: Human Induced Soil Degradation
GLIDE: Global Identifier Number
GRAVITY: Global Risk and Vulnerability Index Trend per Year
GRID: Global Resource Information Database
GTZ: German Technical Co-operation
HDI: Human Development Index
HDR: Human Development Report
HEB: High Energy Biscuits
HIPC: Heavily Indebted Poor Countries
HN: Hazard Net
HPI: Human Poverty Index
IAEA: International Atomic Energy Agency
IASC: Inter Agency Standing Committee
ICRC: International Committee of the Red
ICRC: International Committee of the Red Cross
ICVA: International Council of Voluntary Agencies
IDB: Inter-American Development Bank
IDNDR: International Decade for Natural Disaster Reduction
IDNDR: International Decade for Natural Disaster Reduction
IDP: Internally Displaced Persons
IFI: International financial institution

IFPRI: International Food Policy Research Institute

IFRC: International Federation of Red Cross and Red Crescent Societies

IFRC: International Federation of Red Cross and Red Crescent Societies

IFRC: International Federation of the Red Cross and Red Crescent Societies

IGAD: Intergovernmental Authority on Development

ILO: International Labour Organization

IMF: International Monetary Fund

IOM: International Organisation for Migration

IOM: International Organisation for Migration

IRA: Immediate Response Accounts

IRI: International Research Institute for Climate Prediction

ISDR: International Strategy for Disaster Reduction

ISDR: International Strategy for Disaster Reduction

ISDR: International Strategy for Disaster Reduction

ITU: International Telecommunication Union

IUCN: World Conservation Union

LA RED: Network for Social Studies on Disaster Prevention in Latin America

LCAs: Logistics Capacity Assessments

LDC: Least Developed Country

MANDISA: Monitoring, Mapping and Analysis of Disaster Incidents in South Africa

MDGs: Millennium Development Goals

MOFTEC: Ministry of Foreign Trade and Economic Co-operation

MSF: Médecins sans Frontières

NCEP: National Center for Environmental Prediction

NCGIA: National Center for Geographic Information and Analysis
NGO: Non-Governmental Organisation
NGO: Non-Governmental Organization
NOAA: National Oceanic and Atmospheric Administration
OAS: Organization of American States
OCHA: Office for the Coordination of Humanitarian Affairs
OCHA: Office for the Co-ordination of Humanitarian Affairs
ODS: Official Development Assistance
OECD: Organisation for Economic Co-operation and Development
OECS: Organization of Eastern Caribbean States
OFDA: U S Office of Foreign Disaster Assistance

OHA: Office of the Humanitarian Adviser
OSOCC: On Site Operations Co-ordination Centre
PADF: Pan American Development Foundation
PAHO: Pan American Health Organisation
PAHO: Pan American Health Organization
PEMC: Pacific Emergency Management Centre
PhExp: Physical Exposure (if not specified, for drought)
PPP: Purchasing Power Parity
PRSP: Poverty Reduction Strategy Paper
SADC: The Southern African Development Community
SAR: Search and Rescue
SDRU: The Swiss Disaster Relief Unit
SIDS: Small Island Developing States
SNPMAD: System National para la Prevention, Mitigación y Atención de Desastres
SOPAC: South Pacific Applied Geoscience Commission
SRSG: Special Representative of the Secretary-General

U5MORT: Under five years old mortality rate
UNAIDS: Joint United Nations Programme on HIV/AIDS
UNCRD: United Nations Centre for Regional Development
UNCTAD: United Nations Conference on Trade and Development
UNCTAD: United Nations Conference on Trade and Development
UNDAC (OCHA): United Nations Assessment and Co-ordination
UNDAF: United Nations Development Assessment Framework
UNDG: United Nations Development Group
UNDMT: United Nations Disaster Management Team
UNDP: United Nations Development Programme
UNDP: United Nations Development Programme
UNDP: United Nations Development Programme
UNEP/GRID: United Nations Environment Programme, Global Resource Information Database
UNESCO: United Nations Educational, Scientific and Cultural Organisation
UNESCO: United Nations Educational, Scientific and Cultural Organization
UNFCCC: United Nations Framework Convention on Climate Change
UNFPA: United Nations Population Fund
UNHABITAT: United Nations Human Settlements Programme
UNHCHR: United Nations High Commissioner for Human Rights
UNHCR: Office of the United Nations High Commissioner for Refugees
UNHCR: UN High Commissioner for Refugees
UNICEF: United Nations Children's Fund
UNOPS: United Nations Office for Project Services
UNRW: A United Nations Relief and Work Agency

UNSECOORD: Office of the United Nations Security Co-ordinator
UNV: UN Volunteers
UNV: United Nations Volunteers
USAID/OFDA: United States Agency for International Development, Office of U.S. Foreign Disaster Assistance
USG: Under-Secretary-General
USGS: United States Geological Survey
VAM: Vulnerability and Analysis and Mapping Project
WATRUR: Percentage of population having access to improved water supply in rural area
WATTOT: Percentage of population having access to improved water supply
WATURB: Percentage of population having access to improved water supply in urban area
WB: World Bank
WFP: World Food Programme
WFP: World Food Programme
WFP: World Food Programme
WFP: World Food Programme
WHA: World Health Assembly
WHO: World Health Organisation
WHO: World Health Organisation
WMO: World Meteorological Organisation
WMO: World Meteorological Organization
WRI: World Resources Institute
WTO: World Trade Organization
ZENEB: Zentrum für Naturrisiken und Entwicklung (Center for Nature Risks and Development)

1

UN Disaster Management Team and Training Programme

An Introductory Overview

THE DISASTER MANAGEMENT TEAM

Before we go further into describing the nature of disasters, we will introduce part of your role in the management of them. One of the primary purposes of this overall training programme is to introduce the concept of managing disasters as a team. The objectives of disaster management through teamwork include:

- A forum for communication, information exchange and developing consensus
- A format for coordination, eliminating duplication and reducing gaps in services
- The possibility of being more effective through pooled resources

The UN Disaster Management Team

The United Nations General Assembly believes that the objectives of team management are applicable to the UN agencies oriented to emergencies. They have mandated that a standing UN Disaster Management Team (UN-DMT) be formed in each disaster-prone country, convened and chaired by the UN resident coordinator. The composition of the UN-DMT is determined by taking into account the types of disaster to which the country is prone and the organizations present, but should normally include a core group consisting of the country-level representatives of FAO, UNDP/UNDRO, UNICEF, WFP, WHO and, where present, UNHCR. It may be enlarged to include additional representatives or project personnel from other relevant agencies when an emergency arises.

The original and primary purpose of the UN-DMT is to ensure a prompt, effective and concerted response by the UN system at country level in the event of a disaster. The team should also ensure similar coordination of UN assistance to the Government in respect to post-disaster rehabilitation and reconstruction, and relevant disaster mitigation measures through long-term development programmes. It should be emphasized that for all aspects of disaster management the UN-DMT is in a support role of the government. The UN-DMT recognizes and in no way supersedes the mandates and specific functions of the various organizations in the exercise of those mandates. It supports and assists the office of the resident coordinator in the exercise of its system-wide functions. In line with General Assembly resolution 46/182, the latter will maintain close contact with, and receive leadership from the Emergency Relief Coordinator.

Country Disaster Management Team

Most disaster prone countries already have a formal or informal disaster management team. It is typically headed by a national disaster focal point body. This body functions in liaison with the Office of the President or Prime Minister, with civil defense organizations, key government ministries, the Red Cross/Red Crescent, and other NGOs and major donors. The UN-DMT needs to interface with this team and, where practical, to be a team member. Where national officials do not participate in UN-DMT meetings or activities, the resident coordinator should ensure that they are consulted and briefed on all relevant matters. In practice it is vital that the policies of the DMT relate to those approved by the Government even under the pressure of event.

Tasks, Roles and Resources of the UN

This part of the chapter is condensed from Chapter 1 of the UNDP/UNDRO Disaster Management Manual. It describes the role of the UN system and its agencies in disaster management.

Organizational Tasks and General Roles

Primary responsibility for all aspects of disaster management rests with the Government of the affected country. This includes: planning and implementing long-term risk reduction and preparedness measures; requesting and administering disaster relief and rehabilitation operations, requesting international assistance if required; and coordinating all disaster-related assistance programmes, both nationally and internationally-funded.

Each UN organization or agency is responsible for providing advice and assistance to the Government of a disaster-prone or disaster-affected country, in accordance with its mandate and the resources available to it. In so doing, each agency is accountable to its own governing body, but it is also called upon to act as a member of a united team. In the case of refugee emergencies, UNHCR remains responsible for their protection and the coordination of international assistance for the refugees.

In relation to disaster relief and other post-disaster assistance, each organization and agency of the UN system is called on to:

- Mobilize and provide timely technical assistance and material support to disaster-affected countries, according to its own mandate and the resources available to it.
- Co-operate with the UN resident coordinator, UNDRO, or any other coordination mechanism established by the Secretary-General to ensure—appropriate, coordinated UN system assistance in the context of a concerted plan and programme.

Roles and Resources of UNDP, UNDRO, and other UN Agencies

The Role of UNDP

UNDP focuses primarily on the development-related aspects of disaster risks and occurrences, and on providing technical assistance to institution building in relation to all aspects of disaster management. Its emphasis is therefore on:

(a) Incorporating long-term risk reduction and preparedness measures in normal development planning and programmes, including support for specific mitigation measures where required.
(b) Assisting in the planning and implementation of post-disaster rehabilitation and reconstruction, including the definition of new development strategies that incorporate risk reduction measures relevant to the affected area.
(c) Reviewing the impact of large settlements of refugees or displaced persons on development and seeking ways to incorporate the refugees and displaced persons in development strategies.
(d) Providing technical assistance to the authorities managing major emergency assistance operations of extended duration (especially in relation to displaced persons and the possibilities for achieving durable solutions in such cases).

In addition, UNDP provides administrative and operational support to the resident coordinator function, particularly at country level, but also at headquarters.

In the event of a disaster, UNDP may grant a maximum of $50,000 from SPR funds to provide immediate relief. UNDP is not otherwise involved in the provision of "relief using any of its own resources or other funds administered by the Programme.

Where a major emergency substantially affects the whole

development process within a country, IFF resources may be used to provide technical assistance to plan and manage the operation, with the agreement of the Government.

Technical and material assistance in support of long-term risk reduction and preparedness measures is included in the country programme, and may be funded from IFF resources or from other UNDP-administered funds. The same can also be used to assist rehabilitation and reconstruction. Special additional grants (up to $1.1 million) may be made from SPR funds for technical assistance to such post-disaster recovery efforts following natural disasters.

The particular responsibilities of the UNDP resident representative are summarized in the following panel.

Disaster Management Responsibilities of the UNDP Resident Representative

The resident representative is responsible for:

(a) Ensuring that all concerned in planning development programmes are aware of any known or potential hazards and their likely effects, and that these are appropriately taken into account in the country programme.

(b) Designating a "disaster focal point", and ensuring that the field office is adequately prepared to respond to an emergency.

(c) In the event of a disaster:
- Mobilizing UNDP staff and technical assistance personnel and other resources that meet the needs of the situation, particularly those needed for the initial assessment and immediate response.
- Ensuring that UNDP assistance is used to good effect, and the capacity of the office is strengthened if necessary to ensure effective response.

In all disaster-prone country field offices, a senior national officer is designated a "disaster focal point" for all disaster-related matters including mitigation, response and international UN/UNDP preparedness. Section3A and appendix 3 A of the UNDP/UNDRO Disaster Manual provide detail on the duties and qualifications of the disaster focal point.

In a major or complex emergency of extended duration (typically involving displaced populations), UNDP may temporarily assign an additional deputy resident representative. That deputy may either manage normal UNDP business while the resident representative concentrates on the resident coordinator functions, or may take day-today responsibility for matters relating to the emergency which are within the UNDP mandate. In the countries with the most severe or prolonged emergencies UNDP has established UN Emergency Units. These units are able to focus exclusively on addressing the emergency and are often staffed by person seconded from sister UN agencies that are operational in the country.

In the event of a sudden influx of refugees into a country in which there is no UNHCR representation, the resident representative immediately notifies UNHCR and initiates the assessment process on behalf of the UNHCR.

The Role of UNDRO

UNDRO is the focal point for disaster management in the UN system (except in those countries where a UN Emergency Unit is established). In relief it provides a framework for coordination of assistance by the UN agencies and helps to coordinate such assistance with that from other sources. In addition, UNDRO has an important role in mobilizing external assistance and serving as a clearing house for information concerning disasters. In the area of mitigation, UNDRO promotes long-term measures to reduce disaster-related risks and enhance preparedness in disaster-prone countries. UNDRO is represented at country level on a permanent basis by the resident coordinator/representative.

Coordination at headquarters level is often effected by

contacts between the Head of Agencies concerned at the beginning of a relief operation, and through frequent ongoing contacts between the relevant focal points. At the country level, coordination is undertaken by the resident coordinator who is also the UNDRO representative. Whenever possible and required, UNDRO supports the resident coordinator by dispatching an UNDRO delegate or emergency assistance team.

UNDRO concentrates on problems related to natural hazards and sudden disasters, but as its mandate covers all kinds of emergencies UNDRO may also offer its services and advice in situations including droughts, and cases of war and civil conflicts, unless and until the Secretary-General makes other arrangements.

Following a disaster, UNDRO, acting on behalf of the Secretary-General, offers its services to the Government of the disaster-stricken state in assessing the need for external relief assistance, and communicating that information to prospective donors and others concerned. (Contacts with The Government are conducted through the resident coordinator /representative and the country's mission in Geneva or New York.) Where international assistance is required or requested, UNDRO:

- Helps to identify priority needs on the basis of information from the Government, the resident coordinator/representative, UN-DMT, and other competent bodies.
- Issues international appeals and acts as a clearing house for information on needs and contributions, the assistance extended or planned by all donors, and the progress of relief operations.
- Seeks to mobilize resources and coordinate relief assistance by various UN organizations and agencies, bilateral donors, and inter-and non-govern mental organizations and administers funds channeled through it.

Depending on the particular situation after consultations,

wherever possible, with the Government or the resident coordinator/ representative, UNDRO may:

- Assign one or more delegates on mission to assist the national authorities in organizing the assessment and administering relief operations, and assist the resident coordinator/representative in information management, the local coordination of international relief assistance, and in his reporting responsibilities to UNDRO.
- Provide logistic support to ensure the timely arrival of relief supplies and their prompt delivery to the affected population. This may include organizing shared or joint relief flights.

The Coordinator may approve a grant of up to US$50,000 per disaster from funds available to UNDRO, subject to certain conditions. In some situations, UNDRO can release supplies from the emergency stockpile it administers in Pisa, Italy.

UNDP/UNDRO Collaboration

UNDP and UNDRO complement each other. UNDP has a wealth of experience in development planning and administration, and well-established field offices. UNDRO has specific knowledge and experience in disaster management, and established contacts with relevant specialist bodies. The fact that the UNDP resident representative also represents UNDRO helps to ensure fruitful cooperation between the organizations.

At the country level UNDP field offices generally administer funds and resources channeled through UNDRO, following normal inter-agency procedures. This includes the local procurement of supplies and services, and the recruitment and appointment of temporary staff.

Disaster-related Roles of the Core Members of the UN-DMTs

FAO Provides technical advice in reducing vulnerability and helps in the rehabilitation of agriculture, livestock, and fisheries, with emphasis on local food production. Monitors food production, exports and imports, and forecasts any requirements of exceptional food assistance.

UNDP Promotes the incorporation of disaster mitigation in development planning, and funds technical assistance for all aspects of disaster management. Provides administrative support to the resident coordinator and UN-DMT.

UNDRO Mobilizes and coordinates international emergency relief assistance, issuing consolidated appeals. Assists in assessments and relief management if required. Provides advice and guidance on risk assessments and in planning and implementing mitigation measures.

UNHCR Assures the protection of refugees and seeks durable solutions to their problems. Helps to mobilize and assure the delivery of necessary assistance in the country of asylum if it is a developing country.

UNICEF Attends to the well-being of children and women, especially child health and nutrition. Assistance activities may include: social programmes; child feeding (in collaboration with WFP); water supplies, sanitation and direct health interventions (in collaboration with WHO). Provides related management and logistical support.

WFP Provides "targeted" food aid for humanitarian relief, and to support rehabilitation, reconstruction, and risk-reducing development programmes. Mobilizes and coordinates the delivery of complementary emergency and "programme" food aid from bilateral and other sources.

WHO Provides advice and assistance in all aspects

of preventive and curative health care, including the preparedness of health services for rapid response to disaster.

Role of other UN Organizations and Agencies

A number of other UN organizations and agencies have specific responsibilities, organizational arrangements, and capabilities relating to disaster mitigation, and/or relief or recovery assistance. UNDP, UNDRO, and resident coordinators must respect the mandates and skills of these agencies, and seek to ensure that all work together in harmony. All should use their expertise and resources to best effect in helping people in disaster-prone and disaster-affected areas.

UN System Resources Available to Initiate Responses to Disasters and Emergency Needs

FAO	Up to $20,000 at discretion of FAOR within the context of an ongoing emergency or long-term aid project.
UNDP	Up to $50,000 per occurrence for immediate relief; approved by the Director DOF following a request from the resident representative. Up to $1.1 million for technical assistance for rehabilitation and reconstruction; approved by the Administrator or Governing Council. IPF funds for technical assistance to emergency management Is major operations agreed with Government; approved by Director PCO.
UNDRO	Up to $50,000 per disaster, subject to the availability of resources; approved by the UNDRO coordinator following a request by the Government and proposal by the resident representative or other UN organization or agency.
UNHCR	Allocations from a global emergency reserve

	for assistance to refugees, approved by the High Commissioner.
UNICEF	Up to $25,000 diversion of existing programme funds or In-country supplies at discretion of the country representative In agreement with Government. Larger amounts from global emergency reserve ($4 million per year); approved by Executive Director following a specific proposal by the country representative. Possibility of diverting some existing country programme funds In case of a major national catastrophe.
WFP	Possibility of borrowing food aid commodities from ongoing WFP-assisted development projects, governmental or other donor' stocks, subject to headquarters approval to assure replacement. Up to $50,000 for local purchases of commodities at the discretion of the Director of Operations where there are no other means of arranging timely deliveries. Allocations primarily from the International Emergency Food Reserve (IEFR), managed by WFP, and from WFP general resources ($45 million annually).
WHO	Global reserve from which allocations can be made for priority medical needs in anticipation of special donor contributions; approved by the Director ERO.

Coordination: the Resident Co-ordinator and the UN-DMT

The national Government is ultimately responsible for requesting and coordinating all international assistance. It also approves all programmes and emergency work in the country. However, the UN system stands ready to assist upon request. At the country level, the resident coordinator/representative and the UN disaster Management Team (UN-DMT) are the essential UN coordinating institutions. Their responsibilities apply to all situations which require significant interventions from more than one UN organization or agency. At the international level, UNDRO promotes the coordination of responses to particular disaster situations, both within the UN system and in the wider international community, essentially through information-sharing.

Coordination

Coordination as used in the manual means:

- The intelligent sharing of information and the frank, constructive discussion of issues and possible courses of action.
- Achieving consensus on objectives and an overall strategy.
- The voluntary adoption by those concerned of specific responsibilities and tasks in the context of the agreed objectives and strategy. Coordination is based on mutual respect for the competencies and agreed responsibilities of each party, and willingness to co-operate in addressing and solving problems in pursuit of a common aim.

Role of the UN Resident Coordinator

The resident coordinator, also representing UNDRO, is both the UN system's team leader at country level, and chairman of the UN-DMT. Following the occurrence of a major disaster, the resident coordinator/representative must be ready to give absolute priority to this coordination role, which also includes helping to ensure the coordination of all international emergency assistance.

The resident coordinator should fulfill the general responsibilities indicated in the panel on the next page.

Coordination Arrangements for Emergencies

The Secretary-General of the United Nations has appointed

an Emergency Relief Coordinator at the level of the Under Secretary-General, who has been entrusted with the responsibility for the coordination of emergency assistance as outlined in General Assembly Resolution 46/182 of 19 December,1991. The Emergency Relief Coordinator is in charge of the Central Emergency Revolving Fund, which has been established as a cashflow mechanism of US$ 50 million to ensure the rapid and coordinated response of the organizations of the system. He has direct access to the Secretary General in New York and maintains contacts with, and provides leadership to, the field Resident Coordinators.

Disaster Management Responsibilities of the Resident

On an ongoing basis, the resident coordinator must:

- Ensure that the UN organizations and agencies active In a disaster-prone country are collectively 'prepared" to offer appropriate technical and material assistance as part of an overall International response In the event of a disaster.
- Ensure that the same agencies take account of disaster risks in their long-term development programmes, and provide concerted assistance In relation to disaster mitigation. In consultation with any national IDNDR committee.

In the Event of a "Multi-Sectoral" Disaster:

- Bring the various agendas of the UN system together and ensure the provision of prompt, effective, and concerted multi-disciplinary advice and assistance.
- Maintain contact with the government authority responsible for conducting relief operations. Ensure concerted UN assistance to that authority in assessing the situation and the requirements for International assistance.
- Keep UNDRO Informed of the situation and needs for

International assistance. Provide a clear statement of priority needs for International assistance rapidly to UNDRO for distribution internationally, and provide similar Information to the local representatives of the International community. Update the Information continuously to keep it current.

- Recommend that the UN team be reinforced by the appropriate agencies at the country level when necessary.
- Help to secure co-operation and coordination between all International assistance bodies, the government, and other national organizations to ensure proper management of International assistance.

In Case of a Refugee Influx or "mono-sectoral" Disaster

- Consult with the local representative of the competent UN organization or agency (UNHCR or other) to determine what the resident coordinator and UN-DMT should do to support that agency.

THE UN DISASTER MANAGEMENT TEAM (UNDMT)

Learning Objectives

After completing this part of the module, you will be able to:

- Describe how the UNDMT is structured and functions
- Identify the concept and purpose of the UNDMT

Beginning in 1989, all UNDP offices in disaster and emergency prone countries were requested to set up UN Disaster Management Teams (UNDMTs). The composition and leadership structures of these teams have evolved since that time. UNDMTs have often been formed only after a disaster has struck, while others have become active in the preparedness stage. In the first part of this chapter we present the current recommendations for structuring a UNDMT and the primary activities for the Team in all phases of disaster/emergency management.

Structure

In consultation with the host Government and the UN country Team, the UN Resident Coordinator is expected to form a UN **Disaster Management Team (UNDMT),** which will prepare a disaster management plan. The UN Resident Coordinator acts also as the focal point for disaster reduction and mitigation, as well as ensures the effective dovetailing of relief assistance into rehabilitation and reconstruction programmes.

Though not yet implemented everywhere, in disaster and emergency prone countries the UN Resident Co-ordinator heads a Disaster Management Team (UNDMT) consisting of UN agencies concerned with response to humanitarian emergencies. The composition of the UNDMT is determined by taking into account the types of disaster to which the country is prone and the organisations present. The country representatives or most senior resident staff members of the following organisations constitute the core membership of the UNDMT: FAO, UNDP, UNHCR, UNICEF, WFP and WHO. Depending on the particular types of disasters to which the country is prone and the kinds of intervention which might therefore be required, representatives or senior project personnel of other agencies may be included as regular members or invited to attend specific meetings when appropriate. The managers/chief technical advisers of any disaster mitigation projects should automatically be included, along with the representative of the IFRC. Representatives of key government bodies, donors, NGOs, IOM, ICRC, and National Red Cross and Red Crescent Societies should be invited when ever possible. When a delegate or support team, of a member agency of the UNDMT and/or OCHA, is assigned, the delegate or leader of the team will automatically become a member of the UNDMT. The team should work in close association with the host government, the diplomatic missions of donor countries and regional organisations.

As a general rule the UN Resident Coordinator, who also represents OCHA, is Chairperson of the UNDMT. In some cases a Co-chairperson may be decided on and selected from the Team members, taking account of personal experience in emergency management and the level of disaster-related resource inputs of the agencies represented. If the disaster clearly falls within the competence and mandate of a UN agency, then a representative of that agency would normally be the Co-chairperson for all discussions relating specifically to that situation.

The UNDMT recognises and in no way supersedes the mandates and specific functions of the various organisations. It supports and assists the office of the UN Resident Co-ordinator in the exercise of its system-wide functions. In line with General Assembly Resolution 46/182, the UN Resident Co-ordinator will maintain close contact with, and receive leadership from the Emergency Relief Co-ordinator.

Terms of Reference

A primary purpose of the UNDMT is to ensure a prompt, effective and concerted country-level response by the UN system in the event of a disaster. The team should ensure co-ordination of UN assistance to the receiving government in respect to rehabilitation, reconstruction, and disaster mitigation. The team should co-ordinate all disaster-related activities, technical advice and material assistance provided by UN agencies, as well as take steps to avoid wasteful duplication or competition for resources by UN agencies. It is vital that the policies of the UNDMT relate to those approved by the receiving government.

On an on-going basis, in anticipation of disaster risks and potential emergencies, the Team combines to:

(a) compile, evaluate, and keep up-to-date information about disaster risks and preparedness arrangements in the country, the resources likely to be available for use in an emergency, and the kinds of international assistance likely to be required in particular situations

(b) draw up and regularly review an action/preparedness plan for the UN system at country level so that all members know in an emergency what to do, when and how, in order to complement each other and provide concerted UN assistance to the Government and affected populations which is timely, coherent and effective

(c) ensure that appropriate elements of the plan are reflected in the UN Security Plan so that appropriate measures can be invoked under different security phases to protect UN staff and property and also ensure the operationally of the UNDMT

(d) Review the implications of known and potential hazards for the development process in the country and:

- Co-ordinate the assistance of the various UN organisations/agencies in relation to risk reduction measures and national disaster preparedness arrangements
- identify opportunities for collaboration in joint and/or parallel projects in various sectors that can directly or indirectly contribute to risk reduction and preparedness, particularly at the local level
- Act as a focal point for co-operation between the UN system and other disaster-related co-ordination mechanisms at country-level and the national ISDR committee (where one exists)

In the event of an emergency or disaster that does not fall within the mandate and overall competence of given UN organisations, the UNDMT collaborates with the UN Resident Coordinator and OCHA in helping to:

(a) arrange assistance to the Government, mobilising and co-ordinating international assistance and in assessing the situation and the practical possibilities for meeting the priority needs. (For more information, see the DMTP training module, *Disaster-Assessment*.)

(b) establish a consolidated UN assessment of the requirements for international assistance, incorporating the conclusions of any expert assessment missions organised by the headquarters of the competent agencies

(c) develop an integrated plan and consolidated appeal for the provision of concerted assistance by the UN system, taking account of the resources expected to be mobilised from national and other sources. (For more information, see the "Guidelines for Implementing the Consolidated Appeals Process.")

(d) co-ordinate the dissemination of the UN assessment results, plan an appeal to OCHA as well as the headquarters of other agencies and local representatives of potential donors and operational organisations

(e) co-ordinate the delivery of assistance by UN agencies and their resource mobilisation efforts at country level, including approaches to the local representatives of potential donors

(f) arrange the provision of consistent and coherent operational support and technical assistance to the Government, where required, possibly including the establishment and operation of an Emergency Information and Co-ordination Support Unit ***(On-Site Operations Co-ordination Centre)*** or through assistance to OCHA's UN Disaster Assessment and Co-ordination Team (UNDAC)

(g) integrate risk/vulnerability analysis into the CCA. This initiates an interagency planning process at the country level. The process is the vehicle, through which comparative response capabilities are identified, gaps or overlaps avoided, and scarce resources more effectively allocated. This joint effort enhances the likelihood for a timely and effectively response by the system as awhile to any impending future crisis.

Procedures/Guidelines

The UNDMT should interface with, and be a member of, country disaster management teams, when practical. Most disaster prone countries already have a formal or informal disaster management team—typically headed by a national disaster focal point body. This body often functions in liaison with the Office of the President or Prime Minister, with civil defence organisations, key government ministries, the Red Cross/Red Crescent, NGOs and major donors. Where national officials do not participate in UNDMT meetings or activities, the UN Resident Coordinator should ensure they are consulted and briefed on all relevant matters. In practice it is vital that the policies of the UNDMT relate to those approved by the Government even under the pressure of events.

A disaster focal point officer (normally a senior national officer from one of the member agencies) serves as secretary to the UNDMT unless a given situation requires an international staff. The team as a whole should make the decision. The field office of one of the co-chairpersons provides the venue for meetings and the basic administrative support.

The UN Resident Co-ordinator informs the relevant government authorities and OCHA of the membership of the UNDMT and the identity, addresses and telephone numbers of the co-chairperson and the secretary, and of any changes thereto.

Meetings are convened by either of the co-chairpersons. Any member of the team may ask for a meeting at any time. The frequency of meetings depends upon various factors:

- In a country subject to potentially damaging seasonal phenomena (notably floods and tropical storms), the UNDMT should meet formally just before the start of the threat season, and at regular intervals during that season.
- Where the incidence of disaster hazards cannot be predicted, the Team should meet at regular intervals throughout the year, but not less than twice a year, and

more frequently where slow-onset emergencies are possible and early warning systems provide information that needs to be considered at regular intervals.

- The Team is immediately convened when a warning of the imminent impact of a disaster hazard is received.
- Once a disaster has occurred, frequent regular meetings take place.

The secretary prepares and circulates copies of summary minutes including any significant new information presented, decisions and recommendations made, any differences of opinion (with reasons), and matters to be followed up (specifying by whom). The co-chairperson sends OCHA copies of the minutes of meetings when there are aspects likely to be of interest or concern to OCHA.

UNITED NATIONS DISASTER MANAGEMENT TRAINING PROGRAMME (DMTP) CONCEPT BRIEF: 2000-2003

Background

1. The concept of the DMTP was developed in 1989 and conceived, from the outset, as a multi-agency undertaking. At that time, it was jointly managed by UNDP and UNDRO, later DHA, in co-operation with a core group of United Nations agencies, international organisations and non-governmental organisations (NGOs) with a role in crisis and disaster management. In the context of the UN Programme for Reform and pursuant to General Assembly resolution 52/12B, the DMTP was fully divested to UNDP in March, 1998.
2. In developing the DMTP, it was recognised that crisis and disasters world-wide continued to occur at an alarming rate, diverting substantial human and material resources into emergency response. At that time, disaster management had been widely regarded

as being focussed primarily upon those aspects that pertained to the response phase-immediate preparedness for, and co-ordination of, crisis and disaster response. It was agreed that the DMTP would seek to foster the notion that the roles and responsibilities of crisis and disaster managers, politicians and decision-makers should, in addition to response preparedness, embrace prevention, mitigation and the transition to sustainable recovery, ensuring that recovery was viewed within the context of the development requirements of affected communities.

3. DMTP established itself as a system-wide training and capacity building tool for addressing crisis and disaster management demands comprehensively. In this, it has also maintained a primary focus of clarifying the role and functions of United Nations Disaster Management Teams (DMT) and of strengthening their performance capacities. The Programme has been an inter-agency activity in every way, however difficult such an undertaking might be. The overall findings in an Evaluation of the DMTP Phase One, (1990-1996), concluded that DMTP had been an essential international initiative, which had succeeded in placing the concept of disaster management more firmly into the global dialogue on sustainable human development at the levels of both national governments and the international community.
4. Over the past decade, political, economic, social and institutional processes have significantly changed the risk scenario in many sub-regions. Globalisation, economic transformation, regional integration/ disintegration and social exclusion, amongst others, have reset the parameters for crisis and disaster risk and vulnerability reduction. At the same time, the number of institutional, organisational and individual stakeholders now involved has increased enormously. Civil society organisation, municipalities, financial

institutions and private sector concerns have joined national authorities, international organisations and NGOs in assuming a growing role and interest in crisis and disaster response as well as risk reduction.

5. Over the same period, violent conflicts and disasters of increased number and severity have drawn the attention and active involvement of a broader range of humanitarian actors. The complexity of these events, the need to consider a wider range of political, security and human rights issues and the addition of new actors has highlighted the need for co-ordination, joint strategies and collaborative action well beyond existing frameworks and capacities.
6. Many agencies now implement disaster and conflict related capacity-building activities in their particular fields of competence and a number of training modules now exist to support these efforts. However, many of these organisation-specific initiatives are isolated from each other and large areas of need remain unmet. The need for cross-fertilisation and filing the gaps between these efforts is greater than ever.

Future Direction

7. A Consultation with DMTP Partner Organisations, held on 29 July, 1999, initiated an exchange of suggestions on the need for further evolution of the Programme. As a result of this consultation and further dialogue with individual organisations, it is proposed that: (a) the activities of the Programme be more closely linked with broader capacity building initiatives; (b) the overall Programme be refined to strengthen its catalytic role in jointly developing human resources of international organisations and national authorities at the country level, and (c) the inter-agency nature of the DMTP is strengthened by establishing a broad-based Advisory Committee and ensuring implementation through collaboration between

humanitarian and development organisations.

Objective and Beneficiaries

Development Objective

8. The DMTP is foreseen to contribute to a long-term development objective consisting of the following components: Reduced incidence and impact of crisis and disaster occurrences in programme countries; a reduction of risks and vulnerability to such events; effective national and regional strategies in crisis and disaster prevention, preparedness, mitigation, response and recovery, and efficient co-ordination and collaboration at all phases of crisis and disaster management, between and among national and international partners. Beyond the contribution of the DMTP, It is expected that achieving this development objective will require significant international support in the formulation and implementation of broad-based capacity building programmes supported by the United Nations system.

Immediate Objective

9. Improved capacities of national and international partners for enhanced co-ordination and collaborative efforts in risk management and crisis/disaster response. Achievement indicators include measured strengthening of capacities in the formulation and implementation of comprehensive and appropriate crisis and disaster management policy, legislation, strategies, systems, plans and programmes as well as in the formulation and implementation of inter-related national and community level frameworks for early warning, public awareness and sound disaster management practice.
10. In contributing to this objective, the DMTP has

established itself as a platform for applied learning; providing professional and structured learning and skill-building programmes which also serve to: (a) support and create synergies among Partner Organisations' capacity building efforts; (b) apply collective and individual resources with increased efficiency; (c) raise the profile and visibility of disaster management in areas of particular risk; (d) promote awareness raising and motivation, adaptability, increased ownership and responsibility, common values and a principled approach, and (e) facilitate mobilising the commitment of people, local and international resources, technologies and funding.

Country Specificity of Outputs

11. Selection of particular countries for support by DMTP is based upon the following criteria: (a) nature and extent of risk to crisis and disaster; (b) overall level of development; (c) extent of existing crisis and disaster management capacity; (d) receptivity and commitment of host Government, and (e) current DMT capacities and commitment of the UN Country Team.
12. A capacity-building analysis of individual country or sub-regional situation indicates the particular nature of outputs to be provided by DMTP activities. Each DMTP programme is tailored to provide knowledge and skills reflecting priority emphasis on one or more of the following areas of need: (a) mapping risks and vulnerabilities; (b) formulating policy and strategy; (c) addressing substantive and technical requirements; (d) strengthening institutional frameworks and capacities, and (e) developing human resources.
13. DMTP emphasises approaches for effective collaboration, co-operation and co-ordination and attend to refining/developing and implementing learning platforms and events to strengthen national

and community authorities as well as staff of international agencies who are country-based (UNDMTs) and those who undertake country support missions. The DMTP focuses on two key components: (a) disaster risk management/reduction, response and recovery, and (b) risk management, humanitarian response and recovery requirements in the context of crisis resulting from violent conflict.

14. Specific activities pertaining to country level workshops proposed under these components generally follow a two step process as indicated below: (a) conduct, with or through participating agencies or implementing partners, joint learning and skill-building need assessments in selected countries or regions/sub-regions; define gaps and duplications in coverage; conduct and/or commission relevant research as necessary, and conduct a review of DMT capacity building requirements in selected countries, and (b) based upon these assessments, develop and/or revise training materials and conduct, jointly with participating agencies, workshops or seminars to improve inter-action between national international stakeholders, share experience acquire additional knowledge and skills, and to jointly plan for crisis and disaster-management capacity building efforts.
15. In support of these programme components, and in order to facilitate networking and exchange of experience between international organisations, national and sub-regional training institutions to provide effective human resource development programmes, service products of the DMTP include development and maintenance of a web-site data base comprising: (a) an inventory of additionally relevant training institutions and programmes; (b) a calendar of events and reports of completed activities as well as training materials and guidelines, and (c) an on-line distance learning training facility.

Management and Organisational Arrangements

16. The proposed management arrangement aims to ensure that the DMTP is designed and implemented as a fully-fledged multi-agency initiative in the context of IASC collaborative efforts. It also provides for a clear structure and policy framework to ensure high quality substantive products, effective direction and implementation as well as accountability through regular monitoring and reporting.

Advisory Committee

17. Membership of the Advisory Committee (AC) remains open to all agencies that are a part of the IASC mechanism. It is planned that the AC meets at least twice a year to: (a) review and advise on broad policies and approaches of the DMTP; (b) review and advise on criteria for the selection of countries and/or sub-regions for DMTP activities; (c) provide guidance on proposed annual plan of action; (d) ensure the support of their organisations in the implementation of the Programme; (e) review and promote synergy between DMTP and related capacity building activities, and (f) recommend and support resource mobilisation strategies.

Technical Committees

18. Led by designated Task Managers, Technical Committees (TCs) are established to supervise and co-ordinate agreed activities within their designated subject area of responsibility. TCs have the following general terms of reference. (a) determine priority topic areas and propose countries and/or sub-regions for DMTP attention; (b) identify an expert cadre of institutions and individuals available to provide substantive support to priority topic areas (undertake research, prepare technical documentation, etc);

(c) define specific capacities that need strengthening in co-operation with the UN resident/humanitarian co-ordinator and respective DMT and propose agenda for agreed upon training events; (d) as necessary, propose and provide guidance to missions and consultancies arranged support the implementation of DMTP support, and (e) provide substantive inputs to the development or revision of workshop documents, case studies and training materials and provide resource persons for training events.

19. Creation of the following Technical Committees has been agreed:

Disaster Management

(a) Disaster Reduction and Recovery (i) Subject areas of primary focus include risk, hazard and vulnerability assessment; risk reduction; disaster mitigation; disaster economics; disasters and the environment; rehabilitation and reconstruction. (ii) Proposed Task Manager UNDP-DRRP

(b) Disaster Response (i) Subject areas of primary focus include disaster response preparedness; disaster assessment; co-ordination of international response; disaster response ethics and evaluation; logistics; emergency information management and telecommunications. (ii) Proposed Task Manager: OCHA-DRB

Crisis Management

(a) Risk Reduction and Recovery (i) Subject areas of primary focus include such topics as conflict transformation by peaceful means; reconciliation; disarmament, demobilisation and reintegration; crisis risk analysis; resettlement/reintegration of refugees and internally displaced persons; area-based recovery programmes; rehabilitation and reconstruction, etc. (ii) Further consultations are required in order to determine appropriate topic areas and proposed task manager(s).

(b) Crisis Response (i) Subject areas of primary focus include such topics as humanitarian principles and operational dilemmas in war zones; international law of disasters and armed conflict; co-ordination among international organisations in complex emergencies, etc. (ii) Further consultations are required in order to determine appropriate topic areas and proposed task manager(s).

20. The TCs on Disaster Reduction and Recovery and on Disaster Response liaise closely on development of required guidelines and materials. They have joint responsibility for developing materials that provide an overview or introduction to various training programmes. They also work in collaboration to ensure consistency and harmony between the two perspectives of disaster reduction/recovery and response in developing materials and programmes, which address particular hazards.

21. Within this framework and specifically relating to the development of appropriate training materials for DMTs, the DMTP Secretariat serves as the focal point, in collaboration with the TCs on Disaster Reduction and Recovery and on Disaster Response in order to prepare: (a) "best practices" and lessons learned for the improved DMT performance; (b) guidelines and support materials to clarify roles and responsibilities for DMTs, and (c) training materials and provide support to UN system training initiatives for resident and humanitarian co-ordinators on the topic of managing DMTs.

Ad hoc Group on Training Methodology

22. While the TCs ensure the professional integrity of the substantive elements of the DMTP, the Ad hoc Group on Training Methodology (AGTM) contributes to ensuring that, pedagogically, the DMTP employs

innovative, high quality training approaches. The AGTM is responsible for: (a) advising on appropriate training technologies to effectively implement the DMTP; (b) reviewing DMTP documentation and materials and recommending pedagogical revisions; (c) identifying candidates to serve as facilitators for training events, and (d) developing and supporting the implementation of a Training-of-Trainers programme for resource persons and facilitators.

UNDP Emergency Response Division

23. In meeting the provisions of decision 52/12B of the UN General Assembly pertaining to the United Nations Programme for Reform, UNDP has designated ERD the following responsibilities: (a) maintains overall responsibility for the management of the DMTP and its financial administration; (b) based on advice from the Advisory Committee and Joint UNDP-OCHA Working Group, determines overall approach and annual programme targets and selection of countries for DMTP activities; (c) co-ordinates resource mobilisation activities and manages DMTP trust funds; (d) provides funding to assist the Technical Committees to fulfil their responsibilities; (e) consults with the IASC-WG to ensure linkages between DMTP and other training programmes of IASC members, and (f) remains accountable for meeting DMTP goals and objectives.

Joint UNDP-OCHA Working Group

24. In order to ensure close collaboration on matters pertaining to co-ordination of humanitarian and development action, a Joint UNDP-OCHA Working Group (JWG), consisting of UNDP-ERD/Geneva Operations and OCHA CERB/DRB, is established with the following functions: (a) ensure that DMTP activities

effectively promote linkages between humanitarian and development strategy and action; (b) provide direct oversight to the further development of and implementation of policy, guidelines, training materials and training activities focusing on the functioning of UN Disaster Management Teams (UNDMTs); (c) ensure synergy of effort among Technical Committees (TCs) and with the Ad hoc Group on Training Methodology; (d) review and endorse/amend proposals of the AGTM for implementation by the Secretariat and TCs; (e) agree on the establishment and terms of reference for TCs, review and endorse/amend proposals of the TCs; (f) propose annual programme targets, priority topic areas and countries/sub-regions for DMTP support and, in this respect, review presentations for the Advisory Committee; (g) agree on the focus, substantive balance and overall agenda of particular DMTP events, and (h) in support of implementing particular DMTP events, agree on division of labour between UNDP and OCHA within existing mandates, monitor and follow-up on the deployment of UNDP and OCHA organisational resources.

DMTP Secretariat

25. The DMTP Secretariat is established as a component of UNDP/ERD. The Secretariat principally serves to support and co-ordinate the implementation of training activities and provides central information services through management of the DMTP website towards building human resource capacities for disaster and emergency management. These activities and services are based upon recommendations of the Advisory Committee (AC), Technical Committees (TCs) and Ad hoc Group on Training Methodology (AGTM) comprised of representatives of the UN System, International Organisations and NGOs.
26. In this regard, the Secretariat:

(a) facilitates linkage and co-ordination between activities of the AC, TCs and AGTM;
(b) prepares overall DMTP work plans, drawing upon advice of the AC and TCs;
(c) receives requests for DMTP activities from UN resident/humanitarian co-ordinators, seeks advice on new requests with relevant partner agencies, submits proposals for consideration by Advisory Committee and decision by ERD;
(d) announces the Programme activities and ensures necessary agreements with the UN resident/humanitarian co-ordinator;
(e) co-ordinates communications on DMTP matters with UN resident/humanitarian co-ordinators (and UNDP organisational units);
(f) prepares necessary background papers, annual and periodic progress reports for the Advisory Committee and inputs to documentation for UN bodies as required;
(g) organises donor consultations and prepares reports, documents and presentation materials in support of resource mobilisation activities;
(h) prepares budget proposals to for agreed activities and maintains financial records;
(i) administers project(s) established for implementation of the DMTP—co-ordinates and monitors the implementation of agreed activities, ensuring that specified products are achieved and initiates/facilitates evaluation as required;
(j) arranges for the contracting and oversees the work of consultants and institutions engaged in support of the development and implementation of the Programme;
(k) identifies and maintains an inventory on relevant training programmes, training materials, curricula and methodologies;
(l) ensures the development/revision and distribution of the DMTP training materials;

(m) drawing upon TCs and AGTM inputs, identifies and maintains a roster of substantive experts, resource persons and training facilitators as well as specialised institutions;

(n) provides facilitation/resource person services, as required, to selected training events, and

(o) establishes and maintains DMTP web-site and database.

THE UNITED NATIONS DISASTER MANAGEMENT TRAINING PROGRAMME (DMTP)

DMTP is a learning platform addressing crises, emergencies and disasters for the UN Member States, the UN System and international and non-governmental organisations.

The Programme was launched by the United Nations Development Programme (UNDP) and the Office of the United Nations Disaster Relief Co-ordinator in co-operation with UN Agencies in 1990 and has been endorsed by the Resolution of the General Assembly 46/182 at its 78th Plenary Meeting on 19 December, 1991. DMTP has raised awareness of the need for a more effective crisis and disaster management to reduce risks and vulnerabilities.

In 1997, the United Nations Programme for Reform undertook to redistribute operational aspects of responsibilities of the Emergency Relief Co-ordinator (ERC) to other parts of the UN System. In this context, the General Assembly decided at its 52nd session to transfer to UNDP the responsibilities of the ERC for operational activities for natural disaster mitigation, prevention and preparedness. As part of this transfer, the DMTP was divested to UNDP, Bureau for Crisis Prevention and Recovery (BCPR), formerly Emergency Response Division (ERD), which ensures the management of the Programme on behalf of twenty-five UN Agencies and international organisations. Since 2002, the DMTP is located in the Disaster Reduction Unit (DRU), BCPR.

DMTP's long-term development objective is: To reduce incidence and impact of crisis and disaster occurrences in programme countries; and eliminate of risks and vulnerability to such events; promote effective national and regional strategies in crisis and disaster prevention, preparedness, mitigation, response and recovery, and encourage efficient co-ordination and collaboration at all phases of crisis and disaster management, between and among national and international partners. The Programme supports ongoing capacity building efforts of the United Nations System, international organisations and Member States in the field of disasters and crises resulting from violent conflict. Its focus is on promoting co-operation and co-ordination among the UN Agencies, national counterparts, NGOs and donor governments. It has demonstrated that the UN can run a quality-training programme with a joint, inter-agency approach for the benefit of international and national partners in crisis and disaster management and successfully extract the knowledge and the experience in this field into useful learning tools. The DMTP has also been successful in establishing synergies between development and humanitarian responses in crisis- and disaster situations and in creating a culture of people and agencies that embrace crisis- and disaster-management issues within the scope of their overall concern.

The DMTP has conducted more than 70 workshops benefiting approximately 6,000 participants in Africa, Latin America and the Caribbean, Asia and the Pacific, the Middle East and the Commonwealth of Independent States. The workshops have been catalytic in supporting the revision of the national disaster management plans, the adoption of relevant laws and regulations and the creation and strengthening of the national and the UN Disaster Management Teams. They often generate follow-up training events cascading down learning to community levels and initiate technical projects supported by UNDP, other partner agencies and donor governments.

UN Agencies have developed, through the DMTP, a wide range of crisis and disaster related training modules available in English, French and Spanish, Russian, Bahasa Indonesian.

DMTP Member Agencies/Organisations

Multilateral and UN System: FAO, IBRD, ILO, IOM, OCHA, OHCHR, UNCHS, UNCTAD, UNDP, UNEP, UNESCO, UNFPA, UNHCR, UNICEF, UNITAR, UNOPS, UNSC, UNV, WFP, WHO and WMO. Other Organisations: ICRC, ICVA, IFRC, NRC and SCHR.

2

Disaster Preparedness, Rehabilitation and Reconstruction

DISASTER PREPAREDNESS

The concept of disaster preparedness is quite straightforward. Its objective is to ensure that in times of disasters appropriate systems, procedures and resources are in place to assist those afflicted by the disaster and enable them to help themselves.

The aims of disaster preparedness are to minimize the adverse effects of a hazard through effective precautionary actions, and to ensure timely, appropriate and efficient organization and delivery of emergency response following the impact of a disaster.

This definition establishes the broad framework for disaster preparedness, but it is worth dwelling on some of the points implicit in the definition.

"to minimize the adverse effects of a hazard"

Disaster risk reduction is intended to minimize the adverse effects of a hazard by eliminating the vulnerabilities which hazards otherwise would expose and by directly reducing the potential impact of a hazard before it strikes. Disaster preparedness in its starkest form assumes that certain groups of people will nevertheless remain vulnerable, and that preparedness will have to address the consequences of a hazard's impact.

"through effective precautionary actions"

It is important to note that the term used is "precautionary actions", for all too often the end product of disaster preparedness is seen as a static plan to be devised and then filed until it is needed. Disaster preparedness, to the contrary, must be seen as an active and continuing process. Of course, both plans and strategies are required, but they both must be dynamic ventures, which are frequently reviewed, modified, updated and tested.

"To ensure timely, appropriate, and efficient organization and delivery"

Perhaps one of the most difficult aspects of disaster management is that of timing. Timing also impinges upon the concept of disaster preparedness. Speed and timeliness have often been treated synonymously, a major conceptual flaw. Decisions related to timing must consider the relationship between relief inputs and their effects. In some types of disasters, flood, for example, there are certain basics such as shelter and clothing that may be required immediately. In terms of alleviating immediate distress, speed is critical. However, there are other forms.

Similarly, appropriate assistance demands careful scrutiny. The issue goes beyond the standard stories of canned pork and high heeled shoes to flood. Muslim communities. The issue goes to the important and natural link between disaster preparedness, recovery and rehabilitation. Ultimately we need to ask if one of the key objectives of disaster preparedness—the provision of appropriate assistance—is designed merely to ensure the immediate survival of affected communities or, in ensuring immediate survival, to simultaneously pave the way for recovery?

"Efficient organization and delivery"

Efficient organization and delivery suggest obvious criteria for effective disaster preparedness. Systematic planning, well executed distribution, clear cut roles and responsibilities are all vital. However, too often disaster situations create conditions of chaos. The best laid plans can mitigate but not eliminate the chaos. To the extent possible, preparedness plans should seek to anticipate the sources of chaos and equally as important should try to anticipate what to do when plans go awry. However, where a criterion of efficiency becomes particularly important is in the context of distribution. The key here is to ensure that efficiency is measured in terms of the ability to deliver needed assistance to those most vulnerable. All too often in disaster relief situations, food and non-food relief arrives at the scene of a disaster, but no system or structure has been established to ensure that those in greatest need are the beneficiaries. In the final analysis, the most important test of efficiency is that those in need are adequately provided for.

Components of Disaster Preparedness

There are nine major components involved in disaster preparedness which provide a framework upon which a national disaster preparedness strategy can be developed.

Assessing Vulnerability

Fundamental to all aspects of disaster management is information. It is a point that may appear obvious, but it is frequently overlooked. The disaster manager may know that a particular geographic region or community is susceptible to the impacts of sudden or slow-onset hazards. However, in reality, until a decision is made on systematic ways to compile and assess information about disaster vulnerabilities, the manager is and will be working in a void.

Developing and compiling vulnerability assessments is one way of approaching a systematic means of establishing an essential disaster management tool. There will be more on this subject in the next chapter.

Planning

Throughout all the activities designed to promote disaster

preparedness, the ultimate objective is to have plans in place that are agreed upon, that are implement able and for which commitment and resources are relatively assured. The plan itself will have to address other points in this framework.

Institutional Framework

A coordinated disaster preparedness and response system is a prerequisite to any disaster preparedness plan. Each system design will depend upon the traditions and governmental structure of the country under review. However, without ensuring that there is horizontal coordination" at central government levels among ministries and specialized government bodies and "vertical coordination" between central and local authorities, apian will rapidly disintegrate. This requires a structure for decision-making, inter-ministerial committees to coordinate the plan, focal points within each ministry to be responsible for the plan implementation and communication, as well as regional and community structure to implement the plan at the local level.

Information Systems

The preparedness plan must have an information system. For slow onset disasters this should consist of a formalized data collection process, and early warning system (especially for regions prone to famine), and monitoring system to update the early warning information. For sudden onset disasters a similar system must be in place for production, warning, and evacuation communication.

Resource Base

The requirements to meet an emergency situation will clearly depend upon the types of hazards the plan anticipates. Such requirements should be made explicit, and should cover all aspects of disaster relief and recovery implementation. The range of relief requirements is too extensive to put in this module, but this list indicates some of the major requirements:

- Shelter
- Medicines
- Food
- Supplementary food
- Communications systems
- Logistics systems
- Relief workers
- Clearance equipment

Warning Systems

For most types of rapid onset disasters, a warning system can save many lives. By giving a vulnerable population adequate notice of an impending disaster, they can either escape the event or take precautions to reduce the dangers. However, you must assume that functioning communications systems, such as telephones and telexes, may not be available in times of a major disaster. Begin to plan a warning system around that assumption. Consider what type of communications equipment will be needed and sustainable if power lines and receiving stations are destroyed. Preparedness plans should include provisions for access to alternative communication systems among police, military and government networks.

Warning is also critical for slow onset disasters and population displacements. In this case it is called early warning and has to do with information audits distribution regarding either:

Giving timely notice of an impending world crisis in the supply of food making ready for or preventing forced migrations of people.

Response Mechanisms

The plan's ultimate test is the effectiveness of response to warnings and disaster impacts. At a certain stage in the warning process, various responses will have to be mobilized. The staging of responses becomes an essential factor in designing a preparedness plan. Chapter 9 lays out the required responses.

Public Education and Training

The focus of a disaster preparedness plan should be to anticipate, to the extent possible, the types of requirements needed for action or responses to warnings and a disaster relief operation. The plan should also specify the most effective ways of ensuring that such requirements are met. Yet, the process will only be effective if those who are the ultimate beneficiaries know what to do in times of disasters and know what to expect. For this reason, an essential part of a disaster preparedness plan is the education of those who may be threatened by disaster. Such education takes many forms, such as:

1. Public education in schools for children and young adults, emphasizing what actions should be taken in case of a disaster threat (for example, earthquake tremors);
2. Special training courses, designed for an adult population either specifically or as an extra dimension of on-going programmes such as Preventive Health Care or Maternal and Child Health programmes;
3. Extension programmes, in which community and village-based extension workers are instructed to provide relevant information and trained for the tasks they should undertake during the event;
4. Public information, through mass media, be they television, radio or the printed word, will never really replace the impact of direct instruction. However, if sensitively designed and presented, mass media may provide a useful supplement to the overall educational process.

Rehearsals (drills)

As military maneuvers cannot fully portray the reality of battle, neither can disaster preparedness rehearsals portray the full dynamics—and potential chaos—of a disaster relief operation. However, that fact should provide no excuse for avoiding the need to rehearse the disaster preparedness plan. Not only will rehearsals reemphasize points made in separate training programmes, but they will also test the system as a whole and, invariably, reveal gaps that otherwise might be overlooked.'

PREPAREDNESS OF THE UNDMT

Learning Objectives

This part of the module is designed to help you understand:

- The main preparedness actions the UNDMT needs to take
- What the UNDMT needs if there is earning or occurrence of a disaster

Preparedness Actions

The ability of the UNDMT to respond effectively depends mainly on certain actions being taken in advance. This must be a collective, team effort between the member agencies of the UNDMT.

To the extent possible, preparedness arrangements within the UNDP office and the UNDMT must be integrated with and designed to complement national preparedness arrangements. Each member of the UNDMT should have established relationships with appropriate Government bodies responsible for disaster management, and be aware of the Government's plans and capacities for responding to emergencies of various kinds. The nature and extent of UNDMT preparedness arrangements will depend on the disaster profile of the country and the state of national preparedness.

Similar arrangements need to be made with respect to interaction with international bilateral, multilateral, and NGO representatives likely to be active in disaster response.

Where national preparedness plans and systems are ell-developed, the UNDMT's emphasis will be on knowledge of: the hazards and their typical effects; the national arrangements; how the UN agencies, individually and collectively, should work with the national authorities in the event of an emergency; and the sources of supplies and services (including expertise) which may need to be provided by the UN agencies.

Where sudden disasters constitute a major threat and national preparedness arrangements are in an early stage of development, the field office and the UNDMT must be ready to provide more substantial management support to the Government. In addition, preparedness within the UNDMT should then include compiling a wide range of relevant baseline data on the disaster-prone areas and establishing arrangements to set up an emergency information and co-ordination centre on short notice.

The UNDMT will compile basic data on preparedness measures that exist or can be developed in advance of emergencies. This information will include: the types of food, clothing, shelter, medical and other supplies which are appropriate for local use—noting those which are available for local purchase; communication and transport arrangements; ports, airports and airstrips; and all other facilities relevant to a rapid and effective response to emergencies. The UNDMTs will progressively move toward the standardisation of supplies and equipment appropriate for their area, giving priority to harmonising communications equipment, then to standardisation in other sectors.

The UNDMT should meet at regular intervals to:

- Review prevention and preparedness arrangements within the country, including the progress of any relevant ongoing development projects
- Review preparedness arrangements within the UN team of agencies
- Discuss the analysis and interpretation of data from in-country and external early warning systems
- Decide on any specific actions to be taken by members of the group individually and/or collectively
- Get copies of national disaster preparedness plans. Keep up-to-date information on the disaster-prone areas and likely disaster scenarios, and baseline data on the most disaster-prone areas

- Establish and maintain working relationships with government bodies responsible for disaster preparedness and response
- Establish links with forecasting and warning systems for natural phenomena, and systematically monitor famine early warning indicators where there is a risk of famine
- Establish links with the embassies, aid missions and NGOs that are likely to furnish emergency assistance
- Define a UNDMT action plan, and keep it up-to-date. This includes:
  - Defining the functional responsibilities of each member of the UNDMT in the event of a disaster
  - Establishing, in advance, the systems and procedures that will be needed to manage the UNDMT response to potential disasters, including arrangements for assessments, information management, communications and co-ordination
  - Making arrangements to establish a UNDMT co-ordination centre that can be established at short notice. This includes designating suitable offices and earmarking computing, communications and other necessary equipment
  - Documenting all operating procedures fully and clearly, and making this documentation readily available to all concerned
  - Sending OCHA (the Office for the Co-ordination of Humanitarian Affairs) copies of government and UNDMT preparedness plans and any other relevant documents.

The work of the UNDMT should feed into the CCA process.

Receipt and Monitoring of Warnings and Indicators

Ideally, warnings and indicators of impending—or occurring—potentially disastrous events should be available quickly to national authorities, on whom rests the responsibility for alerting the populations and response mechanisms concerned. In practice this may be the case, but information may also reach the authorities slowly, in fragmented form, or not at all. However, to the extent possible, procedures must be established for the UNDMT to receive promptly all forecasts and consequent public warnings of imminent floods, storms, volcanic eruptions, and tsunamis. These forecasts and warnings should be obtained from the responsible national authorities, through the appropriate (and specifically designated) member agency.

OCHA routinely receives warning directly from international sources and may contact the UN Resident Co-ordinator for preliminary consultation.

In any country where the food supply is uncertain, especially where crops are vulnerable to drought or pest attack, the UNDMT must not only promote the establishment of famine early warning systems but also receive and review relevant data. These include official government channels, out-posted and travelling UN staff, NGOs' and other observers' reports, including those from journalists and the news media.

The UNDMT must determine who is responsible for obtaining particular data and bringing it to the attention of the team.

Up-to-date Knowledge and Information

As part of their preparedness activities, members of the UNDMT should make arrangements to ensure that the team and each individual member agency:

1. Is aware of the possible disaster scenarios that might arise in different parts of the country. Each agency should have a common, documented "disaster profile" of the country, which includes: the history of the incidence of particular types of disasters in different areas; the impacts on the population and the economy; the types of assistance provided from all sources in the

past; the effectiveness of that assistance; and the problems faced and the "lessons learned."

2. Knows the kinds of material and other assistance that are likely to be required from the international community in particular types of disasters—and the types of assistance which would almost certainly *not* be required.
3. Has relevant, up-to-date information to facilitate a rapid and appropriate response in the event of a disaster. This includes:
   - Baseline data on the most disaster-prone areas
   - Lists of potentially useful in-country human resources within the UN system (including project personnel), and from other sources including national bodies, bilateral agencies and NGOs. These lists normally include practical expertise in public health, water supplies, agronomy, civil and irrigation engineering, and logistics.
   - Lists of potential in-country sources of the kinds of supplies that might be needed on short notice to meet emergency needs.
   - Details of the means of transport that may be available to move both personnel and supplies. This could include commercial transports and volunteer organisations such as flying clubs.
4. Keeps a readily accessible collection of publications and other documents pertinent to all aspects of disaster management, including the handbooks, manuals, and relevant technical guidelines of all concerned organisations.

The Government should keep information that is typically needed in order to expedite a rapid and appropriate disaster response within the framework of a national disaster preparedness plan. Such information should be readily available at all times. If any of this information is not available, or not up-to-date, the UNDMT should compile and maintain it as a team effort, normally in collaboration with national counterparts. Team members must determine who is responsible for obtaining particular data and bringing it to the attention of the team. Arrangements must also be made to discuss possible remedial or preventive measures with the relevant national authorities, if necessary. The UN Resident Co-ordinator should make sure that all sectors are covered.

"Electronic" Sources of Information

Relief Web (http:/vww.reliefweb.int). Relief Web's purpose is to strengthen the response capacity of the humanitarian relief community through the timely dissemination of reliable information, on response, preparedness and disaster prevention. This includes access to time-critical reports, maps, consolidated inter-agency appeals and financial contributions for complex emergencies and natural disasters, and to specific sections on emergency telecommunications, country and sectoral links, early warning, contact directories and site links, a training inventory, and library of reference, policy and research documentation. Several hundred sources of information include UN agencies, governments, international and non-governmental organisations, scientific and academic institutions and the media.

Systems, Procedures and Facilities

As part of the UNDMT action plan, contingency arrangements must be made to ensure that the team will be able to rapidly perform the functions required in case of an emergency. This will depend on the national systems and capacity and the extent to which the UN system is likely to be called to support the Government in information management, co-ordination and other functions. As a minimum, the UNDMT must have:

- assured means of communications
- mechanisms to receive and gather information
- Information management systems for recording and tracking needs for international assistance

The UNDMT needs to meet regularly both to review these arrangements and ensure that the necessary tools and facilities will be available and in good working order when needed.

One practical way to do this is to periodically arrange for a simulation exercise around a simulated disaster, with team members assuming various roles and responsibilities.

STRENGTHENING PREPAREDNESS AMONG NEIGHBOURS (SPAN)

SPAN is a preparedness programme designed to help you and your neighbors better prepare for disasters! Founded in 1987, SPAN is recognized internationally as one of the industry's leading neighborhood disaster preparedness programmes.

Major disasters stretch city resources to their limits. It is estimated that regular emergency services will be unable to respond to most calls during the first 72 hours following a major disaster, such as a severe earthquake. The number of people who will need help, and the inaccessibility of many neighborhoods due to damage and debris will prevent immediate aid.

If individuals and their neighborhoods are prepared to mutually assist each other during thee critical hours, lives can be saved, property can be spared, and emergency services can be freed to respond to the most devastated areas.

SPAN's overall purpose is to enable neighborhoods to be self sufficient for a minimum of 72 hours following a major disaster. This will be accomplished by:

- encouraging each individual and home to become personally prepared at home
- organizing block groups into seven disaster response teams:
    - Block Coordination
    - Communications
    - Damage Assessment
    - First Aid
    - Safety and Security

- Light Search and Rescue
- Sheltering and Special Needs
- utilizing the skills and knowledge the neighborhood currently possesses

While the overall purpose of the SPAN programme is to teach neighborhoods self sufficiency during times of disaster, preparedness efforts must also focus on individuals and families in their homes. A city whose population is prepared at home will see a significant reduction in the need for police, fire and ambulance support.

The SPAN programme encourages and supports individual citizens in completing one preparedness activity each month.

Some SPAN sites:

- Peninsulas Emergency Preparedness—State of Washington
- Seattle Disaster Aid and Response Teams (SDART) Programme

REHABILITATION AND RECONSTRUCTION

Disaster Impact

Rehabilitation and reconstruction comprise most of the disaster recovery phase. This period following the emergency phase focuses on activities that enable victims to resume normal, viable lives and means of livelihood. It also includes the restoration of infrastructure, services and the economy in a manner appropriate to long-term needs and defined development objectives. Nevertheless, after some disasters, there also may be a need for continuing humanitarian assistance for selected vulnerable groups.

This chapter provides brief guidelines concerning assistance to rehabilitation and reconstruction following a disaster. Although presented here as a separate chapter, rehabilitation and reconstruction must, in fact, be planned for either at the same time as relief, or built up during the relief operations.

Rehabilitation

For some agencies it is important to distinguish between rehabilitation and reconstruction. Specifically, rehabilitation is the actions taken in the aftermath of a disaster to enable basic services to resume functioning, assist victims' self-help efforts to repair dwellings and community facilities, and facilitate the revival of economic activities (including agriculture).

Rehabilitation focuses on enabling the affected populations (families and local communities) to resume more-or-less normal (pro-disaster) patterns of life. It may be considered as a transitional phase between (i) immediate relief and (*ii*) more major, long-term reconstruction and the pursuit of ongoing development.

Reconstruction

Reconstruction is the permanent construction or replacement of severely damaged physical structures, the full restoration of all services and local infrastructure, and the revitalization of the economy (including agriculture). Reconstruction must be fully integrated into ongoing long-term development plans, taking account of future disaster risks. It must also consider the possibilities of reducing those risks by the incorporation of appropriate mitigation measures. Damaged structures and services may not necessarily be restored in their previous form or locations. It may include the replacement of any temporary arrangements established as a part of the emergency response or rehabilitation.

Under conditions of conflict, however, rehabilitation and reconstruction may not be feasible. For obvious reasons of safety and security, activities in rehabilitation and reconstruction may need to wait until peace allows them.

Priorities and Opportunities in Rehabilitation and Reconstruction

The disaster occurred be cause the society was vulnerable to the impact of the hazard concerned. Rehabilitation and reconstruction must therefore not be seen as a process of simply restoring what existed previously. The need is rather to develop strategies and modalities to reconstitute services and renovate or replace essential structures such that vulnerability is reduced. These strategies must include long-term development policies and plans which take account of the current situation including any basic changes resulting from the disaster.

The disaster may, in fact, have created new opportunities for development by changing the environment and the point of departure, both in terms of physical structures and/or social patterns and attitudes. It will certainly have heightened awareness concerning disaster risks, and both the local populations and national authorities are likely to be especially receptive to proposals for risk reduction and preparedness measures. Such opportunities must be recognized and seized in the planning of rehabilitation and reconstruction projects, as well as in the formulation of new, long-term development programmes.

Assistance to rehabilitation and reconstruction must therefore be planned on the basis of a thorough assessment and appraisal of the technical and social issues involved. While the planning of such assistance cannot be unduly rushed, it must be accomplished as expeditiously as possible. There are two reasons for this:

- Certain rehabilitation and reconstruction measures, if organized rapidly enough, can shorten the period for which emergency relief assistance is needed and eliminate the need to invest resources in temporary measures.
- The "window of opportunity" may be short for the incorporation of risk reduction measures in reconstruction (of housing, for instance) or for new development initiatives (especially social aspects).

Seasonal factors must be considered and may determine the needed timetable for reconstruction, for example, the replacement of emergency shelter or the rehabilitation of irrigation systems in time for the next crop.

The aim is to promote and assist recovery. Assistance during the post-disaster phase must be planned and implemented with this clearly in mind. Damaged structures and services which are essential to the society must be repaired or replaced, duly protected against future risks. At the same time, and no less important, ways must be found to help people recover, particularly those people who have the least resources to call on.

As noted earlier, "the majority of people affected are the poor." For the poor, disasters represent lost property, jobs, and economic opportunity. In real terms that can represent an enormous economic setback. Therefore, reconstruction assistance should be designed to:

- relieve economic constraints and reduce the cost of reconstruction
- inject capital into the community
- create employment opportunities
- support and strengthen existing economic enterprises."

Timely and imaginative planning is therefore required to dovetail rehabilitation and reconstruction with short-term "relief" measures, and to make the most effective use of external financial resources, materials, and technical assistance in achieving development gains while satisfying humanitarian needs.

The Danger of Planning and Conducting Reconstruction in Haste

"Post-disaster programmes—even reconstruction programmes, are often planned and carried out in haste. The rush may occur because of the reconstruction planners' perceived need to return the community to "normal" as soon as possible or because of time constraints on donor funding. Thus the sort of careful planning and community involvement necessary for development planning is ...

(Contd.)

(Contd.)

The Danger of Planning and Conducting Reconstruction in Haste

...often overlooked. Without such planning, these programmes may infringe on longer-term development efforts or delay their implementation. Reconstruction programmes that are ill-planned and merely return communities to the status quo may leave them almost as vulnerable again to a future disaster, while at the same time creating a sense of complacency because something has been seen to have been done."

3

Disaster Declaration, Response and Command System

DISASTER DECLARATION, RESPONSE

Introduction

In the complexity of disaster situations, international disaster and emergency managers have many difficult ethical decisions to make which affect millions of lives each year. Economics, power, politics, racism, sexism, and classis are intricately interwoven in causes of disasters as well as in decision-making processes that declare certain emergencies as disasters while others go unrecognized and without support from international response networks.

Vulnerable people worldwide and particularly those in developing countries are affected disproportionately by most disasters. The resources available are not keeping up with emergency response needs. Disaster managers have the responsibility to strive for the purest ethical standards for asserting the rights of individuals and communities to receive assistance and to utilize their own resources in equitably planning and implementing humanitarian assistance. In this context, disaster and eminency decision-makers must turn vision into reality with the highest degree of personal and institutional integrity.

Some Ethical Issues and Exploration of Responses

Seven major ethical issues are discussed here with regard to disaster declaration and response.

1. *Disaster Managers Need to Achieve Balance in Disaster Response—Recognizing the Local Capacities While Also Recognizing the Need*: The international community has amoral duty to assist when a disaster causes damage of sufficient severity and magnitude that the needs of individuals and families, community, region, or country are beyond the capabilities of the region and of the national government. If needed resources are available in the region, however, it is not appropriate to import them. Cash infused into the local area to purchase resources stimulates the economy. This in turn helps integrate relief and recovery into long-term development and economic sustainability.

For disaster response efforts to be most effective, participation from all levels of society must be involved in the pre-disaster planning. Awareness of the racial and socio-economic status of a given community is critical in planning. Individuals and communities must be encouraged to assert their rights to both receive and give assistance. "Traditional" disaster response must be redefined to include issues of social justice so as to assist with a dignified emotional and physical recovery.

2. *A Second Ethical Issue in Disaster Response Involves Identifying the Vulnerabilities, Needs and Abilities of Marginalized Populations*: A crisis or an emergency event must affect vulnerable people to be a disaster. Levels of vulnerability are determined by capacities to resist disaster emotionally and physically, as well as to rebuild family and community after disaster strikes.

The International Federation of Red Cross and Red Crescent Societies define vulnerability as "...those at greatest risk from situations that threatens their survival or their capacity to live with a minimum of economic and social security and human dignity." Those already least able to cope are usually even further marginalized. Women, children, minorities, refugees, and others are doubly or even triply vulnerable.

Certain ethnic or cultural traditions tend to keep some disaster survivors out of the formal aid network.

Disenfranchised groups may be routinely denied access to vital information and resources that others take for granted. The policies and standards that guide organizations must be re-examined to eliminate social inequities in aid access including the exclusion of minorities, women and the poor. Institutional neglect and resistance to providing information is likely to be greater for groups such as women and minorities who have low income and poor housing, education and health.

3. *A Third Ethical Issue Related to Power Indecision-making:* Who has the right to determine acceptable levels of risk and vulnerability as well as whether and at what level humanitarian assistance is provided? Many international disaster relief organizations fail to recognize that local people know what they need and that they are the first to respond to an emergency. The mandate of assistance organizations should be to supplement the efforts of those affected and their available local and regional resources. International assistance should be sought only when regional and national resources are likely to be exhausted.

When individuals and communities are involved in assessing risk and vulnerability, they can collaborate in prevention, mitigation, and preparedness activities in cooperation with their government and other organizations. This has proven helpful with planning and resource management. Empowerment is the key to transforming the widening gap between needs and resources to sustainable development. When people are empowered to fully participate in planning and decision-making:

- there is ownership in the plan and initiative to seek out their own cultural resources
- assistance may arrive from nearby through an expedient, culturally acceptable, and usually less expensive process
- there is potentially less unmet need, and therefore less need for national and international assistance

4. *A Fourth Issue Involves National Sovereignty versus Individuals' Human Rights*: National governments reserve the sole right to issue an international appeal through the U.N. A problem arises when governments give priority to their political considerations over the needs of the people. All people within national borders, including displaced people and refugees, have the right to decent, humane treatment, as well as to protection and assistance when needed. When governments blatantly violate human rights, the international community has amoral duty to intervene.

An aware, knowledgeable, self-sufficient population that participates in government structures is able to determine its own acceptable levels of risk, vulnerability, and need for assistance. When the affected population is not aware of risk and vulnerability nor sufficiently empowered to prevent or mitigate disaster, it is unlikely to have a say in disaster response and reconstruction needs.

5. *Of Fundamental Humanitarian Concern is the Safeguarding of Human Rights and the Protection and Welfare of the Individual*: In the area of human rights, it is not sufficient to be a neutral intermediary. Disasters have their greatest impact on those least likely to claim their human rights. Because vulnerable populations are more burdened in recovery, decision-makers must actively advocate for the effective implementation of human rights for all. This advocacy is key to disaster relief and rehabilitation. Without these safeguards, disaster survivors cannot recover either emotionally or physically.

The usually hidden pattern of discrimination and violence against women is brought into sharp focus in disaster situations. Frequently, personnel from national and international organizations hastily interact with local and regional traditional people, assuming that the leaders who emerge first represent and serve the entire population.

International disaster and emergency management personnel have a responsibility to become aware of, include and help others recognize the contributions, human rights and special needs of women.

All women, men and children have the right to be free from

violence including: verbal and physical assault, rape, female infanticide, genital mutilation, and sex tourism as well as discrimination in health care, employment, social, economic, and political opportunities. While the 1948 Universal Declaration of Human Rights is understood to include women, violence and the abuse of women have been minimized or even dismissed as common practice. Men who perpetuate patterns of violence against women sometimes claim that these patterns should not be subject to public or international jurisdiction.

The right of an individual to receive equitable disaster relief and recovery aid that is culturally and gender-appropriate should be an inalienable right and not subject to negotiation. If there is a duty to bring relief aid to disaster survivors, then that duty must include non-discrimination on the basis of race, religion, gender, class, and political affiliation.

6. A Sixth Ethical Issue Facing the International Disaster Management Community Involves the Utilization of Military Force Provided by Another Government: The military brings logistics, skills and resources that may meet immediate needs. The military, however, directly represents the foreign policy of its government and is specifically trained to perform a confrontational role. Development issues of the local people and region must be considered. It may be more culturally appropriate and cost-effective to stimulate the local and regional economy by contracting with local civilian entities rather than paying for military or other international services from abroad. Culturally appropriate responses bolster the survivors' will to recover. Cost-effective responses leave more resources to meet other needs. Well-planned stimulation of the local and regional economy fosters long-term sustainable development.

The U.N. Security Council took a historical decision in December, 1992 to allow the use of all necessary means to halt famine and anarchy and to establish a safe environment for humanitarian relief operations. It is important to establish safe corridors for transport, security, and distribution of relief aid, including protection of relief personnel and supplies.

7. *Disaster Managers Face a Seventh Issue when Donor Nations*

and Nations Impacted by Disaster have Conflicting Standards of Justice and National Public Policy: Whose values count? How are differences negotiated? Many nations contend that Western standards of justice and fairness do not necessary apply to them. In some cases, these countries accuse donor countries of using their standards as an excuse not to give aid. When disaster strikes, these countries will want assurances that industrialized countries will not withhold aid contingent on a "democratic" system, human rights records, or "prudent" economic policies set by Western and Northern standards. The perspectives of diverse opinions must be considered when working to resolve these issues.

Some Goals and Priorities for Disaster Response

Focus on Prevention and Mitigation and Preparedness

Disaster and emergencies, many of which are complicated and multi-faceted, call for a close look at root causes with the focus on prevention. New preventive measures must be sought by all people and organizations. Emphasis must be on peace-making and weapons reduction to prevent initial conflicts. Prevention of human-caused, technological and environmental disasters must be given the highest priority at local, national and international levels.

Disaster preparedness and response involves a matrix of evolving education and awareness building, resource planning and sharing, and communication at all levels: from village councils to regional and national governments, and to international coordinating bodies. More sophisticated diplomatic and political skills are needed at all levels. The effectiveness of the response depends on the level of mitigation and preparedness, involving representatives of all people, from the village to the national level.

For disasters that cannot be prevented, mitigation and preparedness must be the highest priority. When catastrophe occurs, effective cultural and gender-appropriate responses must be carried out. These responses must be fully integrated into sustainable development.

Improved Criteria for Organizational Funding and Accountability

To receive funding, organizations should focus on the above priorities and assist those most in need: those vulnerable before the disaster occurred, such as the children, women, elderly, developmentally disabled, physically challenged, and others with special needs.

Priority funding for disaster response should go to groups with a high priority on social justice that work with and emerge from vulnerable grassroots communities. Programme priorities should include awareness-building and prevention of human-caused disasters, including peace-making, low-cost disaster mitigation measures, leadership training and exchange, and communication linkages that cut across geographic, class, and political boundaries. All programmes must be planned integrally within long-term sustainable development systems.

Each organization's accountability is of vital importance. Many times, however, the groups that are well organized and have a "track record" of public relations receive the lion's share of funding in disaster situations. Their commitment to relate culturally or geographically to those most in need is essential to consider. International organizations have special responsibilities to upon the highest ethical standards in their roles as enablers, coordinators and facilitators to meet human need.

"No longer are just food, clothing and blankets provided to disaster victims; often an entire range of goods that would make a department store owner envious are shipped to the scene. When the distribution system is setup, it is almost always controlled by the relief agency acting through its representatives in the community.

When disaster strikes a community, the economic systems of the community are also affected. Physical facilities may be destroyed or damaged, and the distribution of goods and services disrupted. If the community is to return to normal, it is essential that these systems be restored as quickly as possible. But just as these systems are smuggling to recover, new systems in the form of relief and reconstruction programmes appear and compete directly with them. A recent example occurred on Fiji. One island group was severely affected by an intense hurricane that destroyed much of the agricultural production of the country and approximately 80 per cent of the housing. Massive relief efforts were organized by the government. To qualify for the relief, family members had to show they were unemployed as well as being disaster victims. During the period that the aid continued, the normal economic systems (such as small stores, material suppliers, and their respective distribution networks) were bypassed. The aid, in effect, became a competing system. Thus the victims were denied much-needed capital that would have enabled them to recover more quickly. Several of the smaller stores eventually closed, and a number of suppliers put off reordering stock.

The relief programme delayed recovery of the normal economic systems within the community."

> Most disaster organizations and managers probably accept at a theoretical level the many goals enumerated in "Ethical Dilemmas in Disaster Declaration and Response." In an ideal world, they would seek to implement them all. When major disasters are involved, however, the world is anything but ideal. The situation is difficult enough in "natural disasters." Complex emergencies escalate the challenges further still.

It may be tempting to debate overarching objectives such as empowering people "to participate fully in planning and decision-making," adopting an inclusive approach to the special needs of "minorities, women and poor," or functioning according to "the highest ethics of human values." However, it is more productive to focus on the obstacles-institutional, political, financial, or professional-which complicate putting such eminently praiseworthy objectives into practice.

In the area of empowerment, for example, agencies firmly committed to strengthening local institutions frequently mount programmes first and address empowerment issues later. In practical terms, they give higher priority to saving lives than to institution-building. But is the trade-offs as stark as frequently presented? Could more ingenuity not produce the best of both worlds, or at least do better by both?

As **regards neutrality,** the materials suggest that "it is not sufficient to be a neutral intermediary." Disaster managers, we are told, must be concerned about underlying causes of emergencies and become advocates for durable solutions. What about those who believe that being other than a neutral intermediary can undercut effective disaster response? How can shared concerns about the underlying causes of disasters and shared desires to see changed government policies be most effectively expressed?

Concerning **objectivity,** the Cold War which infiltrated the declaration of and response to disasters is now past. However, as the materials suggest, the international community still lacks uniform and consistent ways of proceeding to establish and respond to such crises. What are the sources—political, commercial, or otherwise which continue to impede responses based on the severity of the need? What criteria can be agreed upon to help assure more businesslike action in the future?

There are probably divergent views about what constitute the "purest ethical standards" **of accountability.** The idea that disaster assistance should be accountable to the beneficiaries suggests that it may be more than "gifts" bestowed by outside "donors." The new approach, in addition to shifting greater power to disaster-prone areas and institutions, would demand better performance from outsiders. The suggestion that funds should seek out organizations "which focus on the above priorities" also raises questions, given the multiple sources of existing funds and the diverse agendas of those who provide them.

Action in these areas would have wide-ranging implications for the current disaster management system as we know it. The existing division of labor, for example, would be overturned. Such implications deserve review.

DISASTER RESPONSE

After reading the material and completing the exercises in Part 3 you should be able to:

- identify the major categories of activities and responsibilities of disaster response
- identify the objectives of disaster assessment and how assessment data is used
- describe the role of your UN organization in the various disaster response activities
- identify key points for action in coordination and information management
- describe development opportunities within the disaster reconstruction phase

Disaster response is the sum total of actions taken by people and institutions in the face of disaster. These actions commence with the warning of an oncoming threatening event or with the event itself if it occurs without warning. Disaster response includes the implementation of disaster preparedness plans and procedures, thus overlapping with disaster preparedness. The end of disaster response comes with the completion of response comes with the completion of disaster rehabilitation programmes.

This chapter identifies the principal activities of disaster response. Each activity is, formally or informally governed by a set of policies and procedures, and each activity is typically under the auspices of a lead agency. In the end, disaster response activities are implemented by a myriad of government organizations, international and national agencies, local entities and individuals, each with their roles and responsibilities.

A full discussion of disaster response would, for each activity, identify:

- Who is responsible for its implementation, who supports it

- What means are required for its implementation?
- When are its activities implemented?
- What is its scope?
- Why does it need to be done?

Aims of Emergency and Post-Disaster Assistance

The overall aims of emergency and post-disaster assistance are:

- To ensure the survival of the maximum possible number of victims, keeping them in the best possible health in the circumstances.
- To re-establish self-sufficiency and essential services as quickly as possible for all population groups, with special attention to those whose needs are greatest: the most vulnerable and underprivileged.
- To repair or replace damaged infrastructure and regenerate viable economic activities. To do this in a manner that contributes to long-term development goals and reduces vulnerability to any future recurrence of potentially damaging hazards.
- In situations of civil or international conflict, the aim is to protect and assist the civilian population, in close collaboration with the International Committee of the Red Cross (ICRC) and in compliance with international conventions.
- In cases involving population displacements (due to any type of disaster), the aim is to find durable solutions as quickly as possible, while ensuring protection and assistance as necessary in the mean time.
- The following are typical activities of emergency response. There are important differences, however, between sudden and slow onset disasters. Differences also emerge when comparing the specific geographical situation and the disaster's socio/ political context.

Warning

SUDDEN ONSET Warning refers to arrangements to rapidly disseminate information concerning imminent disaster threats to government officials, institutions and the population at large in the areas at immediate risk. These warnings normally relate to tropical storms and floods.

SLOW ONSET Early warning is the term used regarding slow-onset disasters, especially famine. Early warning activities include the process of monitoring the situation in communities or areas known to be particularly vulnerable to the effects of droughts, crop failures and/or changes in economic conditions. An adequate warning will enable remedial measures to be initiated before hardships become acute. Early warning is a disaster response activity only if it has failed to detect the warning signs or where such signs were ignored.

Evacuation/Migration

SUDDEN ONSET Evacuation involves the relocation of a population from zones at risk of an imminent disaster to a safer location. Evacuation is most commonly associated with tropical storms but is also a frequent requirement with technological or industrial accidents. For evacuation to work there must be a timely and accurate warning system, clear identification of escape routes, an established policy that requires everyone to evacuate when an order is given, and a public education programme to make the community aware of the plan.

SLOW ONSET The movement of people from the zone where they are at risk to a safer site is not, in fact, evacuation but crisis-induced migration. This movement is usually not organized and coordinated by authorities but is a spontaneous response to the perception by the migrants that food and/or security can be obtained elsewhere.

Search and Rescue

SUDDEN ONSET Search and rescue, often known by the acronym SAR, is the process of identifying the location of disaster victims that may be trapped or isolated and bringing them to safety and medical attention.

In the aftermath of tropical storms and floods, SAR usually includes locating stranded flood victims, who may be threatened by rising water, and either bringing them to safety or providing them with food and first aid until they can be evacuated or returned to their homes.

In the aftermath of earthquakes, SAR normally focuses on locating people who are trapped and injured in collapsed buildings.

Post-disaster Assessment

SUDDEN AND SLOW ONSET: The primary objective of assessment is to provide a clear, concise picture of the post-disaster situation, to identify relief needs and to develop strategies for recovery. It determines options for humanitarian assistance, how best to utilize existing resources, or to develop requests for further assistance. The post-disaster assessment must distinguish among pro-disaster chronic conditions, the needs of disaster survivors and their resources.

This activity is so vital that we will devote the next chapter exclusively to disaster assessment.

Emergency Relief

SUDDEN ONSET Emergency relief is the provision on a humanitarian basis of material aid and emergency medical care necessary to save and preserve human lives. It also enables families to meet their basic needs for medical and health care, shelter, clothing, water, and food (including the means to prepare food}. Relief supplies or services are typically provided, free of charge, in the days and weeks immediately following a sudden disaster.

SLOW ONSET Emergency relief may need to be provided for extended periods in the case of neglected or deteriorated slow-onset emergency situations and population displacements (refugees, internally and externally displaced people). The impact of the disaster may be mitigated for these populations through additional assistance to the host community as well.

Logistics and Supply

SUDDEN AND SLOW ONSET The delivery of emergency relief will require logistical facilities and capacity. A well-organized supply service is crucial for handling the procurement or receipt, storage, and dispatch of relief supplies for distribution to disaster victims. The logistical system is perhaps more vital and of higher priority for slow onset emergencies.

Communication and Information Management

SUDDEN AND SLOW ONSET: All of the above activities are dependent on communication. There are two aspects to communications in disasters. One is the equipment that is essential for information flow, such as radios, telephones and their supporting systems of repeaters, satellites, and transmission lines. The other is information management: the protocol of knowing who communicates what information to whom, what priority is given to it, and how is disseminated and interpreted.

Survivor Response and Coping

SUDDEN AND SLOW ONSET: In the rush to plan and execute aisle operation it is easy to overlook the real needs and resources of the survivors. The assessment must take into account existing social coping mechanisms that negate the need to bring in outside assistance. On the other hand, disaster survivors may have new and special needs for social services to help adjust to the trauma and disruption caused by the disaster.

Participation in the disaster response process by individuals to community organizations is a key to healthy recovery. Through them appropriate coping mechanisms will be most successfully utilized.

Security

SUDDEN ONSET: Security is not always a priority issue after sudden onset natural disasters. It is typically handled by civil defense or police departments.

SLOW ONSET: The protection of the human rights and safety of displaced populations and refugees can be of paramount importance requiring international monitoring.

Emergency Operations Management

SUDDEN AND SLOW ONSET: None of the above activities can be implemented without some degree of emergency operations management. Policies and procedures for management requirements need to be established well in advance of the disaster. More attention is given to this subject in the following chapter on *Responding to a sudden disaster.*

Rehabilitation and Reconstruction

Rehabilitation and reconstruction complete the disaster response activities. As much of this activity is within the scope of UNDP's concern.

UN RESPONSE TO DISASTERS

Principal Elements and Actions in Response to a Sudden Disaster

The vast majority of international emergency and post-disaster assistance is funded by special contributions to the UN agencies, or is delivered bilaterally or through NGOs. Action by UNDRO, the resident coordinator/representative and the UN-DMT is therefore extremely important: information management and exchange, coordination, preparation of appeals, and the mobilization of resources. The extent to which the resident coordinator/representative and the UN-DMT are involved in these activities, and in the provision of direct operational support to the Government, will depend on the nature and scale of the emergency situation, on the capacity and wishes of the national authorities, and on the resources which can be mobilized.

The above applies in emergency situations which require action by a number of UN organizations/agencies (possibly including UNDP) and, in consequence, coordination by the resident coordinator and UNDRO. In situations which fall entirely within the mandate of one specific organ of the UN system (e.g. and epidemic or crop pest attack), primary responsibility rests with the appropriate agency (e.g. WHO, FAO) although the country-level UN Disaster Management Team may, if required, play a role in support of that agency. (The information dissemination services of UNDRO may also be made available to the agency concerned at the international level.)

The following is a list of the principal actions to be taken by the resident coordinator/representative and the UN-DMT immediately before and during a disaster.

Actions to be Taken on Receipt of a Disaster Warning

On receipt of a warning of an imminent disaster threat:

- Contact and exchange information with UNDRO: review need for precautionary measures.
- Contact the relevant government authorities: confirm readiness of UNDRO and UN-DMT to assist, if needed.
- Convene the UN-DMT, review preparedness arrangements, alert personnel and review the UN security plan.

Actions to be taken following the Occurrence of a Disaster

Immediate action in all cases:

- Ensure the security of all UN personnel: activate the security plan, if necessary.

- Ensure reliable telecommunications between the field office and Geneva, New York and the affected areas.
- Contact and exchange information with UNDRO: send an alert message and then regular field satraps, and maintain telephone contact, if possible.
- Contact the government emergency management authorities: get information, offer UN assistance and reaffirm the capabilities of the various agencies; confirm arrangements for ongoing contacts and collaboration.
- Determine whether the Government requires international assistance and wishes UNDRO to launch and international appeal. Consider needs for:
  - Search and rescue (SAR), or other specialist assistance
  - Relief assistance.
- Convene the UN-DMT: review whatever information is available; confirm/define responsibilities within the team; arrange follow-up meetings and information-sharing.
- Gather and collate information on the situation; participate in initial reconnaissance visits to the affected areas. Mobilize and provide technical assistance for the assessment process.

If International Emergency Assistance is Required

1. Immediate needs and action
   - Determine, on a provisional basis, the specific functions to be undertaken by the UN at country level in the light of the particular situation and the capacity of the Government.
   - Define any needs for SAR teams or other specialist assistance; inform and consult with UNDRO immediately.
   - Consult with UNDRO concerning the possible assignment of one or more UNDRO delegates.
   - Ensure the convening of an early, broad-based

coordination meeting to coordinate immediate responses and arrangements for assessment.

- Institute necessary organizational arrangements and systems within the field office: redeploy staff, define work priorities, and ensure the availability of office equipment and clerical and administrative support to staff engaged in emergency activities.
- Put information systems into operation to record and track needs and contributions of international assistance.
- Consider and, where appropriate, make recommendations for the provision of emergency grants by UNDRO and UNDP, and/or the release of supplies by UNDRO from Pisa.

2. Continuing action during the early days of emergency assistance operations:
   - Maintain close contact and exchange information with the Government and other concerned parties (donors, NGOs); participate in and support in-country coordination mechanisms.
   - Maintain a dialogue and frequent information exchanges with UNDRO (through field sitreps and by telephone).
   - Help to define priority needs for international assistance:
   - Participate in the overall assessment
   - Make an independent judgement of the priority needs for international emergency assistance
   - Help in formulating and screening requests
   - Develop a concerted programme of assistance and a consolidated UN appeal including the proposals and requirements of all UN agencies.
   - Disseminate information on needs for international assistance to local representatives of donors and NGOs, and help to mobilize resources to cover unmet needs.
   - Help to monitor assistance operations, and provide operational assistance, where required.

- Make arrangements for relations with the news media, and the reception and servicing of visiting missions.
- Undertake a review (post mortem) of the UN assistance to the emergency operation as it draws to a close.

If there are political complications or humanitarian needs which are not being met, advise the Secretary-General through the office of Emergency Relief Coordinator.

Additional Support Functions (On a Continuous Basis) Depending on the Need and the Capacity of the Government

- Convening and providing secretariat services to broad-based coordination meetings.
- Providing operational support to management information systems, logistics, or communications.

Assistance to Rehabilitation and Reconstruction

Help to plan and introduce assistance to rehabilitation and reconstruction in phases from the earliest possible moment.

Assistance to Populations in Areas of Conflict

At present the UN has little role in active conflict areas for .people in need caught in the conflict. This role is mainly left to the ICRC and certain NCOs.

Sitreps-exchanging Information with UNDRO

This section describes the responsibilities of the resident coordinator/representative in respect of reporting to UNDRO, and provides guidelines for the preparation of the required field sitreps. It describes UNDRO's reporting (information dissemination) system in the context of international information flows.

Contacting UNDRO, Geneva

UNDRO maintains a 24-hour duty system,
365 clays-a-year. To contact:

Telephone	(4122)-7332010	(Direct line for use in case of an emergency: Out of office hours the call is received by Air Call answering service which conveys the message to the UNDRO duty officer who then calls back)
or	(4122)-7346011	(United Nations Office Geneva switchboard: ask for UNDRO duty officer)
Telex	414242 DRO CH	
Fax	(4122)-7335623	
Electronic Mail	UNX008	Use the UNDP E-mail facility. (Message is delivered to UNDRO via UNIENET)

Alert Message and Field Sitreps

To ensure a timely, appropriate, and coordinated international response, it is essential that the rest dent coordinator report rapidly to UNDRO any disaster occurrence, with an early assessment of damage and needs, however tentative. This must then be followed up by regular and systematic reporting of increasing detail.

Send an alert message to UNDRO as soon as information of a disaster occurrence is received, or an occurrence in a remote area is confirmed. This serves to let UNDRO know that something has happened and that the field office is following up. Do not delay while waiting to get more information.

Send the first field sitrep as quickly as possible, and in any case not more than 24 hours after the disaster occurrence. Send whatever relevant information is available: do not delay because certain information's lacking. Send information as it becomes available, indicating what additional information is anticipated and arrangements made to gather more.

Send field sitreps regularly, at least daily during the initial emergency period (typically 10-20 days) and until a reduced frequency is agreed with UNDRO. Always follow the basic format but, if necessary, adapt the sub-headings of the individual sections depending on the needs of the particular situation.

Send sitreps by fax (or Email) when possible. This takes full advantage of word processing facilities in preparing and updating the reports.

Involve the UN-DMT in the preparation of the sitreps to help ensure comprehensive reporting and a unified UN system presentation to the Government and the international community. The UNDP disaster focal point should normally be responsible for collating information from the various agencies and preparing the first draft. Arrange for copies of the field sitreps to be sent promptly to the headquarters of the UN agencies most directly concerned.

Main Headings for Field Sitreps

1. General situation
2. National response
3. Country-level International response
4. Requirements for International assistance
5. Channels for delivery of International aid
6. International pledges and contributions
7. Other Information

The Importance of Coordination and Information

Coordination is even more important in emergency assistance operations than in development work: lives might be at risk, logistic and other resources are likely to be limited, and decisions are made quickly. There are many possibilities for duplicating effort, wasting resources, and leaving gaps in both geographic and sectoral coverage.

Timely, reliable information is crucial to planning and implementing emergency and post-disaster assistance operations, and to mobilizing national and international resources. The regular dissemination of relevant information is a precondition for effective coordination and co-operation-at national and local levels-between sectors and between Government, operational agencies, and donors.

Key Action Points in Co-Ordination and Information Management

- Maintain frequent, direct contacts with government focal point, operational departments, donors, and NGOs.
- Review within the UN-DMT and discuss with the government focal point whether help from the resident co-co-ordinator or UN-DMT is required in:
  - Compiling and analyzing Information and preparing reports on needs for and use of International assistance
  - Establishing and operating more comprehensive management information systems in support of the responsible government authorities
  - Convening information and co-ordination meetings Involving government bodies, donors, NGOs, and the UN organizations and agencies.
- Ensure the convening of regular, broad-based co-ordination meetings (probably weekly), encourage constructive discussion, promote consensus on actions by all concerned, provide secretnat service, if required.
- Specify the information management functions to be fulfilled by the resident co-ordlnator and UN-DMT, and the resources (staff, equipment, office space, and budget) required.
- Initiate the needed Information systems and services using existing staff facilities, Inform UNDRO, the regional bureau, and local donor representatives of requirements to develop and continue.

- Establish and emergency Information and co-ordination (EIC) support unit, where needed, as a collaborative UN-DMT effort, encourage all UN-DMT members to second staff, co-operate in mobilizing other needed resources, and use the facilities.
- Disseminate information regularly to all concerned government departments, donors and NGOs, fax copies to UNDRO.
- Encourage all concerned to be consistent in the use of agreed catena, standards, and terminology, and to harmonize reporting periods to the extent feasible.
- Help direct the attention of NGOs to areas and activities where they can make the greatest contribution (not necessarily in the most affected areas).

FAQ—INCIDENT COMMAND SYSTEM (ICS)

The incident Command System (ICS) is the model tool for command, control, and coordination of a response and provides a means to coordinate the efforts of individual agencies as they work toward the common goal of stabilizing the incident and protecting life, property, and the environment. ICS uses principles that have been proven to improve efficiency and effectiveness in a business setting and applies the principles to emergency response.

When is ICS Used?

ICS has been proven effective for responding to all types of incidents, including:

- Hazardous materials (HAZMAT) incidents
- Planned events (celebrations, parades, concerts, official visits, etc.)
- Response to natural hazards
- Single and multi agency law enforcement incidents
- Lack of comprehensive resource management strategy
- Fires

- Incidents involving multiple casualties
- Multijurisdictional and multi agency incidents
- Air, rail, water, or ground transportation accidents
- Wide-area search and rescue missions
- Private sector emergency management programme

ICS History

ICS was developed in the 1970s in response to a series of major wildland fires in southern California. At that time, municipal, county, State, and Federal fire authorities collaborated to form the Firefighting Resources of California Organized for Potential Emergencies (FIRESCOPE). FIRESCOPE identified several recurring problems involving multiagency responses, such as:

- Nonstandard terminology among responding agencies.
- Lack of capability to expand and contract as required by the situation.
- Nonstandard and nonintegrated communications.
- Lack of consolidated action plans.
- Lack of designated facilities.

Efforts to address these difficulties resulted in the development of the original ICS model for effective incident management. Although originally developed in response to wildfires, ICS has evolved into an all-risk system that is appropriate for all types of fire and non-fire emergencies. Much of the success of ICS has resulted directly from applying:

- A common organizational structure
- Key management principles in a standardized way

ICS Components

No single agency or department can handle an emergency situation of any scale alone. Everyone must work together to manage the emergency. To coordinate the effective use of all of the available resources, agencies need a formalized management structure that lends consistency, fosters efficiency, and provides direction during a response. The ICS organization is built around five major components:

- Command
- Planning
- Operations
- Logistics
- Finance/Administration

These five major components are the foundation upon which the ICS organization develops. They apply during a routine emergency, when preparing for a major event, or when managing a response to a major disaster. In small-scale incidents, all of the components may be managed by one person, the incident Commander. Large-scale incidents usually require that each component, or section, is set up separately.

RESPONSE OF THE UNDMT

Learning Objectives

This part of the module is designed to help you understand:

- What the UNDMT needs to do, should a disaster occur

Principal Elements and Actions

Much of what needs to be done should be anticipated and pre-planned as part of the UNDMT preparedness as covered in the preceding section. Where this has indeed been done, the response will be more rapid, effective and efficient.

The role of the UN Resident Co-ordinator and the UNDMT, working with OCHA and the agencies represented on the team, is to:

- Assist the Government, as required, in assessing the situation and assistance needs arising
- Provide the international community with reliable information, an independent assessment of the priority

needs for international assistance (taking account of local and national capacities and resources), and a consolidated statement of requirements of the various UN organisations and agencies

- Mobilise and provide international assistance, and do everything reasonably possible to ensure its timely delivery to victims in order to save lives, minimise suffering, and promote recovery
- Strengthen the management capacity of the responsible government institutions, where required, and provide operational support to help ensure the reception, transportation and distribution of relief supplies
- Ensure the effective use of internationally supplied resources and report to the international community on the use of those resources

In this process, attention must be given to:

- Identifying and exploiting possibilities for obtaining needed supplies and services locally
- Monitoring the situation and operational performance continuously, and being responsive to new information and changing needs
- Introducing rehabilitation, reconstruction, and further development activities in phases from the earliest possible moment
- Anticipating the time when the international emergency response should be scaled down or end, and in particular when "external" international aid staff are present, when and how an "exit" strategy should be conducted

The vast majority of international emergency and post disaster assistance is funded by special contributions to the UN agencies, or delivered bilaterally (usually the highest percentage of external aid) or through NGOs. Actions by the UNDMT are therefore critical in the areas of coordination, information management and exchange, and mobilisation of resources. The extent, to which the UN Resident Co-ordinator and the UNDMDT are involved in these activities, and in the provision of direct operational support to the Government, will depend on the nature and scale of the emergency situation, on the capacity and wishes of the national authorities, and on the resources which can be mobilised.

Actions on Receipt of a Warning or Unconfirmed Report

Immediately on receipt of a warning of an imminent disaster threat or unconfirmed report of a disaster occurrence in a remote part of the country, the following actions need to betaken:

- Contact OCHA:
  - Exchange information with OCHA on the disaster that threatens (or may have occurred) and ensure that the UNDMT as a whole is on the alert and following up
- Contact the relevant government authorities:
  - Seek confirmation and any additional information that might be available
  - Confirm the preparedness of the UN system to assist, and establish arrangements for the exchange of further information, as it becomes available
  - Determine whether specialist assistance is required to plan and implement precautionary measures
- Convene the UNDMT to:
  1 Exchange information
  - Review UN preparedness arrangements including base line information on facilities and resources in and near the threatened areas
  - Ensure that necessary communications and information systems are ready and operational
  - Ensure that all relevant personnel in all agencies are on standby and that responsibilities for all

aspects of UNDMT response are clearly defined and assigned

- Determine whether any UN personnel are in or near the areas concerned, whether there is need to inform them or take other action to assure their safety, and whether they can provide information if a disaster does occur

These actions should be undertaken more-or-less simultaneously. The precise sequence will depend on the situation and local logistics. Exchanging information promptly with OCHA is important for three main reasons. First, to ensure that the UNDMT and OCHA have similar information and take complementary measures. Second, to enable OCHA to respond appropriately to questions from potential donors at the international level. Third, to get advice from OCHA concerning preparatory action to be taken.

Actions to be taken following the Occurrence of a Disaster

The following actions need to be taken rapidly—in the first few days—in some cases simultaneously:

- Ensure the security of all UN personnel and activate the security plan, if necessary
- Ensure reliable telecommunications between the field office and Geneva, New York and the affected areas
- Contact and exchange information with OCHA: send an alert message, regular field sitreps, and maintain telephone contact, if possible
- Contact the government emergency management authorities: get information, offer UN assistance and reaffirm the capabilities of the various agencies; confirm arrangements for ongoing contacts and collaboration
- Determine whether the Government requires international assistance and wishes OCHA to launch an international appeal. Consider needs for:

    - Search and rescue (SAR), or other specialist assistance
    - Relief assistance
- Confirm/define responsibilities within the team; arrange follow-up meetings and information-sharing
- Gather and collate information on the situation; participate in initial reconnaissance visits to the affected areas. Mobilise and provide technical assistance for the assessment process

Any requirement for any external teams such as UNDAC (United Nations Disaster Assessment and Co-ordination Teams) or SAR (Search and Rescue Teams), or other specialist inputs to save lives, must be identified and specified within hours. Rapid judgement must also be made concerning the precise functions that the UN system should be ready to undertake in the light of the particular situation.

Assessment and the UNDMT

This section describes what the UN Resident Co-ordinator and UNDMT should do during the initial assessment phase following the occurrence of a disaster.

The Assessment Process

Assessment is the process of determining the impact that a disaster has on a society; the needs for immediate, emergency measures to save and sustain the lives of survivors; the resources available; and the possibilities for expediting recovery and development. Assessment involves on-the-spot surveys and the collation, evaluation, and interpretation of information from various sources concerning both direct and indirect losses, and short and long term effects. It involves determining not only what has happened and what assistance might be needed, but also defining specific objectives and how relevant assistance can actually be provided to the victims.

The fundamental questions that must be answered are:

- What has happened? Has there really been a "disaster"? Is the situation one that requires exceptional measures to be taken?
- Is there a need for international assistance? If so: What? When? How?
- How is the situation likely to evolve: How long is the need for international assistance likely to last?

In situations involving displaced persons, it includes questions of security and protection, the possibilities for durable solutions, and the situation and needs of the host populations.

In some cases, days or even weeks might be required before these questions can be fully and accurately answered. However, early (provisional) value judgements need to be made to establish a framework for providing emergency assistance where needed and making arrangements for undertaking a detailed assessment and planning major emergency and rehabilitation programmes.

Role of the UN in Relation to Assessments

Where there is a likelihood of international assistance being required following the occurrence of a disaster, the UN system is expected to be capable of:

- providing advice and assistance to the Government as required, in conducting an assessment of the situation, defining appropriate intervention strategies, specifying needs for assistance
- making an independent judgement concerning the priority needs for international assistance, and providing potential donors and the international community as a whole with objective statements of those needs
- including a developmental perspective in the planning of emergency and post-disaster assistance

Each agency is responsible for assessments in accordance with its own competence and mandate, and is expected to contribute its information and conclusions in the overall UNDMT effort. All aspects should be covered and the information of all concerned consolidated, while respecting the individual agencies' mandates.

The precise role of the UN system in general and of the UNDMT in particular in the assessment process will depend on the Government's policies, and on its capacity in relation to the scale and nature of the situation. Consultations with the Government, members of the UNDMT and other concerned parties should be held as soon as possible to determine what, if any, additional technical assistance is required for the assessment.

Where the Government (possibly with the collaboration of the national Red Cross/Red Crescent Society and other operational agencies) has a proven capacity to conduct a thorough and objective assessment, the UN Resident Co-ordinator and the UNDMT, possibly assisted by assigned specialists, will only need to satisfy themselves of the validity of the assessment, and the stated priorities. This may be done by means of carefully planned field visits, discussions with survivors, and discussions with officials at various levels.

- In some cases direct UN assistance is solicited by the authorities undertaking the assessment and determining priorities. In such cases, the UN Resident Co-ordinator, the UNDMT and any additional assigned international expertise need to: Work with the Government and others to organise the assessment, including specifying the technical expertise required to supplement existing local capacity
- Clearly define the role of each individual agency in the overall, collaborative assessment effort, and the role of individual UN staff in each field survey visit
- Mobilise the expertise and experience—of both national and international staff- available in the various UN agencies, including that of project personnel

- Help to mobilise and integrate relevant expertise available elsewhere in the country—from national bodies, bilateral organisations and NGOs
- Inform OCHA and concerned aid organisations locally of the arrangements being made, and any requirements for additional technical or logistical assistance needed for the assessment

In some cases, it may be necessary to bring together and dispatch multi-agency assessment teams to the stricken area to conduct an independent assessment, associating national and other international experts to the extent possible. In both cases the UNDMT should ensure coherence between its own assessment and that of the Government.

Gathering and Interpreting Assessment Information

The UN Resident Co-ordinator and the UNDMT need to ensure that

- Assessment activities are co-ordinated, well organised and carefully planned in order to:
    - Obtain information that is consistent and comparable; obtain all needed information; avoid effort being wasted on gathering unnecessary information; and avoid duplication of effort
    - The assessment focuses on determining how to support local coping mechanisms and recovery processes
    - The assessment goes beyond the simple listing of needs; it must explicitly consider implementation means and capacities, and the possibilities of obtaining needed supplies and services locally
    - An initial assessment is completed rapidly in all areas to identify immediate needs and aspects on which the detailed follow-up assessment should follow, identifying more substantial requirements sector-by-sector

- All communities in the affected area are covered systematically, and differences between areas and distinct population groups are identified
- Information is shared as effectively as possible between all concerned parties, and the greatest possible consensus achieved among the national and local authorities, the donor community, and operational agencies concerning the situation, any assistance requirements, and proposed interventions

A multi-sectoral approach to the assessment in which agencies and sectoral entities collaborate and agree on findings and response strategies is important. Sectoral assessments which are undertaken independently and in isolation from each other are likely to result in duplication of effort, and gaps in coverage and information. There will be a need to try to piece together an overall assessment, reconcile different viewpoints, and determine inter-sectoral priorities. Similarly, consensus should be pursued between national and local authorities, the donor community and operational agencies.

The UNDMT should collectively follow the objectives, assessment procedures and standards for planning and providing assistance which have been defined by the various UN agencies in their respective areas of competence. Respective government bodies should be encouraged to apply similar standards in requests for international assistance. The UNDMT should maintain close contacts with all embassies, bilateral agencies, and other institutions involved in making or evaluating assessments.

Assessment information needs to be analysed carefully to ensure consistency and plausibility and avoid possible biases and exaggeration, erring on the safe side or the underplaying of needs. National or international vested interests and political pressures should be watched for and resisted. Information provided from various sources is likely to vary in quality and precision, and should be evaluated in terms of the experience and proven competence of the organisations and individuals concerned. Where necessary, it should be cross-checked against other reports and available baseline data on the area.

Field Survey Visits

Field visits by experienced observers and technical experts are an essential part of any assessment although a simple visit in itself does not constitute a complete "assessment", which is a broad process. Adequate visits are also important as part of the monitoring of progress, performance and effectiveness of assistance operations (the UNDMT has to be vigilant in preventing "humanitarian tourism").

Each field visit needs specific, pre-defined objectives and is planned to ensure that the visiting team meets those objectives without wasting the time of all concerned (including the disaster victims, relief workers and local officials). When possible the initiative should be taken to arrange joint visits by UN personnel with government personnel and personnel of other organisations involved in the response.

Overflights (aerial missions) can be valuable in the immediate aftermath of a disaster, an earthquake or a flood for example, to determine the extent of the area affected and gain an impression for the relative intensity of the impact in different areas. But to produce useful information, they must be carried out by experienced professionals who know the area and are equipped with appropriate tools.

Requirements and Appeals for International Assistance

The UN Resident Co-ordinator will need to discuss the situation with the responsible government authorities and determine whether:

- There are any unmet needs
- Any international assistance is required
- If these needs should be announced at the international level

A verbal request from the Government is sufficient in the

first instance, but when the Government wants OCHA to disseminate a request or appeal, it should be confirmed rapidly in writing. Requests may be received from various bodies, for example: the Prime Minister's Office, the Ministry of Foreign Affairs, and the national disaster management authority, the Ministry of Health. Requests could be received from different government bodies. These should be crosschecked, in particular with any designated focal point for international emergency assistance.

OCHA needs to be quickly informed of the nature of the unmet needs, if international assistance is needed, the source and nature of the request, and whether it should be considered official or not.

Any request to an individual UN agency should be brought to the attention of the UNDMT. If a Government's mission in Geneva or New York approaches OCHA directly, or through the Secretary-General, the UN Resident Co-ordinator will be informed promptly.

When a Government does *not* want international assistance, or addresses specific requests to particular bilateral donors or international organisations but does not want to make any general international appeal, the UN Resident Co-ordinator should inform OCHA accordingly. This enables OCHA to reply to queries at the international level and inform interested donor governments and organisations.

In some instances, for political or cultural reasons, a Government may indicate that it "does not wish to make an international appeal, but would welcome offers of assistance." In such cases, the UN Resident Co-ordinator should nonetheless strive to define with the Government the specific types and quantities of assistance which would be valuable and those which would not be needed, and inform OCHA accordingly.

Formulating and Screening Requests for International Emergency Assistance

When international assistance is needed, the UN Resident Co-ordinator and the UNDMT should work with the Government in formulating an aid request or appeal which is based on an agreed assessment, and is as accurate and specific as possible. Within their spheres of competence, each UN agency should assist the Government to formulate relevant requests and review those that are received. This will be done in accordance with the standing instructions of the agency concerned. (An in dependent judgement should be formed on the priority needs for international assistance. In general, the only supplies and personnel which should be sought from the outside are the ones which are not available in the country.) Precise specifications must be provided for all supplies, services, and personnel required; otherwise time will be lost or inappropriate supplies or personnel will be provided.

The UN Resident Co-ordinator and the UNDMT should carefully review all requests received, before communicating them to OCHA or to local donor representatives. Where necessary:

- Relationships between different requests should be clarified with the responsible authorities, and specifications, priorities, quantities and required delivery schedules should be reviewed and refined
- Vague, exaggerated or even underestimated requests should be advised against, as skeptical donors may be discouraged from responding or an oversupply of certain relief goods and personnel may result
- Initiatives can be taken to help bring together separate government bodies having overlapping or closely-related interests (in particular, the Ministry of Foreign Affairs and the operational departments) to ensure co-ordination and consistency in their separate proposals and requests

On a continuing basis, UN Resident Co-ordinator and the UNDMT should review with the Government available information concerning pledges and scheduled deliveries and up-to-date statements of unmet needs. This implies keeping track of contributions delivered, expected schedules for the delivery of additional confirmed pledges and any changes in the assessed needs.

There should also be ongoing consultation with the Government as to whether and when announcements should be made by OCHA at the international level concerning unmet needs and those that have been satisfied.

Funding, Programming and Appeals in Complex Emergencies

An effective and well co-ordinated response to complex emergencies depends heavily on the ability of the international community to raise the necessary resources. For specific complex emergencies OCHA solicits donor support mainly through the **Consolidated Appeals Process (CAP)** that encompasses the emergency relief requirements of all relevant operational agencies, and to a much lesser extent through the Central Emergency Revolving Fund (CERF).

The CAP is based on an overall strategy that enables the UN system to set clear goals and define priorities in a given country and provides a framework for joint programming, common prioritisation and joint resource mobilisation. The CAP provides a framework for humanitarian organizations—including UN agencies, international organisations and NGOs—to prepare appeals and to monitor the receipt and use of contributions. The CAP also provides a framework for the **Common Humanitarian Action Plan (CHAP),** which is a collaborative effort between UN agency field offices and their headquarters, as well as between agencies and OCHA in the field (for which the primary responsibility lies with the Resident/Humanitarian Co-ordinator).

The CHAP is a co-ordinated programme of interventions based on an agreed strategy designed to achieve shared goals. This strategy is made through common analysis of the political economic and security constraints; analysis of projected humanitarian needs both in the short and longer term, based on sectors, identifying any potential gaps; analysis of the competencies and capacity of the humanitarian community;

and a statement of the sectoral goals and objectives of the humanitarian community. The strategy also includes a common analysis of how the transition will be made from relief activities to reconstruction, rehabilitation and development activities carried out by development agencies. Prioritisation of needs is essential in the CHAP. An updated CHAP becomes the starting point for the actual Consolidated Inter-Agency Appeal document.

The Consolidated Inter-Agency Appeal itself derives from the CHAP and is normally launched on a yearly basis. The in-country team usually prepares the CAP with external assistance if necessary.

In the case of an unusually urgent situation, it may sometimes become necessary to launch "Flash" or Interim Appeals to generate emergency funds, prior to the finalisation of a consolidated inter-agency appeal. These are prepared over the course of a few weeks and usually cover emergency requirements for only a few months.

In order to support urgent funding needs of agencies and organisations in country, the Resident/Humanitarian Co-ordinator, on the advice of the assessment missions (among others), may request that funds from the **Central Emergency Revolving Fund (CERF)** be used.

The CERF is a cash-flow mechanism, under the authority of the Emergency Relief Co-ordinator and administered at the New York headquarters, to enable an immediate response to an emergency. The CERF is used primarily as a funding mechanism by UN operational agencies. The CERF may be used at the very outset of a crisis and, in exceptional cases, during later phases to assist agencies with cash-flow problems before donor contributions are available. The mechanism requires that agencies borrowing from the fund reimburse the amount loaned within a specific target period, not to exceed one year.

Donors are free to channel their response to the various organisations in accordance with their own wishes. In many cases, donors allocate resources for specific activities and channel their contributions directly to the agencies concerned.

Reporting and International Information Dissemination

Alert Message and Field Sitreps

To help ensure a timely, appropriate and co-ordinated international response, the UN Resident Coordinator needs to report rapidly to OCHA any disaster occurrence, with an early assessment of damage and needs, however tentative. Regular and systematic reporting of increasing detail in field Sitreps should then follow up such an alert message.

The first field SITREP should be sent as quickly as possible—at least within 24 hours after the disaster occurrence. It should include whatever relevant information is available and not be delayed because certain information is lacking.

Field Sitreps should be sent regularly and often—possibly daily during the initial emergency period. The basic format to be followed is given in the Annex to Part 1 of this module.

The UNDMT needs to be involved in the preparation of the Sitreps to help ensure comprehensive reporting and unified UN system presentation to the Government and to the international community.

OCHA Sitreps

Situation Reports are issued by OCHA when the Government of a disaster-affected country has requested OCHA to launch an international appeal for relief assistance. These reports are based largely on information provided by the UN Resident Co-ordinators but also include and take account of information and appeals received in Geneva from other sources. In the immediate aftermath of a disaster, frequent sitreps are issued from Geneva, providing the international community with the best possible information, as it becomes available. As necessary and feasible, OCHA crosschecks the information with the headquarters of the other UN agencies and donors.

The reports are sent directly to the capitals of the main donor countries and the headquarters of the UN agencies, inter-governmental organisations (e.g. EEC) and major NGOs, as well at the New York and Geneva missions to the UN of the stricken country. They are typically distributed to over a hundred addressees involved in making decisions in providing international disaster relief and related assistance.

Depending on the quality and timeliness of the information available to OCHA, these sitreps can be of vital importance in mobilising international resources and ensuring that those are resources allocated to the priority sectors and activities. The UN Resident Co-ordinator and the UDMT should see to it that copies of the OCHA sitreps are distributed rapidly to Government focal points concerned, the local representatives of donors and of the major NGOs, and other UN agencies. The sitreps can be complemented with useful information available locally, such as actual deliveries of assistance.

Co-ordination of sitreps should be consistent with those issued by the UNDMT, the Government Team as well as with sitreps issued by IFRC, ICRC and others.

Co-Ordination, Information Management and Resource Mobilization

This section describes what the UN Resident Co-ordinator and the UNDMT should do in relation to co-ordination and information management at the national level, and in working with donor representatives to mobilised resources.

The Importance of Co-ordination and Information

Co-ordination is critically important in emergency assistance operations; lives may be at risk, logistic and other resources are likely to be limited, and decisions are made quickly. There are many possibilities for duplicating effort, wasting resources, and leaving gaps in both geographic and sectoral coverage.

Timely, reliable information is crucial to planning and implementing emergency and post-disaster assistance operations, and to mobilising national and international resources. The regular dissemination of relevant information is a precondition for effective co-ordination and co-operation—

at national and local levels—between sectors and between Government, operational agencies, and donors.

Verifiable information must be collected, analysed, interpreted, and used to make informed planning and operational management decisions. Detailed, up-to-date information is required on both the situation and the needs arising. The progress and status of assistance operations must be monitored, as must the resources (both on hand and expected). Similar information in summary form is necessary to support efforts to mobilise and direct the allocation of resources and encourage operational co-ordination. This includes identifying information gaps and unmet needs for assistance.

National level co-ordination and information management are key roles and, in the first instance, the responsibility of the national authorities. In many cases there will be constraints to effective coordination and information management. To some extent these can be anticipated and reduced as part of operational preparedness or during response, possibly with the support of international counterparts, notably the UNDMT.

Tracking Needs, Pledges, and Contributions

The dissemination and exchange of information on international assistance needs and provision is an area in which the UN system and OCHA have a responsibility towards the international community. The UNDMT and OCHA must work in tandem to maintain a common database and ensure that information issued internationally and locally is accurate and up-to-date, so that donors, assistance organisations, and the Government can make sound decisions.

The UN Resident Co-ordinator and the UNDMT need to:

- Actively seek information from the Government, local donor representatives, and other appropriate sources concerning details of the types of supplies and services needed, where and when they are needed, what has been pledged, what has been delivered, and when further deliveries are expected

- Tabulate and continuously up-date this information, taking care to avoid double counting. The information will need to be cross-checked locally and with OCHA
- Keep OCHA informed of the evolving situation, of new information or changes in previous information, and of current unmet needs
- Provide government authorities, local donor representatives, and NGOs with regular summaries of international assistance data, and copies of OCHA sitreps immediately on receipt—complemented with information available locally on what has actually been delivered
- On the basis of the data on needs and contributions for international assistance, and in concert with the Government and OCHA, potential donors should be followed up with locally to secure contributions to cover unmet needs

The UNDMT should keep its records up to date on the nature, quantities, means of transport, and expected arrival times of contributions of which it is informed, so that to the extent possible, at the national and international levels, all have and work on the basis of the same information.

Resource Mobilization; Working with Donor Representatives

The resource mobilisation efforts of OCHA and the headquarters of other agencies at the international level need to be complemented by efforts at country level. On the basis of data on needs and contributions for international assistance, and in consultation with the Government, there needs to be follow-up locally with potential donors to secure contributions to cover unmet needs. These efforts would focus on the embassies and aid office of donor countries and visiting missions from those countries. (In some cases the local representatives of donor governments and other funding organisations have direct authority over certain resources. They also influence in varying degrees, the decisions taken in their home capitals concerning the allocation of resources from emergency and other aid budgets.

At the international level, OCHA informs potential donors and agencies of the status of needs and contributions through its sitreps, and seeks to mobilise contributions to meet priority unmet needs through direct contacts and consultations. In turn donors are asked to keep OCHA advised of pledges and contributions.

At the national level, the UN Resident Co-ordinator provides the same information to local representatives of the international community and to the Government. This information must be up-dated and completed with information available locally on assistance actually delivered. In some cases a Government will ask the UN Resident Co-ordinator and the UNDMT to track international needs and contributions on its behalf, or perform this function in a support or complimentary role to the Government's own tracking efforts.

To be effective, these country-level resource mobilisation efforts require that credibility be established with the local donor community and the operational agencies. This requires a firm grasp of the whole emergency operation, involving:

- The preparation of detailed, well-argued appeal documents, supported by credible, confirmed information
- Sustained formal and informal contacts with local donor representatives and any special visiting missions to ensure that they are fully informed of the UNDMTs assessment of the situation, the unmet needs and the current priorities for international assistance
- Regular exchange of information with OCHA on the substance of discussions with donors and any indications of likely contributions

Joint field visits can be valuable to enable key national and international officials to obtain a firsthand appreciation of the scope and character of a disaster, demonstrate sympathy and acknowledge the priority needs for support.

These efforts need to be done in the context of a common overall strategy determined by the UN Resident Co-ordinator and UNDMT, and in support of the Government's own efforts. Potential donors will need to be kept informed of the status of assessments and of the preparation of proposals and requests for assistance by the Government and various agencies. Unsolicited contributions should be discouraged. In the case of an emergency situation of an extended duration, there will inevitably be a falling off of interest as time passes, and sensitisation and resource mobilisation efforts will have to be intensified during the later stages.

Office Organization and Responsibilities

To be able to provide effective and efficient support to the emergency assistance operation and, maybe, to the Government, the UNDMT and its facilities need to be well organised. This implies that there are clear definitions of responsibility within the UNDMT and between the various member agencies and clear lines of communications between them. Secretariat and other supporting services (especially information management and communications staff) will need to be ensured. Information systems (computerised and manual) need to be set up to record and keep track of needs pledges and deliveries of international assistance. Filing and display arrangements must be established from the outset to keep all information relating to the emergency situation in order and readily accessible. Procedures need to be put in place to ensure that all tasks are covered.

In the case of a major disaster, adequate office space must be set aside together with an office with dedicated office and communications equipment. This is especially important if the UN Resident Co-ordinator and UNDMT will assume significant information management and co-ordination functions. Generators for emergency power supplies and battery packs and surge protectors for computer equipment are necessary wherever electricity supplies are unreliable. Training should be provided to staff for specific tasks. In such cases a UNDMT information and co-ordination centre (along the lines of an operations room) should be set up from the start. The Centre should be equipped with maps and wall boards to display the locations of field operations, transport routes and bottlenecks, the status of in-country operations, and the external supply lines. Briefing materials should be readied for orientation or up dating of international staff and missions. A duty roster system should ensure that the centre is manned continuously through extended working days, at least in the initial phase.

COMMUNITY EMERGENCY RESPONSE TEAM (CERT)

The Community Emergency Response Team concept was developed and implemented by the Los Angeles City Fire Department (LAFD) in 1985. The Whittier Narrows earthquake in 1987 underscored the area-wide threat of a major disaster in California. Further, it confirmed the need for training civilians to meet their immediate needs. As a result, the LAFD created the Disaster Preparedness Division with the purpose of training citizens and private and government employees.

The training programme that LAFD initiated makes good sense and furthers the process of citizens understanding their responsibility in preparing for disaster. It also increases their ability to safely help themselves, their family and their neighbours. The Federal Emergency Management Agency (FEMA) recognizes the importance of preparing citizens. The Emergency Management Institute (EMI) and the National Fire Academy adopted and expanded the CERT materials believing them applicable to all hazards.

Some CERT sites:

British Columbia
Ontario CERV Programme
Los Angeles
USA Directory

Differences between CERT and SPAN

Community Emergency Response Teams (CERT)	*Strengthening Preparedness among Neighbours (SPAN)*
CERT has a broader scope than SPAN. It seeks to develop community response teams—community being comprised of many neighborhoods. When disaster occurs, these responders leave their own neighborhoods to report to a staging area and then respond to wherever in their "area" there is a need.	SPAN works directly with neighborhoods—typically 25 to 50 contiguous homes. The SPAN philosophy is that when disasters occur on your street, of necessity you and your neighbors become the emergency responders. SPAN's goal is to equip the neighborhood with the plan and procedure that will allow this response to occur—efficiently and effectively.
CERT requires 7 week of training—one night a week for 3 to 4 hours. This training is done by the Fire Dept. During each session participants are required to bring safety equipment (gloves, goggles, mask) and disaster supplies (bandages, flashlight, dressings) which will be used during the session. By doing this for each session, participants are building a disaster response kit of items that they will need during a disaster.	SPAN organizes the neighborhood into 6 response teams that take care of the basics: first aid, light search & rescue, a team to shut off leaking natural gas, a team to check on children and the elderly, communications, and damage assessment. These teams do not require much special training. Simple checklists guide their response activity. All that really is required is a willingness to participate. SPAN starts the organization process in one 90-minute meeting.
The community-based nature of CERT allows you to interact with a wider range of individuals in the community. It provides an umbrella organization offering the opportunity for members of various organizations to cross-train	SPAN's fundamental goal is to create stronger neighborhoods. The SPAN approach fosters getting to know those who live immediately around you. This programme uses disaster preparedness as the vehicle to get people talking to each other, knowing each other, trusting each other.

4

Disaster Mitigation, Reduction and Recovery

DISASTER MITIGATION

After reading Part Four and completing the exercises, you should know the basic concepts, aims and elements of disaster mitigation. You will be able to describe:

- The principle objectives of disaster mitigation
- Several available mitigation techniques
- How to consider disaster mitigation as a development theme
- How to appraise a country's capacity to implement disaster mitigation projects
- How to take hazards into account in project identification and formulation

Mitigation

Mitigation is one of the positive links between disasters and development. Agencies, communities, and individuals can use their development resources to reduce the risk of hazards through mitigation projects. They can also ensure that their other development initiatives contain components that militate against future disaster.

In its broadest usage, mitigation has become a collective term used to encompass all actions taken prior to the occurrence of a disaster (pro-disaster measures). This includes long-term risk reduction and preparedness measures.

Many individuals and institutions, however, apply a narrower definition to mitigation. They use mitigation to mean actions taken to reduce both human suffering and property loss resulting from extreme natural phenomena. The concept of mitigation accepts the fact that some hazard event may occur but tries to lessen the impact by improving the community's ability to absorb the impact with minimum damage or disruptive effect. More simply stated, for this group, mitigation is risk reduction.

Mitigation applies to a wide range of activities and protection measures that might be instigated: from the physical, like constructing stronger buildings or agricultural diversification, to the procedural, like standard techniques for incorporating hazard assessment in land-use planning.

In the 1990s, a major effort is underway to encourage the implementation of disaster mitigation techniques in development projects around the world. The General Assembly of the United Nations has adopted the decade of the 1990s as the international Decade for Natural Disaster Reduction. The aim is to make a significant reduction in the losses of life and material damage caused by disasters by the end of the decade.

Disasters have, until recently, been seen in much the same way as disease was in the early 19th century: unpredictable, unlucky and part of the everyday risk of living. Concentrations of people and rising population levels across the globe are increasing the risk of disasters and multiplying the consequences of natural hazards when they occur. However, the "epidemiology" of disasters—the systematic science of what happens in a disaster—shows that disasters are largely preventable. There are many ways to reduce the impact of a disaster and to mitigate the effects of a possible hazard, accident, or conflict.

Just like the fight against disease, the fight against disasters has to be fought by everyone together. It must involve public and private sector investment, changes in social attitudes and improvements in the practices of individuals.

Governments can use public investment to improve their countries' infrastructure and to promote a physical environment where a disaster is less likely to occur. Individuals must also learn how to act to protect themselves. Just as public health depends on personal hygiene, so public protection depends on personal safety.

The type of cooking stove an individual uses, and their awareness that a sudden earthquake could tip it over is more important in reducing the risk of a disastrous fire than having the community maintains a large fire brigade. The type of house individuals build and where they consider a suitable place to live affects the potential for disaster in a community more than large engineering projects to reduce flood risk, or landslide stabilization efforts or sophisticated typhoon warning systems.

Saving Life and Reducing Economic Disruption

The worst effects of any disaster are the deaths and injuries caused to the population. The scale of disasters and the number of people they are capable of killing is the primary justification for mitigation. Understanding the way that people are killed and injured in disasters is a prerequisite for reducing casualties.

Targeting Mitigation Where it has most Effect

Understanding how the occurrence of a natural hazard or an accident turns into a disaster enables us to forecast likely situations where a disaster is possible. For example, some buildings *(elements)* are more *vulnerable* to earthquakes *(hazard)* than others. Identifying these *elements most at risk,* can indicate priorities for mitigation.

The Menu of Mitigation Actions

The range of techniques that an authority might consider in order to assemble an appropriate package for disaster mitigation can be classified into:

- engineering

- spatial planning
- economic
- management and institutionalization
- societal
- conflict reduction

Engineering

Engineering measures are those that result in stronger individual structures that are more resistant to hazards. This is sometimes referred to as "hardening" facilities against hazard forces. Building codes are critical defensive measures for achieving stronger engineered structures. Training techniques to teach builders the practicalities of disaster resistant construction are now well understood and form part of the menu of mitigation actions available to the disaster planner.

Spatial Planning

Many hazards are localized with their likely effects confined to specific known areas. For example, floods affect flood plains, and landslides affect steep soft slopes. The effects can be greatly reduced if it is possible to avoid having hazardous areas used for settlements or as sites for important structures. Urban planning needs to integrate awareness of natural disaster risk mitigation into the normal procedures of planning a city. For populations displaced by hazards or conflict, opportunities to reduce their risk include the identification of safe zones for resettlement in areas with adequate security and resources to support displaced persons.

Economic

Economic development is key to disaster mitigation. A strong economy is the best protection against a future disaster. A strong economy means more money to spend on stronger buildings, safer sites, and larger financial reserves to cope with future losses. Mitigation measures can help a community reduce future economic losses. They can help members withstand losses and improve their recoverability after loss and measures that make it possible for communities to afford higher levels of safety are important elements of an overall mitigation programme. Economic activities which help a community which hosts displaced persons to absorb this population can militate against the development of serious social or political problems. Some aspects of economic planning are directly relevant to reducing disaster risk. *Diversification of* economic activity is an important economic principle. A single-industry economy is always more vulnerable than an economy made up of many different activities. The linkages between different sectors of an economy—the transportation of goods, the flow of information, and the labor market may be more vulnerable to disruption from a disaster than the physical infrastructure that is the means of production.

Management and Institutionalization of Disaster Mitigation

Disaster mitigation also requires certain organizational and procedural measures. The time scale over which a significant reduction can be achieved in the potential impact of a disaster is medium and long term. Changes in location planning, upgrading structures and changes in the characteristics of building stock are process that take decades. The objectives and policies that guide the mitigation processes have to be sustained over a number of years. They have to survive the changes in political administration that are likely to happen within that time, the changes in budgetary priorities and policies on other matters. The institutionalization of disaster mitigation means the acceptance of a consensus of opinion that efforts to reduce disaster risk are of continual importance.

Education, training and the development of professional expertise are necessary components of institutionalizing disaster mitigation.

Societal

The mitigation of disasters will only come about when there is a consensus that it is desirable. In many places, the individual hazards that threaten do not result in disasters, the steps that people can take to protect themselves are not known and the mandate of the community to have itself protected is not forthcoming. Mitigation planning should aim to develop a disaster "safety culture," one in which the general public is fully aware of potential hazards, chooses to protect itself as fully as possible and can readily support protective efforts made on its behalf.

Conflict Reduction

In the disasters and emergencies created by conflict, mitigation must include conflict reduction. Measures at conflict reduction must start with identifying and addressing the root causes of the conflict. Although negotiation will often be the primary tool of conflict reduction, the issues may arise over such causes as land tenure, employment, access to resources, and intolerance of ethnic or religious differences. These issues need to be anticipated through a form of early warning and defused before conflict erupts.

Classification of Mitigation Measures

Developing a mitigation strategy should include a structure to facilitate decision making. The following series of questions suggests such a structure.

- What risk is being reduced?
- To what level should the risk be reduced?
- What criteria are used to reduce the risk?
- Who decides what the criteria are?
- What is the political process to implement the measure?

Mitigation measures may be classified in several ways. The

following list of such classifications includes many categories which overlap in their implementation.

Active and Passive: For active measures, authorities promote desired actions by offering incentives. For passive measures, authorities prevent undesired actions by using controls and penalties.

Structural and Non-structural: Structural mitigation involves physical measures taken to reduce risk by erecting structures (such as dams). Non-structural measures are policies and practices of development whose implementation reduces the risks to development.

Short-term and Long-term: Short-term measures are those which dare taken rapidly and which have a short life or usefulness such as sand bag reinforcements of a dyke. Long-term measures may include a process that is itself long in implementation, consider an extended timeframe, and change public attitudes through education.

Restrictive and Incentive: Restrictive measures result in practices that promote safety by making some actions or development unlawful or prohibitively expensive. Incentive measures provide financial, legal or other advantages to promote activities which are also beneficial in terms of mitigation.

Sectoral Based Activities: Sectoral based activities start from the vantage point of a sector, such as agriculture, and ask: "within this sector, what can be done to reduce risk?" A response might be to introduce hazard resistant crops, or to diversify cropping patterns.

Timing for Mitigation

The risk reduction measures of mitigation are often placed in the pro-disaster time frame. In fact, the most opportune time to implement mitigation is in the period after a disaster. Public awareness of the problems posed by hazards is high and the political will to act may also be at its peak. This period probably will not last for more than two to three years before other development priorities take precedence.

UN ASSISTANCE TO DISASTER MITIGATION: INCLUDING RISK REDUCTION AND PREPAREDNESS IN THE UNDP COUNTRY PROGRAMME

This chapter focuses primarily on promoting disaster mitigation in the context of long-term development planning and programmes, in particular through the UNDP country programme and other projects funded through UNDRO. Mitigation measures must also be actively promoted in the context of post-disaster rehabilitation and reconstruction.

Disaster Mitigation as a Development Theme

Hazards are a part of the natural and human-made environment. Exposure to hazards and the risks of disastrous consequences must be considered in all development planning. They must certainly be considered by UNDP at an early stage of programme and project formulation and design.

An awareness of the relationship between disasters and development must be maintained in the UNDP country programme and project cycles. The needs and options for mitigation must be specifically addressed in:

- The continuing dialogue between UNDP, other UN agencies, the Government, and aid donors.
- The country programme cycle: in the preparation of the UNDP Advisory Note and the Administrator's Note, and in the country programme document, review and evaluation processes.
- The project cycle: in project identification, design and formulation, approval (PAC/A.C), implementation (PPER, TPR), and evaluation.

It is essential that government bodies responsible for development priorities and planning be fully aware of the impact of natural and man-made hazards on societies and economies. This itself may require certain institution-building initiatives during both the preparation and the implementation of the country programme.

The UN-DMT should review the priorities and possibilities for international assistance, especially in cases where technical assistance is anticipated in different sectors and different UN organizations or agencies and expected to be involved or provide financing.

The context for disaster mitigation efforts lies within the policy for UNDP and UNDRO as set forth in the following panel.

Panel2A/1

Disaster-related Policy Goals of UNDP and UNDRO

With the aim of ensuring that developing countries are fully aware of disaster risks and take advantage of the most effective techniques for disaster mitigation, UNDP and UNDRO seek to:

- Strengthen the ability of societies to avoid, or protect themselves, their property and means of livelihood, against the risks associated with natural and human-made hazards.
- Encourage the Integration of disaster risk reduction and preparedness measures in planning and budgetary processes related to development in all sectors.
- Build on local understanding and experience of disaster threats and coping mechanisms.
- Facilitate exchanges between disaster-prone countries of experience, knowledge and skills related to disaster management.
- Ensure that programmes and projects funded by UNDP contribute to lessening of risks, are not themselves subject to major risks and do not exacerbate the potential adverse effects of hazards.

Appraising Disaster Mitigation Needs, Policies, and Capacity

Almost all countries have established some institutional arrangements for the various aspects of disaster management. Many have instituted some risk reduction and/or disaster preparedness measures. Some countries are well-advanced, others less so. This national capacity for risk assessment, mitigation planning, and implementation will need to be determined, based on an appraisal of the Government's mitigation policies, strategies, and measures.

Appraisal is needed and must enable the resident representative to determine, with the Government:

- Whether technical assistance is required for hazard and risk assessments.
- The priority to assign to risk reduction and preparedness in the country programme.
- The extent to which risk reduction measures can be incorporated into projects being planned or undertaken in various sectors.
- The need for "freestanding" risk reduction and/or preparedness projects.

Informed judgments must be made concerning the likely hazard effects, the adequacy and cost-effectiveness of existing risk reduction and preparedness measures, and on the capacity of all concerned to act on these measures. Appendix 2B of the manual lists what to consider in this appraisal.

The appraisal will be the basis for the inclusion of disaster-related concerns in the UNDP Advisory Note and Administrator's Note, which draw on or address the issues listed in **panel 2B/1** of the manual. They may also refer to UNDP's policy with respect to reaching the objectives of the International Decade for Natural Disaster Reduction.

Sources of Information: Needs for Technical Expertise

The integration of all elements involved in risk assessment is a complex, multi disciplinary task. The resident representative, in collaboration with other members of the UN-DMT, should:

(a) Determine whether the relevant government ministries or other organizations have already compiled relevant risk assessment data, or whether they are capable of doing so.

(b) Review the available information, and identify any the gaps or inadequacies in the available information.

Panel 2B/1

Elements to be Explicitly Considered during the Early Stages of Country Programme Development

- The experience of recent disasters.
- The extent to which the relationship between hazards and socio-economic objectives is explicitly addressed in national development plan, sectoral or multi-sectoral studies.
- The effects of natural disasters on past development activities. Including those funded by UNDP through the country programme.
- Discussions in World Bank Consultative Group meetings, and UNDP-assisted Round Tables, that underscored the link between disaster and development.
- The options available for reducing overall socio-economic losses and setbacks to development by integrating risk reduction and preparedness measures into general development activities.
- Specific possibilities for reducing risks and enhancing national and local-level preparedness through technical assistance within sectoral programmes.
- The availability of national and international resources for mitigation.
- The possible usefulness of technical assistance to assess needs in disaster mitigation.
- The institutional arrangements for inter-sectoral co-ordination of disaster mitigation activities.

Where more data collection and analysis is required, resident representative and the UN-DMT should:

(a) Identify in-country and regional institutions that could be approached to gather and consolidate the required data.

(b) Encourage the Government to begin the required studies.

(c) Define requirements for technical assistance in data gathering and analysis, where needed.

Technical assistance from UNDRO should be requested as necessary.

The analysis should be undertaken before the Advisory Note is prepared, where possible. With Government and UNDP Headquarters consent, SPR funds maybe made available for this purpose if required.

The analysis and the consequent discussions with the government and other concerned agencies should lead to the definition of a strategy that addresses disaster-related issues in the country programme.

Project Identification and Formulation

Project identification and selection must take into account hazard-related risks and national mitigation policies and strategies. There are two contexts to consider:

(a) Possible interaction between proposed projects in all sectors, and known hazards in the project areas. The chief aim of such projects is improvement in the sector concerned. But because a project is in a known hazard area, it must:
   - Be protected from the hazard.
   - Not increase the vulnerability of the population to the hazard.
   - Not worsen the existing hazard or create a new one.

(b) Possible need for "freestanding" disaster mitigation projects to reduce the risk of disaster or enhance national preparedness. The chief aim of such projects is to improve some aspect of disaster management-for example to prepare national and local-level preparedness plans, or to equip and train officials and community leaders for effective disaster response.

Freestanding disaster mitigation projects aim at reducing the risk of disaster by reducing or eliminating the hazard or society's vulnerability to it, or by increasing the capacities of organizations, officials, and communities to prepare for and respond to the hazard. Such projects can be placed within one organizational sector, for example a Ministry of Health or Interior. However, the "Multi-sectoral" impact of disasters makes it more appropriate to place the project in more than one sector or under the domain of a lead entity responsible for coordinating multiple sectors.

Typical freestanding disaster mitigation projects are:

(a) Institution-building projects which strengthen the capacity of governmental institutions to incorporate disaster management considerations in the planning process, or to undertake risk assessment.
(b) Projects to prepare national or sub-national disaster preparedness plans, develop warning and response mechanisms, and ensure the necessary training.
(c) Projects to introduce or strengthen particular kinds of protective measures, such as controlling floods or introducing cyclone-or earthquake-resistant construction.
(d) Projects to strengthen famine early warning systems, and the links between these systems and disaster management bodies, in countries prone to drought, crop failure, and uncertain food supply.

Projects which have one or more aspects of disaster mitigation as their principal objective should normally be designed by-or at least be developed in consultation with-UNDRO.

Disaster Risk Appraisal of all Projects in Hazards

Projects whose activities are located in known hazardous areas must be appraised from a disaster risk perspective, regardless of their sectors or institutional framework. This is the same approach used to review projects from an environmental perspective, or from a women-in-development perspective. This applies to the reviews conducted at both field and headquarters levels. While it may be easy to see the necessity for incorporating risk reduction in a project involving the construction of infrastructure, it also applies to institution-building projects. For example, health personnel should be trained in how to deal with the aftermath of a disaster, and school teachers should be involved in organizing their communities' response to warnings.

Appraisals must consider whether the project and its outputs might be adversely affected by, and therefore need to be protected against, a hazard; whether it will increase the vulnerability of the population in the area, or worsen the existing hazard or create a new one.

The appraisal must determine whether adequate safeguards-possibly including specific risk reduction measures—are built into the project, and if not, what further steps should be taken to assure that they are.

The "Disasters and Development" (DAD) Project Review Form (Appendix 2B of the manual) should be completed and attached to the Project Document for use in project reviews and evaluations. The results of the appraisal should be reflected in sections D and J of the PFF, and B6 (f) and F of the Project Document.

If a project can make a significant contribution to risk reduction (directly or indirectly), this should be so noted in sections of both the PFF and the Project Document as a "problem to be addressed." This should also be noted as a project objective, and the corresponding outputs, activities and inputs are specified.

UNDRO should be invited to review and comment, from a risk perspective, on projects whose activities would be located in areas prone to sudden disasters (natural or technological).

Disaster Risk Reduction Planning Checklist

In order to appraise disaster mitigation needs, policies, and capacity, an informed judgement must be made concerning likely hazards and their effects, the adequacy and cost-effectiveness of existing risk reduction and preparedness measures, and the ability of all concerned to act on these measures. This checklist shows what to consider in this appraisal.

National Policies towards Disaster Risks and Development Planning

- Are hazard-related risks considered in development planning? Is there a policy for risk reduction: At national level? For specific disaster-prone areas?
- Are there institutional mechanisms to integrate risk concerns into development planning and ensure inter-sectoral co-ordination?
- If/when new human settlements are planned, are natural hazards and risk of disaster considered, and appropriate measures built into the planning?

Awareness and Analysis of Risks and Options

- What is the level of awareness of the hazard-related risks among officials in central planning and sectoral bodies?
- What impact have disasters (and all forms of hazard impacts) had on development efforts and on the situation of the most vulnerable groups in society?
- Have data on known hazards (natural and human-made) been analysed? Have hazard maps been prepared? Are the data and maps updated as hazard conditions change, or as new populations or economic activities move into the hazardous areas?
- Have the populations. Infrastructure, agricultural and industrial economic assets, essential services, and development programmes and investments at risk been fully identified?
- Have specific estimates been made of the likely social and economic effects of particular hazard impacts on the various elements at risk and on the society as a whole?
- What measures have been taken, or are planned, to reduce the risks? How effective are they? Have additional specific measures been identified as feasible options?
- Why have they not been adopted or implemented yet?

Institutional Arrangements for Disaster Management

- What arrangements exist at national level? Is there an entity in the national government with specific responsibility for all phases of disaster management? Is it adequately staffed, trained, and funded? Is it properly placed within the government structure?
- Are there specific entities at the regional, sub regional, and community levels specifically responsible for disaster management? Are they adequately staffed, trained, and funded?

Warning and Other Preparedness Measures

- Are mechanisms in place that can issue warnings of disaster threats to populations at risk? Are warnings given with sufficient lead time? Do they make clear the risks involved and the action to take?
- Are there established arrangements at local and national levels? Are all concerned aware of their responsibilities, the procedures to follow, and arrangements for coordination? Are these plans widely understood and regularly tested?
- Are there adequate communications systems including back-up systems, for use in disaster response?

Human Resources for Disaster Management

- Is there a training programme for disaster managers?
- Is there public information and education programme?

BESIDES RESPONSE: THE UNDMT'S IN THE CONTEXT OF DISASTER REDUCTION AND RECOVERY

Learning Objectives

After completing this part of the module you should be aware of:

- The linkages between disaster response and disaster reduction and recovery
- The relationship between the UNDMT and the mission of the UN Country Team to develop a broad policy and strategy framework for disaster reduction and recovery

Disaster Reduction and Recovery

When countries fail to factor hazard and vulnerability considerations into their development policies, strategies and plans, economic growth and social welfare become eroded by large-scale disaster loss, while increasing demands are made on national and international humanitarian assistance. The achievement of poverty alleviation, good governance and other sustainable development related goals becomes a mirage if rapidly accumulating disaster risk is not managed and reduced. In particular, when disaster risk considerations are not factored into recovery efforts following major catastrophes, countries invest in "reconstructing risk", rebuilding the conditions for future and worse disasters.

The mainstreaming of disaster reduction into development and post-disaster recovery is therefore an essential component of sustainable human development: a challenge, which must focus the efforts of all the key stakeholders, at the local, national, regional and international levels. In risk prone countries, the UN Country Team should be supporting national authorities to achieve a sustainable reduction in disaster occurrence and loss by factoring risk management and reduction considerations into both development as well as post disaster recovery on a permanent basis.

To do so the UN Country Teams should address three related objectives:

Mainstream Disaster Risk Considerations into All New Development: This means ensuring that appropriate policies, strategies, legislative systems and administrative structures are in place to ensure that disaster risk considerations are factored into all new development in a country. The outcome of such prospective disaster reduction would be that new development, in the public and private, formal and informal sectors explicitly considers disaster risk and includes measures to ensure risk management and reduction. Given projected increases in population and expansion of associated productive and social infrastructure over the coming decades, prospective disaster reduction is essential to avoid further accumulation of risk, worsening levels of disaster occurrence and loss and an increasing number of countries in crisis.

Militate against Loss of Life and Livelihoods in Disasters and Protect Development Gains: Due to extreme risk in many countries, disasters will continue to occur on a continuing basis for the foreseeable future. Increasing disaster occurrence and loss, therefore, is a predictable variable, which must be factored into planning and programming decisions in most developing countries. Reducing existing risk, through compensatory risk reduction is usually difficult and costly. It is necessary therefore to assist countries to strengthen their capacities to minimise loss and suffering when disasters do occur, through mechanisms such as the translation of early warning information into effective disaster preparedness planning and increased capacity of institutions for emergency management at all levels.

Ensure that Disaster Recovery Reduces Risks and Consolidates Sustainable Human Development: When major catastrophes destroy human settlements, infrastructure, productive and social capital, unique opportunities arise to substantially reduce future disaster risk. Political will and resource availability following major catastrophes makes the recovery phase a potentially unique, though transient, window of opportunity to strengthen disaster reduction capacities and to ensure that risk considerations are factored into all recovery and reconstruction activities. Usually, however, there is a significant "gap" in programming between relief and reconstruction, in which this window of opportunity and the momentum for change is lost. Political and economic expediency often undermine attempts to factor risk considerations into reconstruction. The UN Country Team must help countries to seize major disasters as points of inflection, when a new direction can be charted leading to reduced risks and increased sustainability. This in turn requires the development of innovative planning and financial mechanisms, which eliminate the "gap". Recent experiences in Mozambique show that this is not only desirable but also possible.

In this broader context of the work of the UN Country Teams, the mandate of the UNDMT in emergency management and disaster response should no longer be separated functionally and conceptually from development but should become integrated as a component of a broad and comprehensive framework of policies and strategies to manage and reduce disaster risks.

In particular the work of the UNDMT should integrate within the broader mandate of the UN Country Team. The extent to which the UN Country Team has engaged the issues surrounding disaster risk reduction as an ongoing, permanent activity in a country and has assisted countries in the development of a national disaster risk reduction strategy will condition the relevance, effectiveness and efficiency of the work of the UNDMT in responding to a disaster situation. When the UN Country Team has supported the building of capacities for disaster reduction, for example, the compilation of detailed, geo-referenced, up-to-date information on hazards, vulnerabilities and risks and capacities in a country, this information provides vital background information for disaster response. Similarly, when good relationships have been built up between the UN Country Team and the principal stakeholders involved in disaster reduction at the local and national levels, these relationships will facilitate enormously the work of the UNDMT. When early warning systems and disaster preparedness plans are in place at the local and national level, the more effective response to a disaster will be, both from the national authorities and the UN system. The response mechanisms developed by the UNDMT therefore should build on and be integrated with the broader national disaster reduction strategy developed with the assistance of the UN Country Team.

The foundations of sustainable post-disaster recovery and reconstruction are usually laid in the immediate aftermath of a major disaster, while emergency response activities are still on-going. At the local level in particular, decision-making regarding recovery and reconstruction usually begins in a question of hours following a disaster. Sustainable recovery plans should take advantage of the opportunity afforded by a major disaster to further all the goals and objectives set out in a national disaster risk reduction strategy. The UNDMT, therefore, needs to ensure that disaster response and emergency management activities take into account opportunities to reduce future risks. This may include factoring criteria on disaster risk reduction into decision-making on a range of issues, for example: the temporary resettlement of affected communities, support provided for temporary shelter and housing and the potential impact of emergency assistance on the recovery of local economies and livelihoods. At the same time, the experience of responding to a major disaster may galvanize support amongst communities and the local and national authorities for broader disaster reduction and recovery objectives.

The UNDMT, therefore, needs to work closely with the UN Resident Co-ordinator and UN Country Team so as to ensure that its plans and actions are closely integrated with the broader framework of disaster reduction and recovery. The UNDP Disaster Reduction and Recovery Cluster (DRRC) Mailing address: Palais des Nations, CH-1211, Geneva, Switzerland, telephone number: +41-22-917-8198, fax: +41-22-9178060, e-mail: erd.geneva@undp.org, Web: *www.undp.org/erd)* of the Bureau for Crisis Prevention and Recovery can provide guidance and assistance to UN Country Teams in the development of such frameworks.

Three other training manuals of the Disaster Management Training Programme: Disaster *Mitigation, Vulnerability and Risk Assessment and Building Capacities for Risk Reduction* deal with this broader framework and should be consulted by all those involved in UNDMT.

CRISIS PREVENTION AND RECOVERY IN UNDP

Welcome to the Crisis Prevention and Recovery website of UNDP. Our goal is to become a global centre of excellence on crisis prevention and recovery, through attracting the best professionals, providing knowledge and quality services, responding quickly and appropriately to country demands, and building effective partnerships.

Our Mandate

The February, 2001 UNDP Executive Board reaffirmed that crisis prevention and disaster mitigation should be integral parts of sustainable human development strategies.

UNDP helps countries prevent and recover from armed conflicts and natural disasters through advocacy, capacity building, conflict sensitive development, development of tools and methodologies, gender equality, knowledge networking, strategic planning and programming, and policy and standard setting.

Related Links

- Executive Board decision on role of UNDP in crisis and post-conflict situations (5 February, 2001)
- Role of UNDP in crisis and post-conflict situations-document prepared for the Executive Board—First regular session 2001

Speeches of the UNDP Administrator

- Statement by Kemal Dervis, UNDP Administrator, to the Executive Board of UNDP/UNFPA (19 June, 2006)
- Speech of Kemal Dervis, UNDP Administrator at the DPA-UNDP workshop on building national capacities for conflict prevention and transformation, Istanbul, 6-8 March, 2006

- Statement by Kemal Dervis, UNDP Administrator, to the Executive Board of UNDP/UNFPA (24 January, 2006)

UN's Key Documents on Crisis Prevention and Recovery

- Report of the UN Secretary General: Progress report on the prevention of armed conflict (18 July, 2006)
- Report of the UN Secretary General: In Larger Freedom: towards development, security and human rights for all (September, 2005)
- A more secure world: our shared responsibility—Report of the High Level Panel on Threats, Challenges and Change (2 December, 2004)
- Report of the UN Secretary General on the prevention of armed conflict (7 June, 2001)
- Report of the Panel on United Nations Peace Operations—Brahimi report (21 August, 2000)

Our Role

In 2001, the Executive Board of UNDP raised the profile of its work in crisis situations by creating the Bureau for Crisis Prevention and Recovery (BCPR) "to enhance UNDP's efforts for sustainable development, working with partners to reduce the incidence and impact of disasters and violent conflicts, and to establish the solid foundations for peace and recovery from crisis, thereby advancing the UN Millennium Development Goals on poverty reduction."

BCPR is the practice leader for crisis prevention and recovery within UNDP. BCPR provides expertise on crisis issues to UNDP country offices, regional bureaus, and headquarters. The work of the Bureau bridges the humanitarian phase of a post-crisis response and the long-term development phase following recovery. BCPR is also an advocate for crisis sensitivity, working to ensure that all UNDP's long-term development policies and programmes address the risks and opportunities related to disaster reduction and conflict prevention.

With a staff of 100, BCPR can only contribute to crisis prevention and recovery objectives in cooperation with other actors who are present on the ground. BCPR does not design and implement crisis programmes on its own. Instead, BCPR works closely with UNDP country offices, providing technical assistance, best practices, and financial resources in support of their prevention and recovery activities.

BCPR's Mission Statement

Core Purpose To Advance Peace and Development by Strengthening Capacities to Prevent and Recover from Crisis

Core Values

Respect & Commitment

- Integrity, commitment and respect for those with whom we work and for each other.
- Commitment to a rapid and effective response.
- Dedication to peace, human security, development and human rights.

Partnership

- Achievement of common objectives through partnership.

Excellence, Leadership, Innovation

- Excellence through knowledge, innovation and impact.
- Leadership in all we do.

Goals

For UNDP

To become a global center of excellence on crisis prevention and recovery, by attracting the best professionals, providing knowledge and quality services, responding quickly and appropriately to country-level demands, and building effective partnerships.

For BCPR

To transform UNDP into a global leader on crisis prevention and recovery.

Goals

The Bureau for Crisis Prevention and Recovery (BCPR) has developed a 2007-2011 strategy, which identifies two outcome areas: prevention and risk reduction, and recovery. Under these areas, BCPR has identified eight specific development outcomes to which UNDP contributes.

For each outcome, a set of corresponding outputs has been identified. They represent the core set of deliverables that BCPR will promote. Outputs are owned by UNDP country offices working with national partners.

Also included in the strategy are indicative activities that BCPR may undertake in order to support the identified outputs. Through the annual work-planning process and in consultation with country offices, the Regional Bureaus, and the Bureau for Development Policy, BCPR will determine its specific activities for the next five years.

Results

BCPR is developing a process for monitoring and evaluating the initiatives carried out under this strategy. In addition to assessing progress toward the outcomes and outputs that make up the strategy, the evaluation system will consider BCPR's effectiveness in supporting country offices, transparency and accountability in the use of donor funds, and efficiency and cost related to its operations and administration. BCPR will ensure that these indicators are consistent with the new UNDP 2008-2011 Medium Term Strategic Plan.

Currently, results achieved by UNDP in crisis prevention and recovery are captured in the Multi-Year Funding Framework (MYFF) Reports. The MYFF is the main strategic planning instrument for UNDP approved by its Executive Board every four years. MYFF reports are issued on an annual basis. To see recent MYFF reports and the current Framework:

- Multi-Year Funding Framework Report on UNDP's Performance and Results for 2005

- Multi-Year Funding Framework Report on UNDP's Performance and Results for 2004
- Second Multi-Year Funding Framework (2004-2007)

Our Partners

National Governments

National governments are UNDP's most important partners. UNDP supports national governments in achieving their development goals.

Civil Society Organizations

UNDP works closely with civil society organizations (CSOs) at all levels to promote the Millennium Development Goals and help people build a better life. As one example of its work with CSOs, UNDP launched a small grants programme to strengthen partnerships with civil society organizations in post-conflict countries, including Colombia, Liberia and Sri Lanka.

Regional Organizations

UNDP is engaged with regional organizations in a number of activities such as providing technical and financial assistance, and exchanging knowledge and best practices on crisis prevention and recovery. For instance, UNDP collaborates with the Organization of American States and other partners on the publication and dissemination of a Handbook for Dialogue Practitioners. Another example is the partnership between UNDP and the Economic Community of West African States (ECOWAS) to reduce the availability of small arms and light weapons in the West African region.

Bilateral Partners

In addition to providing financial assistance through UNDP's Thematic Trust Fund for Crisis Prevention and Recovery (CPR TTF), bilateral donors are important policy partners. UNDP actively collaborates with donors on a bilateral basis and in donor forums like the Organization for Economic Cooperation and Development/Development Assistance Committee (OECD-DAC).

UN Agencies

UNDP works with a wide range of UN agencies to address disaster and violent conflict issues. These agencies include, among others, the UN Development Group (UNDG), UNICEF, UNIFEM, UN Fund for Population Activities, the World Health Organization, the World Food Programme, UNHABITAT, the High Commission for Refugees, the International Labor Organization, the Office of the High Commissioner for Human Rights, and the Food and Agriculture Organization.

UN Departments

In collaboration with the Department for Political Affairs and the Department of Economic and Social Affairs, UNDP partners with national actors to build capacity for conflict prevention. In the context of peacekeeping missions, UNDP works with the Department of Peace-keeping Operations and others to develop peace-building strategies; plan and implement peace operations; and set UN standards for disarmament, demobilization and reintegration.

Inter-Agency Cooperation

UNDP is vice chair of the provisional International Strategy for Disaster Reduction Management Oversight Board. The ISDR is an initiative of UN and non-UN stakeholders including the World Bank, World Meteorological Organization, International Federation of Red Cross and Red Crescent, the United Nations Environment Programme and the Prevention Consortium. Its main objectives are to increase public awareness to understand risk, vulnerability and disaster reduction globally and to obtain commitment from public authorities to implement disaster reduction policies and actions.

UNDP is actively involved in the Inter-Agency Standing Committee on Humanitarian Affairs and is leading the work on Early Recovery within the new cluster response system.

UNDP's Bureau for Crisis Prevention and Recovery hosts the secretariat for the Inter-departmental Framework for Coordination (Framework Team), the UN's only internal mechanism for addressing long-term and early conflict prevention issues.

Additionally, UNDP assists in the coordinated UN effort to combat avian influenza. (For more information, visit the UNDG's page or WHO's page on avian influenza.)

UNDP seeks opportunities to work with new institutions and mechanisms as they develop. Recent examples include the Peace Building Commission, the Peace Building Support Office and the Peace Building Fund.

World Bank

One of UNDP's key partners is the World Bank. UNDP is actively engaged on a number of issues with the World Bank, including planning and assessment tools such as post-conflict needs assessments, transitional results matrices, and transitional plans. Other joint initiatives concentrate on peace building, repatriation, reintegration, rehabilitation, reconstruction, and the disarmament, demobilization and reintegration of ex-combatants. Recent collaboration is exploring access to aid, best practices in post-conflict state-building, and expedited loans for crisis countries. UNDP and the World Bank also collaborate in post-disaster situations, such as conducting damage and needs assessments.

Prevention and Risk Reduction

Conflict Prevention

UNDP helps address the structural causes of violent conflict through development programmes that promote participation, dispute resolution and gender equality. By integrating a conflict sensitive approach, development programmes can 'facilitate the creation of opportunities and the political, economic and social spaces within which indigenous actors can identify, develop and use the resources necessary to build a peaceful, equitable and just society' (Secretary General's Report on the Prevention of Armed Conflict, UN, 2001).

Armed Violence Prevention

Armed violence can be defined as the use of armed force (usually with weapons) to achieve specific political, social and economic goals. UNDP supports armed violence prevention by focusing on both structural factors (socio-economic inequalities, weak governance systems) and the weapons themselves. UNDP's support for armed violence reduction focuses on both long- and short-term measures, as part of a broader public security approach.

Natural Disaster Risk Reduction

UNDP supports disaster-prone countries in the development of legislative frameworks, operational systems and coordination mechanisms to ensure the integration of risk reduction into human development. UNDP is also engaged at the local, national, regional and global levels in building capacities for assessing natural disaster risks and for developing appropriate plans and programmes.

Recovery

Following disasters and armed conflict, UNDP assists national governments and communities to lay the foundation for sustainable development. UNDP's expertise and resources focus on:

Early Recovery

Recovery focuses on restoring the capacity of national

institutions and communities after a crisis. Early Recovery is recovery that begins in a humanitarian relief setting immediately following a natural disaster or armed conflict. Guided by development principles, the early recovery phase aims to generate self-sustaining, nationally-owned processes to stabilize human security and address underlying risks that contributed to the crisis.

Economic Recovery

Natural disasters and conflicts destroy homes, businesses, markets and communities. Wide socioeconomic discrepancies, marginalization of groups or regions, and competition over natural resources are often the catalysts of conflict.

Recovering from Natural Disasters

UNDP supports countries in damage assessments, strategic planning, programme design and implementation to ensure sound recovery interventions which integrate risk reduction approaches.

Security

Security is necessary for recovery and long-term development. Restoration occurs through very specific programmes such as de-mining of farms and fields, the reduced availability of small arms, and the disarmament, demobilization and reintegration of former combatants. The reinstitution of an effective, transparent and accountable police and corrections system is crucial to safety and security.

Social Cohesion and Reconciliation

Countries in post-crisis recovery must repair the damaged social fabric. Transitional justice mechanisms are an initial step to restoration of citizens' faith in a justice system and rule of law. Prosecution of crimes perpetuated against women can help women recover. The reintegration of internally displaced populations and ex-combatants contribute to reconciliation of the communities.

Transitional Governance

In the immediate aftermath of a crisis, interventions to regenerate national ownership are key. Assisting national stakeholders to gain control of their recovery process is paramount.

How We Do It

Advocacy and Awareness Raising

UNDP raises the visibility of crisis prevention and recovery issues by participating in policy fora at national, regional and international levels. In conjunction with national counterparts, UNDP develops specific programmes in armed violence prevention, mine action, natural disaster risk reduction, and small arms and light weapons control.

Capacity Development

"Capacity" is the ability of individuals, organizations and societies to perform functions, solve problems, and set and achieve goals. UNDP contributes to Capacity development related to reducing the risk of crisis and establishing solid foundations for recovery. See examples in conflict prevention, natural disaster risk reduction and recovery.

Conflict and Risk-Sensitive Development

UNDP develops tools and methodologies for risk analysis, strategic planning and risk sensitive programming for UNDP country offices and national counterparts. In this way, all of UNDPs' development activities benefit from its experience preventing conflict, and reducing the risk of natural disasters. For more information, go to conflict prevention, natural disaster risk reduction or transitional governance.

Gender Equality

UNDP promotes gender equality through gender mainstreaming. Gender mainstreaming is defined by the United Nations Economic and Social Council as "a strategy for making women's as well as men's concerns and experiences an integral dimension of...the policies and programmes in all political, economic and societal spheres so that women and men benefit equally and inequality is not perpetuated."

Knowledge Networking and Good Practices

Knowledge networking helps to connect people through comparative experiences, best practices and expertise. UNDP ensures that its network of country offices, governments and other development partners share knowledge for solving urgent development challenges.

Linking Strategic Planning to Implementation

UNDP provides methodologies and tools to national actors to analyze post-crisis situations, identify priorities, and design adequate programmes. These tools are developed with UN departments, agencies and partners. Examples include post-natural disaster needs assessments and post-conflict needs assessments.

Promoting Consensus Building and Dialogue

UNDP supports participatory and inclusive processes to build trust among conflicting parties, leading to greater agreement on development issues and plans for change. For more information, go to sections on conflict prevention and transitional justice.

Supporting Community-based Approaches

UNDP's approach to reintegration of internally displaced persons, refugees, or ex-combatants and their families focuses on the receiving communities rather than on individual beneficiary groups. Developing programmes that address the needs of the receiving communities is instrumental in establishing the social, economic and human foundations for sustainable recovery and peace building. For more information, see the section on community-based reintegration.

New Initiatives and Special Programmes

CADRI | GRIP | Mainstreaming Disaster Risk Reduction in Africa | Small Grants Programme for Civil Society | Statebuilding | SURGE Project | Urban Risk | Youth and Violent Conflict.

Capacity for Disaster Reduction Initiative (CADRI)

CADRI functions as a knowledge resource and repository for disaster risk reduction capacity development activities to advance thinking, learning and exchange on this issue. This initiative is developing tools for enhancing and sustaining country level capacities. It also seeks to facilitate multi-stakeholder consensus-building processes to agree on priorities for disaster risk reduction.

For more information on the initiative please contact Joanne Burke at mailto:fenella.frost@undp.org

Global Risk Identification Programme (GRIP)

Following the priorities identified in the Hyogo Framework for Action endorsed by governments at the 2005 World Conference on Disaster Reduction. UNDP is launching a new global project. This five-year programme will support national partners in high-risk countries identify the factors that cause natural disasters. Building upon decades of experience, the Global Risk Identification Programme (GRIP) formalizes collaboration among major actors in the area of risk and loss information.

The GRIP consists of five components:

1. capacity development,

2. improved data on global disaster loss,
3. disaster risk analyses in high risk areas through pilot projects,
4. demonstrated use of information to manage risks, and
5. an update on disaster risk, which builds on UNDP's 2004 Global Report on Reducing Disaster Risk.

For more information on the initiative please contact Maxx Dilley at mailto:janthomas.hiemstra@undp.org

Mainstreaming Disaster Risk Reduction in Africa

UNDP is undertaking a global initiative to support country offices and their partners to more effectively integrate disaster risk reduction (DRR) into development at the national level.

Efforts to date have focused on producing guidance on how to integrate DRR into Common Country Assessments (CCA) and UN Development Assistance Frameworks (UNDAFs), and on supporting practical national level capacity development of UNDP, other UN agencies and government staff.

In Africa the initiative has already had substantial national level impacts:

(a) In Malawi, the initiative has supported the UN family to focus on disaster risk reduction in their new UNDAF as a key theme together with social protection. This support has also helped to kick-start discussion with the Malawi Ministry of Finance regarding how disaster risk reduction can provide a sustainable option to addressing the long term challenges of disaster related food insecurity.

(b) In Niger UNDP co-hosted with the government an inter-ministerial workshop on DRR mainstreaming. This resulted in clear recommendations on how to better integrate disaster risk reduction into that country's new Poverty Reduction Strategy Paper.

Future planned activities include:

(a) a new training programme to provide practical

guidance on the integration of disaster risk reduction into all aspects of UNDP and its partners work (policy, planning and programming);

(b) production of toolkit to support UNDP country offices dealing with disaster-conflict interface situations; and

(c) guidance on integration of disaster risk reduction into three of UNDP's practice areas (energy and environment; poverty reduction; and governance).

For more information on the initiative please contact Fenella Frost at fenella.frost@undp.org

Small Grants Programme for Civil Society

Since 2004, UNDP has sponsored on a small grants programme for civil society organizations in conflict and post-conflict situations. This initiative transforms UNDP's engagement with civil society organizations (CSOs) from a relationship of service provision to one of genuine partnership. The programme aimed to develop the capacity of CSOs to build peace through dialogue, recover democratic and civilian institutions, revitalize economies, and build sustainable partnerships with UNDP country offices. Experiences in three pilot countries, Sri Lanka, Liberia and Colombia were documented in "Experiences from the field: UNDP-CSO partnership for conflict prevention" published in 2005.

For more information on the initiative please contact Celine Moyroud at mailto:fenella.frost@undp.org

Statebuilding Initiative

As part of its work on transitional governance, UNDP has developed a two-year initiative on state building with various partners, including the World Bank and USAID. Statebuilding activities seek to ensure that states emerging from crisis are able to provide services effectively, maintain political stability and peace through inclusive and participatory political processes and are accountable to the populations.UNDP and its partners have scheduled a series of workshops and a regional conference on statebuilding to draw on the knowledge of leading reformers and expert practitioners. An evaluation of early state-building support in post-conflict environments is planned to focus on (re)establishing basic state structures and institutions. It will also provide recommendations on how to prioritize support in the first 30 days, six months and one year after a conflict.

Workshop report: Rebuilding post-conflict societies: lessons from a decade of global experience, UNDP/WB, 2005

For more information on the initiative please contact Zoe Keeler at mailto:fenella.frost@undp.org

SURGE Project: Strengthening Operational Capacity in Crisis Prevention and Recovery

In 2006, UNDP launched the 'SURGE' project to enhance its operational capacity to respond quickly and effectively in the recovery phase following a conflict or natural disaster. This initiative began with a workshop that brought together 40 practitioners from UNDP country offices in all five regions of the world. The workshop helped produce an action plan for the project for 2007. Three sets of inter-related outputs were identified: (a) Human Resources SURGE Capacity—establishing mechanisms to get the right people to the right place at the right time; (b) SURGE Standard Operating Procedures—refining the policies and systems governing UNDP's immediate crisis response; and (c) SURGE Toolkit—compilation of best practices, regulations and specific guidance for crisis countries.

For more information on the initiative please contact Janthomas Hiemstra at janthomas.hiemstra@undp.org

Urban Risk

This global initiative is a response to an ever-increasing need for city administrations to consistently factor risk reduction concerns into urban governance approaches and to regulate new construction and the expansion of urban centres in a manner that reduces risk. This initiative promotes urban risk assessments and supports municipal authorities in the strengthening of legislative frameworks and Disaster Risk Management Master Plans for high risk cities.

For more information on the initiative please contact Max Dilley at mailto:fenella.frost@undp.org

Youth and Violent Conflict

Identifying and including the specific needs of youth is essential to design effective responses for conflict prevention and peace building. UNDP has launched an initiative to better understand the interrelations between youth and violent conflict and published a report titled Youth and Violent Conflict: Society and Development in Crisis? In 2006. Based on the report's recommendations, UNDP is now codifying country experiences with youth-related programming to develop practical guidance.

For more information on the initiative please contact Valeria Izzi at mailto:fenella.frost@undp.org

5

Global Initiatives on Disaster Risk Reduction

PREAMBLE

1. The World Conference on Disaster Reduction was held from 18 to 22 January, 2005 in Kobe, Hyogo, Japan, and adopted the present Framework for Action 2005-2015: Building the Resilience of Nations and Communities to Disasters (here after referred to as the "Framework for Action"). The Conference provided a unique opportunity to promote a strategic and systematic approach to reducing vulnerabilities and risks to hazards. It underscored the need for, and identified ways of, building the resilience of nations and communities to disasters.

A. Challenges Posed by Disasters

2. Disaster loss is on the rise with grave consequences for the survival, dignity and livelihood of individuals, particularly the poor and hard-won development gains. Disaster risk is increasingly of global concern and its impact and actions in one region can have an impact on risks in another, and vice versa. This, compounded by increasing vulnerabilities related to changing demographic, technological and socio-economic conditions, unplanned urbanization, development within high-risk zones, under-development, environmental degradation, climate variability, climate

change, geological hazards, competition for scarce resources, and the impact of epidemics such as HIV/AIDS, points to a future where disasters could increasingly threaten the world's economy, and its population and the sustainable development of developing countries. In the past two decades, on average more than 200 million people have been affected every year by disasters.

3. Disaster risk arises when hazards interact with physical, social, economic and environmental vulnerabilities. Events of hydro meteorological origin constitute the large majority of disasters. Despite the growing understanding and acceptance of the importance of disaster risk reduction and increased disaster response capacities, disasters and in particular the management and reduction of risk continue to pose a global challenge.
4. There is now international acknowledgement that efforts to reduce disaster risks must be systematically integrated into policies, plans and programmes for sustainable development and poverty reduction, and supported through bilateral, regional and international cooperation, including partnerships. Sustainable development, poverty reduction, good governance and disaster risk reduction are mutually supportive objectives, and in order to meet the challenges ahead, accelerated efforts must be made to build the necessary capacities at the community and national levels to manage and reduce risk. Such an approach is to be recognized as an important element for the achievement of internationally agreed development goals, including those contained in the Millennium Declaration.
5. The importance of promoting disaster risk reduction efforts on the international and regional levels as well as the national and local levels has been recognized in the past few years in a number of key multilateral frameworks and declarations.

B. The Yokohama Strategy: Lessons Learned and Gaps Identified

6. *The Yokohama Strategy for a Safer World*: Guidelines for Natural Disaster Prevention, Preparedness and Mitigation and its Plan of Action ("Yokohama Strategy"), adopted in 1994, provides landmark guidance on reducing disaster risk and the impacts of disasters.
7. The review of progress made in implementing the Yokohama Strategy identifies major challenges for the coming years in ensuring more systematic action to address disaster risks in the context of sustainable development and in building resilience through enhanced national and local capabilities to manage and reduce risk.
8. The review stresses the importance of disaster risk reduction being underpinned by a more pro-active approach to informing, motivating and involving people in all aspects of disaster risk reduction in their own local communities. It also highlights the scarcity of resources allocated specifically from development budgets for the realization of risk reduction objectives, either at the national or the regional level or through international cooperation and financial mechanisms, while noting the significant potential to better exploit existing resources and established practices for more effective disaster risk reduction.
9. Specific gaps and challenges are identified in the following five main areas:
   (a) Governance: organizational, legal and policy frameworks;
   (b) Risk identification, assessment, monitoring and early warning;
   (c) Knowledge management and education;
   (d) Reducing underlying risk factors;
   (e) Preparedness for effective response and recovery.

These are the key areas for developing a relevant framework for action for the decade 2005-2015.

WORLD CONFERENCE ON DISASTER REDUCTION: OBJECTIVES, EXPECTED OUTCOME AND STRATEGIC GOALS

Objectives

10. The World Conference on Disaster Reduction was convened by decision of the General Assembly, with five specific objectives:
    (a) To conclude and report on the review of the Yokohama Strategy and its Plan of Action, with a view to updating the guiding framework on disaster reduction for the twenty-first century;
    (b) To identify specific activities aimed at ensuring the implementation of relevant provisions of the Johannesburg Plan of Implementation of the World Summit on Sustainable Development on vulnerability, risk assessment and disaster management;
    (c) To share good practices and lessons learned to further disaster reduction within the context of attaining sustainable development, and to identify gaps and challenges;
    (d) To increase awareness of the importance of disaster reduction policies, thereby facilitating and promoting the implementation of those policies;
    (e) To increase the reliability and availability of appropriate disaster-related information to the public and disaster management agencies in all regions, as set out in relevant provisions of the Johannesburg Plan of Implementation.

Expected Outcome

11. Taking these objectives into account, and drawing on the conclusions of the review of the Yokohama Strategy,

States and other actors participating at the World Conference on Disaster Reduction (hereinafter referred to as "the Conference") resolve to pursue the following expected outcome for the next 10 years:

The substantial reduction of disaster losses, in lives and in the social, economic and environmental assets of communities and countries.

The realization of this outcome will require the full commitment and involvement of all actors concerned, including governments, regional and international organizations and civil society including volunteers, the private sector and the scientific community.

Strategic Goals

12. To attain this expected outcome, the Conference resolves to adopt the following strategic goals:
    (a) The more effective integration of disaster risk considerations into sustainable development policies, planning and programming at all levels, with a special emphasis on disaster prevention, mitigation, preparedness and vulnerability reduction;
    (b) The development and strengthening of institutions, mechanisms and capacities at all levels, in particular at the community level, that can systematically contribute to building resilience to hazards;
    (c) The systematic incorporation of risk reduction approaches into the design and implementation of emergency preparedness, response and recovery programmes in the reconstruction of affected communities.

PRIORITIES FOR ACTION 2005-2015

General Considerations

13. In determining appropriate action to achieve the expected outcome and strategic goals, the Conference reaffirms that the following general considerations will be taken into account:
    (a) The Principles contained in the Yokohama Strategy retain their full relevance in the current context, which is characterized by increasing commitment to disaster reduction;
    (b) Taking into account the importance of international cooperation and partnerships, each State has the primary responsibility for its own sustainable development and for taking effective measures to reduce disaster risk, including for the protection of people on its territory, infrastructure and other national assets from the impact of disasters. At the same time, in the context of increasing global interdependence, concerted international cooperation and an enabling international environment are required to stimulate and contribute to developing the knowledge, capacities and motivation needed for disaster risk reduction at all levels;
    (c) An integrated, multi-hazard approach to disaster risk reduction should be factored into policies, planning and programming related to sustainable development, relief, rehabilitation, and recovery activities in post-disaster and post-conflict situations in disaster-prone countries;
    (d) A gender perspective should be integrated into all disaster risk management policies, plans and decision-making processes, including those related to risk assessment, early warning, information management, and education and training;
    (e) Cultural diversity, age, and vulnerable groups

should be taken into account when planning for disaster risk reduction, as appropriate;

(f) Both communities and local authorities should be empowered to manage and reduce disaster risk by having access to the necessary information, resources and authority to implement actions for disaster risk reduction;

(g) Disaster-prone developing countries, especially least developed countries and small island developing States, warrant particular attention in view of their higher vulnerability and risk levels, which often greatly exceed their capacity to respond to and recover from disasters;

(h) There is a need to enhance international and regional cooperation and assistance in the field of disaster risk reduction through, *inter aha:*

- The transfer of knowledge, technology and expertise to enhance capacity building for disaster risk reduction
- The sharing of research findings, lessons learned and best practices
- The compilation of information on disaster risk and impact for all scales of disasters in a way that can inform sustainable development and disaster risk reduction
- Appropriate support in order to enhance governance for disaster risk reduction, for awareness-raising initiatives and for capacity-development measures at all levels, in order to improve the disaster resilience of developing countries
- The full, speedy and effective implementation of the enhanced Heavily Indebted Poor Countries Initiative, taking into account the impact of disasters on the debt sustain ability of countries eligible for this programme
- Financial assistance to reduce existing risks and to avoid the generation of new risks

(i) The promotion of a culture of prevention, including through the mobilization of adequate resources for disaster risk reduction, is an investment for the future with substantial returns. Risk assessment and early warning systems are essential investments that protect and save lives, property and livelihoods, contribute to the sustain ability of development, and are far more cost-effective in strengthening coping mechanisms than is primary reliance on post-disaster response and recovery;

(j) There is also a need for proactive measures, bearing in mind that the phases of relief, rehabilitation and reconstruction following a disaster are windows of opportunity for the rebuilding of livelihoods and for the planning and reconstruction of physical and socio-economic structures, in a way that will build community resilience and reduce vulnerability to future disaster risks;

(k) Disaster risk reduction is across-cutting issue in the context of sustainable development and therefore an important element for the achievement of internationally agreed development goals, including those contained in the Millennium Declaration. In addition, every effort should be made to use humanitarian assistance in such a way that risks and future vulnerabilities will be lessened as much as possible.

Priorities for Action

14. Drawing on the conclusions of the review of the Yokohama Strategy, and on the basis of deliberations at the World Conference on Disaster Reduction and especially the agreed expected outcome and strategic goals, the Conference has adopted the following five priorities for action:

    1. Ensure that disaster risk reduction is a national and a local priority with a strong institutional basis for implementation.

2. Identify, assess and monitor disaster risks and enhance early warning.
3. Use knowledge, innovation and education to build a culture of safety and resilience at all levels.
4. Reduce the underlying risk factors.
5. Strengthen disaster preparedness for effective response at all levels.

15. In their approach to disaster risk reduction. States, regional and international organizations and other actors concerned should take into consideration the key activities listed under each of these five priorities and should implement them, as appropriate, to their own circumstances and capacities.

Ensure that Disaster Risk Reduction is a National and a Local Priority with a Strong Institutional Basis for Implementation

16. Countries that develop policy, legislative and institutional frameworks for disaster risk reduction and that are able to develop and track progress through specific and measurable indicators have greater capacity to manage risks and to achieve widespread consensus for, engagement in and compliance with disaster risk reduction measures across all sectors of society.

Key Activities

(i) National Institutional and Legislative Frameworks

(a) Support the creation and strengthening of national integrated disaster risk reduction mechanisms, such as multi sectoral national platforms, with designated responsibilities at the national through to the local levels to facilitate coordination across sectors. National platforms should also facilitate coordination across sectors, including by maintaining a broad based dialogue at national and regional levels for promoting awareness among the relevant sectors.

(b) Integrate risk reduction, as appropriate, into development policies and planning at all levels of government, including in poverty reduction strategies and sectors and multi sector policies and plans.

(c) Adopt, or modify where necessary, legislation to support disaster risk reduction, including regulations and mechanisms that encourage compliance and that promote incentives for undertaking risk reduction and mitigation activities.

(d) Recognize the importance and specificity of local risk patterns and trends; decentralize responsibilities and resources for disaster risk reduction to relevant sub-national or local authorities, as appropriate.

(ii) *Resources*

(e) Assess existing human resource capacities for disaster risk reduction \at all levels and develop capacity-building plans and programmes for meeting ongoing and future requirements.

(f) Allocate resources for the development and the implementation of disaster risk management policies, programmes, laws and regulations on disaster risk reduction in all relevant sectors and authorities at all levels of administrative and budgets on the basis of clearly prioritized actions.

(g) Governments should demonstrate the strong political determination required to promote and integrate disaster risk reduction into development programming.

(iii) *Community Participation*

(h) Promote community participation in disaster risk reduction through the adoption of specific policies, the promotion of networking, the strategic management of volunteer resources, the attribution of roles and responsibilities, and the delegation and provision of the necessary authority and resources.

Identify, Assess and Monitor Disaster Risks and Enhance Early Warning

17. The starting point for reducing disaster risk and for promoting a culture of disaster resilience lies in the knowledge of the hazards and the physical, social, economic and environmental vulnerabilities to disasters that most societies face, and of the ways in which hazards and vulnerabilities are changing in the short and long term, followed by action taken on the basis of that knowledge.

Key Activities

(i) *National and Local Risk Assessments*

(a) Develop, update periodically and widely disseminate risk maps and related information to decision-makers, the general public and communities at risk in an appropriate format.
(b) Develop systems of indicators of disaster risk and vulnerability at national and sub-national scales that will enable decision-makers to assess the impact of disasters on social, economic and environmental conditions and disseminate the results to decision-makers, the public and populations at risk.
(c) Record, analyse, summarize and disseminate statistical information on disaster occurrence, impacts and losses, on regular bases through international, regional, national and local mechanisms.

(ii) *Early Warning*

(d) Develop early warning systems that are people centered, in particular systems whose warnings are timely and understandable to those at risk, which take into account the demographic, gender, cultural and livelihood characteristics of the target audiences, including guidance on how to act upon warnings, and that support effective operations by disaster managers and other decision makers.

(e) Establish, periodically review, and maintain information systems as part of early warning systems with a view to ensuring that rapid and coordinated action is taken in cases of alert/emergency.

(f) Establish institutional capacities to ensure that early warning systems are well integrated into governmental policy and decision-making processes and emergency management systems at both the national and the local levels, and are subject to regular system testing and performance assessments.

(g) Implement the outcome of the Second International Conference on Early Warning held in Bonn, Germany, in 2003, including through the strengthening of coordination and cooperation among all relevant sectors and actors in the early warning chain in order to achieve fully effective early warning systems.

(h) Implement the outcome of the Mauritius Strategy for the further implementation of the Barbados Programme of Action for the sustainable development of small island developing States, including by establishing and strengthening effective early warning systems as well as other mitigation and response measures.

(iii) *Capacity*

(i) Support the development and sustain ability of the infrastructure and scientific, technological, technical and institutional capacities needed to research, observe, analyse, map and where possible forecast natural and related hazards, vulnerabilities and disaster impacts.

(j) Support the development and improvement of relevant databases and the promotion of full and open exchange and dissemination of data for assessment, monitoring and early warning purposes, as appropriate, at international, regional, national and local levels.

(k) Support the improvement of scientific and technical methods and capacities for risk assessment, monitoring and early warning, through research, partnerships, training and technical capacity-building. Promote the application *of in situ* and space-based earth observations, space technologies, remote sensing, geographic information systems, hazard modelling and prediction, weather and climate modelling and forecasting, communication tools and studies of the costs and benefits of risk assessment and early warning.

(1) Establish and strengthen the capacity to record, analyze, summarize, disseminate, and exchange statistical information and data on hazards mapping, disaster risks, impacts, and losses; support the development of common methodologies for risk assessment and monitoring.

(iv) *Regional and Emerging Risk's*

(m) Compile and standardize, as appropriate, statistical information and data on regional disaster risks, impacts and losses.

(n) Cooperate regionally and internationally, as appropriate, to assess and monitor regional and trans-boundary hazards, and exchange information and provide early warnings through appropriate arrangements, such as, *inter aha,* those relating to the management of river basins. (o) Research, analyse and report on long-term changes and emerging issues that might increase vulnerabilities and risks or the capacity of authorities and communities to respond to disasters.

Use Knowledge, Innovation and Education to Build a Culture of Safety and Resilience at All Levels

18. Disasters can be substantially reduced if people are well informed and motivated towards a culture of disaster prevention and resilience, which in turn requires the

collection, compilation and dissemination of relevant knowledge and information on hazards, vulnerabilities and capacities.

Key Activities

(i) *Information Management and Exchange*

(a) Provide easily understandable information on disaster risks and protection options, especially to citizens in high-risk areas, to encourage and enable people to take action to reduce risks and build resilience. The information should incorporate relevant traditional and indigenous knowledge and culture heritage and be tailored to different target audiences, taking into account cultural and social factors.
(b) Strengthen networks among disaster experts, managers and planners across sectors and between regions, and create or strengthen procedures for using available expertise when agencies and other important actors develop local risk reduction plans.
(c) Promote and improve dialogue and cooperation among scientific communities and practitioners working on disaster risk reduction, and encourage partnerships among stakeholders, including those working on the socioeconomic dimensions of disaster risk reduction.
(d) Promote the use, application and affordability of recent information, communication and space-based technologies and related services, as well as earth observations, to support disaster risk reduction, particularly for training and for the sharing and dissemination of information among different categories of users.
(e) In the medium term, develop local, national, regional and international user-friendly directories, inventories and national information-sharing systems and services for the exchange of information on good practices, cost-effective and easy-to-use disaster risk reduction

technologies, and lessons learned on policies, plans and measures for disaster risk reduction.

(f) Institutions dealing with urban development should provide information to the public on disaster reduction options prior to constructions, land purchase or land sale.

(g) Update and widely disseminate international standard terminology related to disaster risk reduction, at least in all official United Nations languages, for use in programme and institutional development, operations, research, training curricula and public information programmes.

(ii) *Education and Training*

(h) Promote the inclusion of disaster risk reduction knowledge in relevant sections of school curricula at all levels and the use of other formal and informal channels to reach youth and children with information; promote the integration of disaster risk reduction as an intrinsic element of the United Nations Decade of Education for Sustainable Development (2005-2015).

(i) Promote the implementation of local risk assessment and disaster preparedness programmes in schools and institutions of higher education.

(j) Promote the implementation of programmes and activities in schools for learning how to minimize the effects of hazards.

(k) Develop training and learning programmes in disaster risk reduction targeted at specific sectors (development planners, emergency managers, local government officials, etc.).

(1) Promote community-based training initiatives, considering the role of volunteers, as appropriate, to enhance local capacities to mitigate and cope with disasters.

(m) Ensure equal access to appropriate training and educational opportunities for women and vulnerable constituencies; promote gender and cultural sensitivity training as integral components of education and training for disaster risk reduction.

(iii) *Research*

(n) Develop improved methods for predictive multi-risk assessments and socioeconomic cost-benefit analysis of risk reduction actions at all levels; incorporate these methods into decision-making processes at regional, national and local levels.

(o) Strengthen the technical and scientific capacity to develop and apply methodologies, studies and models to assess vulnerabilities to and the impact of geological, weather, water and climate-related hazards, including the improvement of regional monitoring capacities and assessments.

(iv) *Public Awareness*

(p) Promote the engagement of the media in order to stimulate a culture of disaster resilience and strong community involvement in sustained public education campaigns and public consultations at all levels of society.

Reduce the Underlying Risk Factors

19. Disaster risks related to changing social, economic, environmental conditions and land use, and the impact of hazards associated with geological events, weather, water, climate variability and climate change is addressed in sector development planning and programmes as well as in post-disaster situations.

Key Activities

(i) Environmental and Natural Resource Management

(a) Encourage the sustainable use and management of ecosystems, including through better land-use planning and development activities to reduce risk and vulnerabilities.

(b) Implement integrated environmental and natural resource management approaches that incorporate disaster risk reduction, including structural and non-structural measures, such as integrated flood management and appropriate management of fragile ecosystems.

(c) Promote the integration of risk reduction associated with existing climate variability and future climate change into strategies for the reduction of disaster risk and adaptation to climate change, which would include the clear identification of climate-related disaster risks, the design of specific risk reduction measures and an improved and routine use of climate risk information by planners, engineers and other decision-makers.

(ii) Social and Economic Development Practices

(d) Promote food security as an important factor in ensuring the resilience of communities to hazards, particularly in areas prone to drought, flood, cyclones and other hazards that can weaken agriculture-based livelihoods.

(e) Integrate disaster risk reduction planning into the health sector; promote the goal of "hospitals safe from disaster" by ensuring that all new hospitals are built with a level of resilience that strengthens their capacity to remain functional in disaster situations and implement mitigation measures to reinforce existing health facilities, particularly those providing primary health care.

(f) Protect and strengthen critical public facilities and physical infrastructure, particularly schools, clinics, hospitals, water and power plants, communications and transport lifelines, disaster warning and management centres, and culturally important lands and structures through proper design, retrofitting and re-building, in order to render them adequately resilient to hazards.

(g) Strengthen the implementation of social safety—net mechanisms to assist the poor, the elderly and the disabled, and other populations affected by disasters. Enhance recovery schemes including psycho-social training programmes in order to mitigate the psychological damage of vulnerable populations, particularly children, in the aftermath of disasters.

(h) Incorporate disaster risk reduction measures into post-disaster recovery and rehabilitation processes and use opportunities during the recovery phase to develop capacities that reduce disaster risk in the long term, including through the sharing of expertise, knowledge and lessons learned.

(i) Endeavor to ensure, as appropriate, that programmes for displaced persons do not increase risk and vulnerability to hazards.

(j) Promote diversified income options for populations in high-risk areas to reduce their vulnerability to hazards, and ensure that their income and assets are not undermined by development policy and processes that increase their vulnerability to disasters.

(k) Promote the development of financial risk-sharing mechanisms, particularly insurance and reinsurance against disasters.

(1) Promote the establishment of public-private partnerships to better engage the private sector in disaster risk reduction activities; encourage the private sector to foster a culture of disaster prevention, putting greater emphasis on, and allocating resources to, pro-disaster activities such as risk assessments and early warning systems.

(m) Develop and promote alternative and innovative financial instruments for addressing disaster risk.

(iii) Land-use Planning and other Technical Measures

(n) Incorporate disaster risk assessments into the urban planning and management of disaster-prone human settlements, in particular highly populated areas and quickly urbanizing settlements. The issues of informal or non-permanent housing and the location of housing in high-risk areas should be addressed as priorities, including in the framework of urban poverty reduction and slum-upgrading programmes.

(o) Mainstream disaster risk considerations into planning procedures for major infrastructure projects, including the criteria for design, approval and implementation of such projects and considerations based on social, economic and environmental impact assessments.

(p) Develop, upgrade and encourage the use of guidelines and monitoring tools for the reduction of disaster risk in the context of land-use policy and planning.

(q) Incorporate disaster risk assessment into rural development planning and management, in particular with regard to mountain and coastal flood plain areas, including through the identification of land zones that are available and safe for human settlement,

(r) Encourage the revision of existing or the development of new building codes, standards, rehabilitation and reconstruction practices at the national or local levels, as appropriate, with the aim of making them more applicable in the local context, particularly in informal and marginal human settlements, and reinforce the capacity to implement, monitor and enforce such codes, through a consensus-based approach, with a view to fostering disaster-resistant structures.

Strengthen Disaster Preparedness for Effective Response at All Levels

20. At times of disaster, impacts and losses can be substantially reduced if authorities, individuals and

communities in hazard-prone areas are well prepared and ready to act and are equipped with the knowledge and capacities for effective disaster management.

Key Activities

(a) Strengthen policy, technical and institutional capacities in regional, national and local disaster management, including those related to technology, training, and human and material resources.
(b) Promote and support dialogue, exchange of information and coordination among early warning, disaster risk reduction, disaster response, development and other relevant agencies and institutions at all levels, with the aim of fostering a holistic approach towards disaster risk reduction.
(c) Strengthen and when necessary develop coordinated regional approaches, and create or upgrade regional policies, operational mechanisms, plans and communication systems to prepare for and ensure rapid and effective disaster response in situations that exceed national coping capacities.
(d) Prepare or review and periodically update disaster preparedness and contingency plans and policies at all levels, with a particular focus on the most vulnerable areas and groups. Promote regular disaster preparedness exercises, including evacuation drills, with a view to ensuring rapid and effective disaster response and access to essential food and non-food relief supplies, as appropriate, to local needs.
(e) Promote the establishment of emergency funds, where and as appropriate, to support response, recovery and preparedness measures.
(f) Develop specific mechanisms to engage the active participation and ownership of relevant stakeholders, including communities, in disaster risk reduction, in particular building on the spirit of volunteerism.

IMPLEMENTATION AND FOLLOW-UP

General Considerations

21. The implementation of and follow-up to the strategic goals and priorities for action set out in this Framework for Action should be addressed by different stakeholders in a multi-sectoral approach, including the development sector. States and regional and international organizations, including the United Nations and international financial institutions, are called upon to integrate disaster risk reduction considerations into their sustainable development policy, planning and programming at all levels. Civil society, including volunteers and community-based organizations, the scientific community and the private sector are vital stakeholders in supporting the implementation of disaster risk reduction at all levels.
22. While each State has primary responsibility for its own economic and social development, an enabling international environment is vital to stimulate and contribute to developing the knowledge, capacities and motivation needed to build disaster resilient nations and communities. States and regional and international organizations should foster greater strategic coordination among the United Nations, other international organizations, including international financial institutions, regional bodies, donor agencies and nongovernmental organizations engaged in disaster risk reduction, based on a strengthened International Strategy for Disaster Reduction. In the coming years, consideration should be given to ensuring the implementation and strengthening of relevant international legal instruments related to disaster risk reduction.
23. States and regional and international organizations should also support the capacities of regional mechanisms and organizations to develop regional plans, policies and common practices, as appropriate,

in support of networking, advocacy, coordination, exchange of information and experience, scientific monitoring of hazards and vulnerability, and institutional capacity development and to deal with disaster risks.

24. All actors are encouraged to build multi-stakeholder partnerships, at all levels, as appropriate, and on a voluntary basis, to contribute to the implementation of this Framework for Action. States and other actors are also encouraged to promote the strengthening or establishment of national, regional and international volunteer corps, which can be made available to countries and to the international community to contribute to addressing vulnerability and reducing disaster risk.

25. The Mauritius Strategy for the further implementation of the Barbados Programme of Action for Small Island Developing States underscores that small island developing States are located among the most vulnerable regions in the world in relation to the intensity and frequency of natural and environmental disasters and their increasing impact, and face disproportionately high economic, social and environmental consequences. Small island developing States have undertaken to strengthen their respective national frameworks for more effective disaster management and are committed, with the necessary support of the international community, to improve national disaster mitigation, preparedness and early-warning capacity, increase public awareness about disaster reduction, stimulate interdisciplinary and inter-sectoral partnerships, mainstream risk management into their national planning process, address issues relating to insurance and reinsurance arrangements, and augment their capacity to predict and respond to emergency situations, including those affecting human settlements stemming from natural and environmental disasters.

26. In view of the particular vulnerabilities and insufficient capacities of least developed countries to respond to and recover from disasters, support is needed by the least developed countries as a matter of priority, in executing substantive programmes and relevant institutional mechanisms for the implementation of the Framework for Action, including through financial and technical assistance and for capacity building in disaster risk reduction as an effective and sustainable means to prevent and respond to disasters.
27. Disasters in Africa pose a major obstacle to the African continent's efforts to achieve sustainable development, especially in view of the region's insufficient capacities to predict, monitor, deal with and mitigate disasters. Reducing the vulnerability of the African people to hazards is a necessary element of poverty reduction strategies, including efforts to protect past development gains. Financial and technical assistance is needed to strengthen the capacities of African countries, including observation and early warning systems, assessments, prevention, preparedness, response and recovery.
28. The follow-up on the World Conference on Disaster Reduction will, as appropriate, be an integrated and coordinated part of the follow-up to other major conference in fields relevant to disaster risk reduction. This should include specific reference to progress on disaster risk reduction taking, into account agreed development goals, including those found in the Millennium Declaration.
29. The implementation of this Framework for Action for the period 2005-2015 will be appropriately reviewed.

B. States

30. All States should endeavour to undertake the following tasks at the national and local levels, with a strong sense of ownership and in collaboration with civil society and

other stakeholders, within the bounds of their financial, human and material capacities, and taking into account their domestic legal requirements and existing international instruments related to disaster risk reduction. States should also contribute actively in the context of regional and international cooperation, in line with paragraphs 33 and 34.

(a) Prepare and publish national baseline assessments of the status of disaster risk reduction, according to the capabilities, needs and policies of each State, and, as appropriate, share this information with concerned regional and international bodies;

(b) Designate an appropriate national coordination mechanism for the implementation and follow up of this Framework for Action, and communicate the information to the secretariat of the International Strategy for Disaster Reduction;

(c) Publish and periodically update a summary of national programmes for disaster risk reduction related to this Framework for Action, including on international cooperation;

(d) Develop procedures for reviewing national progress against this Framework for Action, which should include systems for cost benefit analysis and ongoing monitoring and assessment of vulnerability and risk, in particular with regards to regions exposed to hydro metrological and seismic hazards, as appropriate;

(e) Include information on progress of disaster risk reduction in the reporting mechanisms of existing international and other frameworks concerning sustainable development, as appropriate;

(f) Consider, as appropriate, acceding to, approving or ratifying relevant international legal instruments relating to disaster reduction, and, for State parties to those instruments, take measures for their effective implementation;

(g) Promote the integration of risk reduction associated with existing climate variability and future climate change into strategies for the reduction of disaster risk and adaptation to climate change; ensure that the management of risks associated with geological hazards, such as earthquakes and landslides, are fully taken into account in disaster risk reduction programmes.

Regional Organizations and Institutions

31. Regional organizations with a role related to disaster risk reduction are called upon to undertake the following tasks within their mandates, priorities and resources:
(a) Promote regional programmes, including programmes for technical cooperation, capacity development, the development of methodologies and standards for hazard and vulnerability monitoring and assessment, the sharing of information and effective mobilization of resources, in view of supporting national and regional efforts to achieve the objectives of this Framework for Action;
(b) Undertake and publish regional and sub-regional baseline assessments of the disaster risk reduction status, according to the needs identified and in line with their mandates;
(c) Coordinate and publish periodic reviews on progress in the region and on impediments and support needs, and assist countries, as requested, in the preparation of periodic national summaries of their programmes and progress;
(d) Establish or strengthen existing specialized regional collaborative centers, as appropriate, to undertake research, training, education and capacity building in the field of disaster risk reduction;

(e) Support the development of regional mechanisms and capacities for early warning to disasters, including for tsunami.

International Organizations

32. International organizations, including organizations of the United Nations system and international financial institutions, are called upon to undertake the following tasks within their mandates, priorities and resources:

(a) Engage fully in supporting and implementing the International Strategy for Disaster Reduction, and cooperate to advance integrated approaches to building disaster-resilient nations and communities, by encouraging stronger linkages, coherence and integration of disaster risk reduction elements into the humanitarian and sustainable development fields as set out in this Framework for Action;

(b) Strengthen the overall capacity of the United Nations system to assist disaster-prone developing countries in disaster risk reduction through appropriate means and coordination and define and implement appropriate measures for regular assessment of their progress towards the achievement of the goals and priorities set out in this Framework for Action, building on the International Strategy for Disaster Reduction;

(c) Identify relevant actions to assist disaster-prone developing countries in the implementation of this Framework for Action; ensure that relevant actions are integrated, as appropriate, into each organization's own scientific, humanitarian and development sectors, policies, programmes and practices and that adequate funding is allocated for their implementation;

(d) Assist disaster-prone developing countries to set up national strategies and plans of action and programmes for disaster risk reduction and to develop their institutional and technical capacities in the field of disaster risk reduction, as identified through the priorities in this Framework for Action;

(e) Integrate actions in support of the implementation of this Framework into relevant coordination mechanisms such as the United Nations Development Group and the Inter-Agency Standing Committee (on humanitarian action), including at the national level and through the Resident Coordinator system and the United Nations Country teams. In addition, integrate disaster risk reduction considerations into development assistance frameworks, such as the Common Country Assessments, the United Nations Development Assistance Framework and poverty reduction strategies;

(f) In close collaboration with existing networks and platforms, cooperate to support globally consistent data collection and forecasting on natural hazards, vulnerabilities and risks and disaster impacts at all scales. These initiatives should include the development of standards, the maintenance of databases, the development of indicators and indices, support to early warning systems, the full and open exchange of data and the use *of situ* and remotely sensed observations;

(g) Support States with the provision of appropriate, timely and well coordinated international relief assistance, upon request of affected countries, and in accordance with agreed guiding principles for emergency relief assistance and coordination arrangements. Provide this assistance with a view to reducing risk and vulnerability, improving capacities and ensuring effective arrangements for international cooperation for urban search and rescue assistance. Ensure that arrangements for prompt international response to reach affected areas are being developed at national and local levels and that appropriate linkages to recovery efforts and risk reduction are strengthened;

(h) Strengthen the international mechanisms with a view to supporting disaster stricken States in the transition phase towards sustainable physical, social and economic recovery and to reducing future risks. This should include support for risk reduction activities in post-disaster recovery and rehabilitation processes and sharing of good practices, knowledge and technical support with relevant countries, experts and United Nations organizations;

(i) Strengthen and adapt the existing inter-agency disaster management training programme based on a shared, inter-agency strategic vision and framework for disaster risk management that encompasses risk reduction, preparedness, response and recovery.

The International Strategy for Disaster Reduction

33. The partners in the International Strategy for Disaster Reduction, in particular, the Inter-Agency Task Force on Disaster Reduction and its members, in collaboration with relevant national, regional, international and United Nations bodies and supported by the inter-agency secretariat for the International Strategy for Disaster Reduction, are requested to assist in implementing this Framework for Action as follows, subject to the decisions taken upon completion of the review process of the current mechanism and institutional arrangements:

(a) Develop a matrix of roles and initiatives in support of follow-up to this Framework for Action, involving individual members of the Task Force and other international partners;

(b) Facilitate the coordination of effective and

integrated action within the organizations of the United Nations system and among other relevant international and regional entities, in accordance with their respective mandates, to support the implementation of this Framework for Action, identify gaps in implementation and facilitate consultative processes to develop guidelines and policy tools for each priority area, with relevant national, regional and international expertise;

(c) Consult with relevant United Nations agencies and organizations, regional and multilateral organizations and technical and scientific institutions, as well as interested States and civil society, with the view to developing generic, realistic and measurable indicators, keeping in mind available resources of individual States. These indicators could assist States to assess their progress in the implementation of the Framework of Action. The indicators should be in conformity with the internationally agreed development goals, including those contained in the Millennium Declaration;

Once that first stage has been completed. States are encouraged to develop or refine indicators at the national level reflecting their individual disaster risk reduction priorities, drawing upon the generic indicators.

(d) Ensure support to national platforms for disaster reduction, including through the clear articulation of their role and value added, as well as regional coordination, to support the different advocacy and policy needs and priorities set out in this Framework for Action, through coordinated regional facilities for disaster reduction, building on regional programmes and outreach advisors from relevant partners;

(e) Coordinate with the secretariat of the Commission on Sustainable Development to ensure that relevant partnerships contributing to implementation of the

Framework for Action are registered in its sustainable development partnership database;

(f) Stimulate the exchange, compilation, analysis, summary and dissemination of best practices, lessons learned, available technologies and programmes, to support disaster risk reduction in its capacity as an international information clearinghouse; maintain a global information platform on disaster risk reduction and a web-based register "portfolio" of disaster risk reduction programmes and initiatives implemented by States and through regional and international partnerships;

(g) Prepare periodic reviews on progress towards achieving the objectives and priorities of this Framework for Action, within the context of the process of integrated and coordinated follow-up and implementation of United Nations conferences and summits as mandated by the General Assembly, and provide reports and summaries to the Assembly and other United Nations bodies, as requested or as appropriate, based on information from national platforms, regional and international organizations and other stakeholders, including on the follow-up to the implementation of the recommendations from the Second International Conference on Early Warning (2003).

Resource Mobilization

34. States, within the bounds of their financial capabilities, regional and international organizations, through appropriate multilateral, regional and bilateral coordination mechanisms, should undertake the following tasks to mobilize the necessary resources to support implementation of this Framework for Action:

(a) Mobilize the appropriate resources and capabilities of relevant national, regional and international bodies, including the United Nations system;

(b) Provide for and support, through bilateral and multilateral channels, the implementation of this Framework for Action in disaster-prone developing countries, including through financial and technical assistance, addressing debt sustain ability, technology transfer on mutually agreed terms, and public-private partnerships, and encourage North-South and South-South cooperation;

(c) Mainstream disaster risk reduction measures appropriately into multilateral and bilateral development assistance programmes including those related to poverty reduction, natural resource management, urban development and adaptation to climate change;

(d) Provide adequate voluntary financial contributions to the United Nations Trust Fund for Disaster Reduction, in the effort to ensure the adequate support for the follow-up activities to this Framework for Action. Review the current usage and feasibility for the expansion of this fund; *inter aha,* to assist disaster-prone developing countries to set up national strategies for disaster risk reduction.

(e) Develop partnerships to implement schemes that spread out risks, reduce insurance premiums, expand insurance coverage and thereby increase financing for post-disaster reconstruction and rehabilitation, including through public and private partnerships, as appropriate. Promote an environment that encourages a culture of insurance in developing countries, as appropriate.

ANNEXURE 1
SOME MULTILATERAL DEVELOPMENTS RELATED TO DISASTER RISK REDUCTION

Among the multi-lateral frameworks and declarations that are of relevance to this document there are the following:

- The International Meeting to Review the Implementation of the Programme of Action for the Sustainable Development of Small Island Developing States, held in Mauritius in January, 2005, calls for increased commitments to reducing the vulnerability of small island developing States, due to their limited capacity to respond to and recover from disasters.
- The Agenda for Humanitarian Action adopted by the International Conference of the Red Cross and Red Crescent in December, 2003 includes a goal and actions to "reduce the risk and impact of disasters and improve preparedness and response mechanisms".
- The Johannesburg Plan of Implementation of the World Summit on Sustainable Development, held in 2002, paragraph 37 requests actions under the chapeau: "An integrated, multi-hazard, inclusive approach to address vulnerability, risk, assessment and disaster management, including prevention, mitigation, preparedness, response and recovery, is an essential element of a safer world in the 21st century", supporting the International Strategy for Disaster Reduction as the first action. The theme of "vulnerability, risk reduction and disaster management" is included in the multi-year programme of work of the Commission on Sustainable Development in 2014-2015, and as a cross-cutting theme throughout the programme.
- The third Action Programme for Least Developed Countries, adopted in 2001, requests action by development partners in view of giving priority attention to these countries in the substantive programme and institutional arrangements for the implementation of the International Strategy for Disaster Reduction.
- The Millennium Declaration of September, 2000 identified key objectives of "Protecting the vulnerable" and "Protecting our common environment", which resolve to "intensify cooperation to reduce the number and effects of natural and man-made disasters". A

comprehensive review of the progress made in the fulfillment of all the commitments contained in the United Nations Millennium Declaration will be held in July, 2005.

- The International Strategy for Disaster Reduction was launched in 2000 by the Economic and Social Council and the General Assembly as an inter-agency framework and mechanism (inter-agency task force on disaster reduction and an inter-agency secretariat) to serve as a focal point within the United Nations system with the mandate to promote public awareness and commitment, expand networks and partnerships, and improve knowledge about disaster causes and options for risk reduction, building on the Yokohama Strategy and Plan of Action and as follow-up to the International Decade for Natural Disaster Reduction.
- The Johannesburg Plan of Implementation of the World Summit on Sustainable Development, held in 2002, requested the Intergovernmental Panel on Climate Change to "improve techniques and methodologies for assessing the effects of climate change, and encourage the continuing assessment of those adverse effects...". In addition, the General Assembly has encouraged the Conference of the Parties to the United Nations Framework Convention on Climate Change, and the parties to its Kyoto Protocol (entering into force in February, 2005) to continue to address the adverse effects of climate change, especially in those developing countries that are particularly vulnerable. The United Nations General Assembly also encouraged the Intergovernmental Panel on Climate Change to continue to assess the adverse effects of climate change on the socio-economic and natural disaster reduction systems of developing countries.
- The Tampered Convention on the Provision of Telecommunication Resources for Disaster Mitigation and Relief Operations of 1998 entered into force on 8 January, 2005.

- The Yokohama Strategy for a Safer World: Guidelines for Natural Disaster Prevention, Preparedness and Mitigation and its Plan of Action (1994), was adopted at the World Conference on Natural Disaster Reduction, building on the mid-term review of the International Decade for Natural Disaster Reduction.
- The United Nations Convention to Combat Desertification in Those Countries Experiencing Serious Drought and/or Desertification, Particularly in Africa, was adopted in 1994 and entered into force in 1996. The United Nations Convention on Biological Diversity was adopted in 1992 and entered into force in 1993.
- The General Assembly (1991) requested strengthening of the coordination of emergency and humanitarian assistance of the United Nations, in both complex emergencies natural disasters. It recalled the International Framework of Action for the International Decade for Natural Disaster Reduction (resolution 44/236,1989), and set out guiding principles for humanitarian relief, preparedness, prevention and on the continuum from relief to rehabilitation and development

ANNEXURE 2
ROLES AND RESOURCES OF UNDMT MEMBERS

The organisations that are typically part of a UNDMT have different mandates and resources, which, in turn, determine their roles and responsibilities in any operation. This part of the module provides information concerning the disaster/emergency management roles, responsibilities and resources of the core members of a UNDMT as well as the International Committee of the Red Cross, the International Federation of Red Cross and Red Crescent Societies and the International Organisation for Migration.

Food and Agriculture Organization (FAO)

Many of FAO's Field Programme activities contribute to

reducing the vulnerability of agricultural communities to disaster. For example, the Organisation provides support for better water control;

higher-yielding crop production technologies; crop and livestock diversification; greater use of drought-resistant crop varieties; improved control of pests and diseases affecting crops and livestock; improved management of soils, range lands and forested areas, including watersheds; better coastal fishing practices; home gardens and nutrition education; and improved on-farm storage, cereal banks and food security reserves.

FAO helps governments and regional organisations plan for disasters, including measures to mitigate their effects and to mobilise rapid relief and rehabilitation assistance, should this prove necessary. As a follow-up to the World Food Summit, FAO is helping member countries develop national food insecurity and vulnerability information and mapping systems. These will build on existing national food security information systems, many of which have been established with FAO assistance.

FAO's Global Information and Early Warning System for Food and Agriculture (GIEWS) monitors food supply and demand around the world. It provides policy-makers and analysts with up-to-date information on crop prospects and gives early warning on imminent food crises. Also important in this regard is the Emergency Prevention System for Trans-boundary Animal and Plant Pests and Diseases (EMPRES), which keeps a global watch for signs of emerging threats from pests and epidemics. The information collected by these systems enables governments and international bodies to take action early in order to prevent emergencies from developing.

To provide the right kind of help in an emergency it is essential to know the nature and extent of the disaster, how many people are affected and what help is needed. In the immediate aftermath of an emergency involving food and agriculture, FAO works together with the World Food Programme (WFP) to assess the situation and outlook for crops, food supplies and agricultural inputs and to estimate immediate needs for food and agricultural relief. As necessary, FAO mounts agricultural relief and rehabilitation missions to determine inputs and measures needed for restoration of productive activity as soon as possible. FAO rapidly produces reports; provide donor countries with crucial information to help them respond swiftly and effectively. Where relevant, this information is disseminated through consolidated inter-agency humanitarian appeals.

Relief efforts are aimed at saving lives in the immediate wake of a disaster. FAO's Director-general shares with the Executive Director of WFP the responsibility for approving large WFP emergency food relief operations. FAO and WFP monitor pledges and deliveries of international food assistance and keep the international community informed of continuing needs. FAO, through its Special Relief Operations Service, arranges to buy and deliver agricultural essentials such as seeds, tools, fertilizers, fishing gear and livestock and veterinary supplies to permit immediate resumption of basic food production. The aim is to restore the assets and production levels of affected communities as soon as possible.

Once emergency relief operations are under way, FAO, on request, helps governments and financing institutions prepare national rehabilitation and reconstruction plans aimed at restoring agricultural support services (extension, animal health, plant protection and input supplies) and rebuilding essential infrastructure.

During implementation of the plans, when the essential agricultural infrastructure is being rebuilt, FAO provides expertise in many areas, for example, rebuilding of fertiliser factories; repair of dams and irrigation systems; resumption of seed production; rebuilding of livestock herds;

restoration of marketing infrastructure; repair of environmental damage, including damage to forests and soil quality; restoration of fishing industries; replanting of tress crops; and development of programmes for the resettlement and reintegration of refugees, the displaces and ex-combatants.

Once the situation has returned to normal, FAO helps governments formulate food and agricultural development strategies which include the framing of programmes and projects aimed at strengthening the resilience of rural communities against future disasters as part of the development process.

Special Resources for Emergencies

Once an emergency situation occurs in a country, FAO procedures require the FAO Representative to provide the FAO's Special Relief Operations Service (TCOR) with an assessment of the impact on the agricultural sector. Depending of the scale of the catastrophe and in agreement with the FAO Representative, funds can be allocated from FAO's own resources to recruit national or international consultants to carry out a detailed impact assessment of the crop and food supply situation and make proposals for rehabilitation activities.

Depending on the assessment of the needs made, FAO contributes to an eventual UN Inter-agency appeal or decide to launch its own appeal. Three main sources of funding can then be used for the proposed interventions: (i) FAO's Director-General can decide, at the request of the beneficiary Government concerned, to make use of the Technical Co-operation Programme resources to immediately respond to the most urgent needs through project(s) which are limited to a maximum ceiling of US$ 400,000 (ii) voluntary donor contributions constitute the bulk of FAO's emergency interventions, while (iii) other UN agencies fund some of the operations. In the second and third cases, the UN Central Emergency Revolving Fund (CERF) is often used in order to immediately start operations even when delays occur in the effective transfer of funds from the donor (or UN agency) to FAO.

United Nations Children's Fund (UNICEF)

UNICEF advocates and works for the protection of children's rights, meeting the young's basic needs, and helping them reach their full potential. UNICEF also acts to ensure special protection for the most disadvantaged children: victims of war including child soldiers, victims of disasters, extreme poverty, all forms of violence and exploitation, and those with disabilities. In all of this it is guided by the Convention on the Rights of the Child (CRC) and other international legal standards.

UNICEF is guided in its emergency actions by a set of *Core Corporate Commitments* that define the organisation's initial response to the protection and care of children and women in unstable situations. These commitments are:

- To undertake a rapid assessment of the situation of woman and children in crisis;
- To be ready to assume a coordinating role for interventions in public health, nutrition, child protection and psychosocial support, unaccompanied children and education;
- To provide the assurance of good nutrition and family food security; access to potable water; environmental hygiene and safe excreta disposal; the provision of essential child health services and reproductive health care for women; and the rapid establishment of education facilities.

Special Resources for Emergencies

UNICEF has four principal sources of emergency financing:

(a) *Country Programme Funds*: The UNICEF country representative can transfer up to $50,000 from country programme resources to emergency activities, or, with government concurrence and headquarters approval, reallocate resources within it;

(b) *Emergency Programme Fund (EPF)*: The EPF is a two-year allocation of $25 million used to start a cash flow as an initial response in complex emergencies, pending the receipt of supplementary funds contributed through consolidated inter-agency appeals;

(c) *Central Emergency Revolving Fund (CERF):* When UNICEF participates as an operational agency in a consolidated inter-agency appeal; it has access to the OCHA-administered CERF.

(d) *Consolidated Inter-agency Appeals*: UNICEF participates in consolidated inter-agency appeals with partner UN agencies to obtain the bulk of its funding for emergency operations.

UNICEF's Office of Emergency Programmes (EMOPS) is the focal point for emergency assistance within the agency; its Operations Centre in New York specialises in field/ headquarters communications, and information management, analysis and retrieval. There is also an Emergency Office in Geneva that liaises with member agencies, donors, NGOs and human rights organisations.

UNICEF is able tore-deploy quickly staff within regions of crisis. These staff in turn has access to a stockpile of relief supplies, and communications, transportation and warehousing equipment. UNICEF also has a number of standing agreements with NGOs and other agencies for the rapid provision of personnel, material and service packages.

United Nations Development Programme (UNDP)

UNDP's mission is to help countries in their efforts to achieve sustainable human development by assisting them to build their capacity to design and carry out development programmes in poverty eradication, employment creation and sustainable livelihoods, the empowerment of women and the protection and regeneration of the environment, giving first priority to poverty eradication.

With respect to Countries in Special Development Situations (CSDS) and disasters, UNDP strives to be an effective development partner for the United Nations relief agencies, working to sustain livelihoods while they seek to sustain lives. It acts to help countries to prepare for, avoid and manage crisis situations and disasters. It assists with a broad range of responses to emergencies that include: planning and programming work for peace and recovery, area rehabilitation to resettle internally displace persons an returning refugees, reintegration of demobilised soldiers, de-mining, rebuilding institutions and improving governance, organising national elections, managing delivery of programme aid, and sometimes carrying out activities of a semi-emergency nature.

UNDP manages funds and supports the UN Resident Co-ordinator system of the United Nations for operation activities for development, and places the system at the disposal of the United Nations as a whole. UNDP also administers the UN Volunteer Programme that provides volunteers for assignments in humanitarian and relief operations and support to United Nations system-wide responses in complex emergencies and natural disasters, and in efforts to accelerate the process of sustainable recovery.

Within UNDP itself, the Bureau for Crisis Prevention and Recovery (BCRP) has the functions of:

1. Facilitating UNDP's participation in the UN System's co-ordination of operational activities between political, peace-keeping, humanitarian and development dimensions;
2. Facilitating internal co-ordination of resources to CSDS,
3. Providing direct guidance and support to UN Resident Co-ordinators/Resident Representatives and Country Offices on crisis prevention, response and recovery issues,
4. Facilitating UNDP's participation in resource mobilisation for CSDS. In these four areas the Bureau engages in policy development with external partners, special procedural regimes for dealing with crisis situations; advancing innovative performance approaches for capacity development; management and deployment of fast track technical services for programme development and Country Office support; information management and exchange with external

partners; and management and mobilisation of special resources to crisis response.

Disaster reduction is an integral component of UNDP's overall planning framework. In particular, in addressing "countries in special development situations" UNDP aims to reduce the incidence and impact of complex emergencies and disasters—natural, environment and technological—and to accelerate the recovery process towards sustainable human development.

To achieve this goal, the Disaster Reduction and Recovery Cluster (DRRC), a component of the Bureau for Crisis Prevention and Recovery (BCPR), pursues activities to build disaster management capacities in disaster-prone countries such as assisting in the establishment of national disaster management systems and promoting disaster reduction approaches and their integration into national policies, planning and legislation.

Also within the BCPR, the United Nations Disaster Management Training Programme (DMTP) aims to support capacity-building activities in the field of crisis and a disaster management. The DMTP is also mandated to provide, in co-operation with partner Organisations, training support for the UNDMTs.

Special Resources for Emergencies

UNDP's Executive Board decision 95/23 (16 June, 1995) on successor programming arrangements led to the earmarking of 5 percent of UNDP core resources for initiatives in Countries in Special Development Situations. TRAC 1.1.3 Resources, as this funding is termed, are intended to help UNDP better address crisis or emergency situations, thus fulfilling its role as a leading United Nations development institution and manager of the UN Resident Co-ordinator system. Priority in allocating TRAC resources has been given to low income and least developed countries. TRAC funds are intended to address the fundamental distortions in political, social, economic and ecological patterns and systems that result in the creation of emergency and crisis conditions, and which must be addressed in support of post-crisis recovery. Noting that development gains are the first to be destroyed during civil conflict or complex emergency situations, UNDP refocuses its development activities to strengthen coping capacities and stabilise communities, by seeking to maintain productive endeavours and social services.

The UNDP resident representative has the authority to approve an allocation from TRAC 1.1.3. (Category II resources) up to a maximum of US$ 100,000, provided the following conditions are met:

(i) A disaster or crisis warranting an immediate response has occurred and the government has issued an international appeal;
(ii) In consultation with UNDMT, the country office forwards to Bureau for Crisis Prevention and Recovery, copies to the regional bureau, the standard disaster situation report normally provided to the United Nations Emergency Relief Co-ordinator.
(iii) The resident representative promptly informs Bureau for Crisis Prevention and Recovery of the activities planned, the amount approved and confirms that the category II funds can be obligated within 30 days.

The practice in the recent years shows that UNDP may provide for such emergency response activities up to US$ 50,000 "in cash", as well as up to US$ 50,000 "in kind" contributions from Category II resources.

The United Nations High Commissioner for Refugees (UNCHR)

UNHCR, the United Nations refugee organisation, is mandated by the United Nations to lead and co-ordinate international action for the worldwide protection of refugees and the resolution of refugee problems.

UNHCR's primary purpose is to safeguard the rights and

well being of refugees. UNHCR strives to ensure that everyone can exercise the right to seek asylum and find safe refuge in another state, and to return home voluntarily. By assisting refugees to return to their own country or to settle in another country, UNHCR also seeks lasting solutions to their plight.

UNHCR's efforts are mandated by the organisation's Statute, and guided by the 1951 United Nations Convention relating to the Status of Refugees and its 1967 Protocol. International refugee law provides an essential framework of principles for UNHCR's humanitarian activities.

UNHCR's Executive Committee and the UN General Assembly have also authorized the organisation's involvement with other groups. These include people who are stateless or whose nationality is disputed and, in certain circumstances, internally displaced persons.

UNHCR seeks to reduce situations of forced displacement by encouraging states and other institutions to create conditions that are conducive to the protection of human rights and the peaceful resolution of disputes. In pursuit of the same objective, UNHCR actively seeks to consolidate the reintegration of returning refugees in their country of origin, thereby averting the recurrence of refugee-producing situations.

UNHCR offers protection and assistance to refugees and others in an impartial manner, on the basis of their need and irrespective of their race, religion, political opinion or gender. In all of its activities, UNHCR pays particular attention to the needs of children and seeks to promote the equal rights of women and girls.

In its efforts to protect refugees and to promote solutions to their problems, UNHCR works in partnership with governments, regional organisations, international and non-governmental organisations. UNHCR is committed to the principle of participation by consulting refugees on decisions that affect their lives. By virtue of its activities on behalf of refugees and displaced people, UNHCR also promotes the purposes and principles of the United Nations Charter: maintaining international peace and security; developing friendly relations among nations, and encouraging respect for human rights and fundamental freedoms.

Special Resources for Emergencies

In 1992 UNHCR implemented Emergency Response Teams in order to ensure rapid response to emergencies. The leaders of these teams, who are on stand-by at all times for deployment, are drawn from a rotating internal roster of UNHCR staff members located in various Field Offices and units within Headquarters. In addition, personnel trained in providing administrative support for emergency operations are also available from an internal stand-by pool. UNHCR internal staff is complemented by staff from other organisations with which UNHCR has stand-by arrangements including United Nations Volunteers (UNV), the Danish and Norwegian Refugee Councils, Radda Bamen (Sweden), Red R (Australia) and the Centers for Disease Control (USA). These stand-by arrangements have allowed UNHCR to establish an early presence in emergencies, which is crucial for the effective implementation of UNHCR's mandate in the protection and assistance of refugees.

In addition to stand-by personnel, UNHCR also maintains a limited central emergency stockpile of support equipment and facilities for staff such as vehicles, office equipment, survival field kits and telecommunications equipment. In addition, UNHCR's suppliers or NGO partners maintain centrally controlled stockpiles of essential non-food items, such as tents, blankets and water tanks. UNHCR also maintains an emergency fund of $25 million.

World Food Programme (WFP)

The World Food Programme is the frontline United Nations agency mandated to combat hunger, and in emergency situations, it provides food to save lives. WFP responds to crises arising from both natural disasters and complex emergencies. Over the last 10 years WFP has had to shift its focus from development to emergency operations. Although emergencies now account for approximately 80 per cent of WFP's expenditures, WFP has the central role in assessing, co-ordinating, delivering, and most importantly, resourcing of food assistance and the associated transport costs.

Advanced Planning and Preparations: WFP emphasises early warning and contingency planning. Early warning mechanisms include collaboration with the Framework Team in New York and WFP's Vulnerability and Analysis and Mapping Project (VAM).

WFP mainstreams its contingency planning mechanisms within the Programme. The office of the Humanitarian Adviser (OHA) is responsible for co-ordinating the overall contingency planning process. While the Augmented Logistics Intervention Team for Emergencies (ALIT) collates specific logistics based contingency planning information such as logistics capacity assessments (LCAs).

Special Resources for Emergencies

Immediate Response Accounts (IRA): The IRA provides WFP with readily available and unrestricted cash to resource new or rapidly evolving emergency operations. The IRA target level is 35 million USD. IRA can be used to start-up new operations, purchase food, and fund special operations that alleviate logistic bottlenecks such as emergency airlifts. Regional managers have been given the delegated authority to approve emergency operations up to 200,000 USAD from the IRA.

Strategic stocks. WFP's strategic stocks include food and non-food items (NFIs) such as logistics and communications equipment. The WFP managed interagency warehouse (UNHD) in Brindisi opened in July, 2000 and is geared toward fast and effective deployment of food and NFIs.

WFP maintains a central stock of High Energy Biscuits (HEB) to be located in Brindisi. Regional stocks of HEB are also tactically located in areas deemed as "hot-spots". Currently, WFP does not maintain large strategic stocks of food reserves centrally. WFP does however have its 'floating' and in-country stocks that can be diverted to other operations with donor consent. In-country stocks can also be transported to another operation if this is the most effective means of responding to a regional crisis.

Human resources. WFP is in the process of developing internal Emergency Response Roster. So as to be able to deploy Emergency Response Teams within 48 hours.

Stand-by Arrangements. In partnership with various governments and international NGOs, WFP has developed a number of standard arrangements for the rapid secondment of staff to WFP for emergency response. In addition, WFP had developed a number of logistics service packages with donor military and civil defence organisations with donor military and civil defence organisations, in conjunction with MCDU.

The World Food Programme (WFP) has a central role in preparing for, assessing, co-ordinating and delivering food assistance in emergency situations. At the start of an emergency, WFP establishes information systems that collect, analyse and disseminate food aid data, to ensure that recipient authorities, donors, agencies and NGOs are regularly updated on overall food aid needs and all food aid contributions scheduled to meet those needs. In the interests of post-emergency recovery, WFP aims to use food aid, not only to ensure the nutritional objective of providing affected people food to eat in the short term, but also to support economic activities to encourage long term food-security, self-sufficiency, and protection or building of productive assets.

Approximately 50 per cent of all food handled by WFP is purchased. WFP purchases locally, regionally and internationally through a tendering process. Food is transported by sea and overland by truck and rail, or if needed, by air. WFP delivers food at extended delivery points (as close as possible to the final destination) from where distribution is carried out by collaborating agencies, including UNHCR and/ or non-environmental organisations.

World Health Organization (WHO)

The ***World Health Organisation (WHO)*** is the specialised agency of the United Nations with responsibility for health. It's role in emergencies— as set out in it's constitution and guided by the World Health Assembly resolution WHA 48.2 adopted in May 1995—is activated by the Department of Emergency and Humanitarian Action (EHA). WHO acts at the global, regional and country levels concerning disaster reduction (i.e. disaster prevention and preparedness) and emergency response as well as humanitarian advocacy in the health sector.

WHO applies the epidemiological method and the public health model to disaster reduction? The organisation works at strengthening the member countries' capacities in analysing hazards and vulnerabilities and managing the ensuing risks, as well as at ensuring that health priorities and best public health practices are reflected in emergency humanitarian relief.

WHO has offices in almost 200 countries worldwide and they enjoy a long-term relationship with their national counterparts. WHO offices are in the countries before an emergency arises and will stay after daily life has returned to normal. This long-term presence means WHO is well placed to respond to the heath aspects of emergencies and strengthen country capacities for disaster response (mitigation, preparedness and response).

The organisation's main executive authority is the WHO Country Representative supported by the Regional Office and Headquarters. At Headquarters level, the disaster focal point is the Department of Emergency and Humanitarian Action (EHA). The two core functions of WHO in disaster reduction are:

- Partnership for Health in Emergencies for a decentralised transfer of public health technologies on the ground
- Intelligence and Capacity Building for Best Public Health Practices in Emergencies and for evidence-based advance planning and early response

- In collaboration with and for the use of its partners at the global level, WHO develops, consolidates, publishes and disseminates best practices, strategies, and guiding principles for emergency health management through *guidelines, manuals, training materials, newsletters and Web pages*

In the area of disaster reduction, WHO:

- advocates the inclusion of disaster vulnerability in general economic and industrial development decisions
- increases public awareness of the risk that hazards pose to modem societies
- Supports health capacity building at national level regarding disaster management through obtaining commitment by public authorities and by creating disaster-resilient communities

When an emergency occurs, WHO:

- **takes the lead** in health information management, rapid health assessments, epidemiological & nutritional surveillance, sector response co-ordination
- addresses all health life saving issues in order to reduce the mortality and morbidity excess from preventable causes such as epidemic-prone communicable diseases, tuberculosis, HIV/AIDS & sexually transmitted diseases, non safe pregnancy, as well as mental health disorders

Within the UNDMT, WHO is the reference agency that addresses health as being both an immediate post-disaster vital need and a continuously cross cutting issue in all sectors phases and areas of disaster reduction.

Other emergency relief activities include:

- establishment of an emergency task force designed

expressly to deal with policy issues arising within the context of complex emergency management

- the organisation of Health Emergency Teams to assess the health status and needs of populations at the start of emergencies
- the establishment of a network of senior Emergency Health Co-ordinators, drawn from WHO and WHO Collaborating Centres for the purpose of co-ordination of health sector responses to complex emergencies
- strengthening of the Emergency Response Fund both at headquarters level and for each WHO region
- stockpiling and maintenance of buffer stocks
- revision of field operational procedures to bring them into agreement with other agencies working in this field
- guidelines, protocols and other technical support to implementing partners.

Its emergency preparedness activities include policy-making and planning, awareness-building, technical advice, publication of related documentation, including guidelines and research on health emergency preparedness issues. Particular attention is paid to emergency preparedness training activities in the health sector and to related national, human resource development priorities. The standardisation of health related equipment and supplies is being expanded.

Special Resources for Emergencies

Each WHO region should maintain its own reserve fund for carrying out emergency response activities. These relatively limited funds are intended to provide the ability for immediate action. In major and complex emergencies these funds may be supplemented through access to the revolving global reserve and by additional resources from the UN Consolidated Appeals Process (CAP) and from the Central Emergency Revolving Fund (CERF) administered by OCHA.

International Committee of the Red Cross (ICRC)

The activities of the International Committee of the Red Cross (ICRC) are aimed at protecting and assisting the victims of armed conflict and internal violence so as to preserve their physical integrity and their dignity and to enable them to regain their autonomy as quickly as possible. ICRC activities include protection of the civilian population, food and non-food relief operations, health activities such as war surgery, water and sanitation programmes, and restoration of family links, visits to prisoners and dissemination of knowledge of international humanitarian law.

International Federation of Red Cross and Red Crescent Societies (IFRC)

The IFRC is part of the International Red Cross and Red Crescent Movement (which include 176 National Societies and the International Committee of the Red Cross) whose purpose is to prevent and alleviate human suffering wherever it may be found, to protect life and health and ensure respect for the human being.

IFRC acts through and with National Red Cross and Red Crescent Societies to co-ordinate emergency response and development activities. IFRC's mandate is inclusive. All "naturally" triggered disasters, such as floods and drought, fall within the scope of its operations in addition to disasters of a technological nature (e.g. Chemobyl and major transport accidents) as well as both chronic and acute pathogen related emergencies (e.g. the Ebola outbreaks in Africa and the re-emergence of Diphtheria in Europe). IFRC also assists many refugees and internally displaced persons fleeing war and plays a considerable post-conflict role in assisting with the rebuilding of war-torn societies.

Operations coordinated by IFRC include provision of shelter, food, water, health services and other forms of assistance to beneficiaries. Delivery of assistance is arranged through the National Red Cross or Red Crescent Society of the affected country, or through Delegations of the IFRC, in agreement with the National Society. The IFRC works closely with other agencies, such as those of the UN system and others, while maintaining its operational, financial and political independence.

The IFRC also works to help strengthen disaster preparedness planning, build effective disaster response mechanisms raise community awareness and public education and promote activities aimed at disaster prevention and mitigation. Regional and country based Disaster Preparedness Delegations provide technical assistance to National Societies to create effective local, national and regional disaster preparedness capacities.

Special Resources for Emergencies

Emergency response activities focus on the capacity of the National Society of the affected country. Hence, institutional development and capacity building programmes with National Societies are a central component of the resources available for emergencies.

The activities in emergency response centre on the "Disaster Response and Operations Coordination Division (DROCT of the Secretariat, and the Delegations managed by this unit. DROC consists of five regional operational departments and a set of technical support units, including Relief Health, Field Personnel, Logistics, Appeals and Reports, and Operations Support Service.

Operations Support Service develops and maintains a system of Emergency Response Units (ERU) which is structured combinations of equipment, trained personnel, procedures and management structures for a variety of purposes. These can be mobilised from National Societies and deployed at short notice. Currently available ERUs include Airport Logistics, Basic Health Care, Information, Mass Sanitation, Mass Water, Referral Hospital, Specialised Water and Telecommunication.

International Organization for Migration (IOM)

The International Organisation for Migration (IOM) is an intergovernmental organisation dedicated to promoting safe and orderly migration throughout the world. IOM is committed to the principle that humane and orderly migration benefits migrants and society. Its acts with its partners in the international community to assist in meeting the operational challenges of migration, to advance understanding of migration issues, to encourage social and economic development through migration, and to work towards effective respect of the human dignity and well-being of migrants. In the context of its Constitution, individuals of concern to IOM include economic migrants, displaced persons, refugees, nationals returning to their home country, and other individuals in need of international migration assistance.

Given the broad definition of migrants, IOM assists not only the displaced population due to humanitarian complex emergencies but also those affected by natural disasters. While involved in helping the evacuation/resettlement or return of victims of most major population displacements over the past five decades, IOM increasingly focuses on the migration aspects of emergencies. IOM engagement in such situations comprises: registration and documentation, emergency transportation (by land, sea or air), provision of health care (emergency health intervention, pre-embarkation screening, medical escorting), temporary shelter, survey and census taking, camp management, immediate temporary settlement support (provision of cash or basic tools and implements), counselling, and information and referral service.

In post-emergency situations, IOM may provide assistance in the following areas: return and reintegration, civilian registration, return of qualified nationals, repatriation of refugees in cooperation with UNHCR, tracing and family reunification in co-operation with ICRC, health assistance (reconstruction of health services, pre-integration health screening, psychosocial and post traumatic response, training of community health personnel), capacity building in migration management, skills training, information and referral service, job referrals and out-placement, micro-projects to facilitate reintegration, and local communal governance to alleviate migratory pressures.

IOM also provides rapid analysis of migratory flows and early warning, develops national population information systems, organises census taking, and provides technical co-operation and support to governments.

Special Resources for Emergencies

IOM maintains a limited emergency revolving fund for emergency assessment use and for initial start-up of emergency operations prior to actual receipt of external operational funding. In its cooperation with the United Nations, IOM participates in co-ordinated international humanitarian response and the consolidated interagency appeal process led by OCHA. IOM maintains a roster of staff who can be called upon for emergency deployment on short notice. In addition, IOM has formal and informal standby agreements with agencies providing emergency personnel (such as the DRC, NRC, UNV, RedR-UK, SDR, JAFI) should IOM's own internal roster not be sufficient. A limited stockpile of emergency office equipment and supplies, survival field kits, medical kits, telecommunications, is also maintained. IOM also maintains standby arrangements with various external suppliers of emergency equipment and services (such as Noreps, SRSA, Emercom, Bukkehave, Bassadone, SOS). IOM has the EPC or the Emergency and Post-Conflict Division which is the focal point of institutionalizing IOM's emergency preparedness and response capacities."

Office for the Coordination of Humanitarian Affairs (OCHA)

OCHA's main mission is to mobilise and co-ordinate the collective efforts of the international community, in particular those of the UN system, to meet in a coherent and timely manner the needs of those exposed to human suffering and material destruction in disasters and emergencies. This involves reducing vulnerability, promoting solutions to root causes and facilitating the smooth transmission from relief to rehabilitation and development.

OCHA's functions focus on three core areas:

- Co-ordination of humanitarian emergency response to complex emergencies and natural disasters, by ensuring that appropriate response mechanisms are established on the ground, notably through consultations of the IASC and ECHA.
- Advocacy of humanitarian issues with political organs, notably the Security Council, the Department of Political Affairs, the Department of Peacekeeping Operations, Governments and the general public.
- Policy development in support of the Secretary-General and the IASC, to ensure that humanitarian issues are addressed.

Specifically with respect to complex emergencies:

Early Warning: OCHA plays a leading role in inter-agency early warning of potential new complex emergencies. This work within a Framework for Co-ordination mechanism that includes OCHA, DPA, DPKO, UNDP, UN Human Rights, FAO, UNICEF and WHO. The Framework Team consultations on countries of concern include promoting in-country contingency planning for higher risk countries, as well as actions that could help or mitigate the conflict. With respect to natural and technological disasters, OCHA has agreements and established procedures with both UN and non-UN monitoring organisations concerned to receive early warning of the occurrence or possible occurrence of potentially disastrous events. While OCHA does not itself issue warnings, it uses these warnings for its own preparedness to respond.

Contingency Planning/Forward Planning: Prior to the onset of a complex emergency, OCHA is responsible for working with the UN Resident Co-ordinator and agencies in-country to carry out contingency planning and preparedness actions—such as developing common inter-agency planning scenarios and assumptions, agreeing on the division of labour at the start of a relief operation, and identifying and positioning standby relief items. OCHA uses the term "forward planning" for the comparable work it undertakes once a complex emergency has actually started.

Inter-agency Situation/Needs Assessment: When a humanitarian crisis appears imminent, or is in the early stages, OCHA, through IASC consultations,. will organise and lead inter-agency assessment missions in order to determine needs and put in place appropriate co-ordination mechanisms.

Field Co-ordination Mechanisms: With respect to complex emergencies, OCHA field coordination mechanisms vary depending on the particular circumstances of the emergency. The Inter-agency Standing Committee (IASC) decides upon the appropriate mechanism on a case-by-case basis. There are three main mechanisms (detailed in Section I): the UN Resident Co-ordinator as Humanitarian Co-ordinator, the Lead Agency and the Humanitarian Co-ordinator distinct form Resident Co-ordinator or Lead Agency. With respect to natural disaster response, the UN Resident Co-ordinator represents and is accountable to the ERC.

Resource Mobilisation: For specific complex emergency situations, OCHA solicits donor support mainly through the Consolidated Appeals Process (CAP) that encompasses the emergency relief requirement of the relevant operational agencies, and to a much lesser extent through the Central Emergency Revolving Fund (CERF). The OCHA Situation Reports are the main means for communicating international resource mobilisation requirements following a natural disaster.

Post-Emergency: When post-conflict or post-disaster rehabilitation becomes a realistic option, OCHA seeks to hand over most of its activities to other agencies that are mandated to co-ordinate such rehabilitation. These would normally include the UN Development Programme, and bodies such as the World Bank. OCHA would then resume responsibility for monitoring humanitarian needs, through the UN Resident Co-ordinator in country.

Specifically with respect to natural disasters:

Natural Disaster Prevention, Preparedness, and Mitigation: Policy positions for OCHA in relation to natural disaster prevention, preparedness and mitigation are developed by the Secretariat of the International Strategy for Disaster Reduction (ISDR). OCHA promotes the inclusion of disaster reduction during the emergency phase and carries out lessons learnt studies of disaster response of disaster response operations that lead to further policy development. OCHA contributes to improving inter-agency and overall response preparedness of the international humanitarian community, as well as national capacity building, through a broad range of international level initiatives.

Specifically with Respect to Environmental Emergencies

OCHA and UNEP have a joint Environment Unit designed to ensure a prompt international response to environmental disasters—such as industrial/technological accidents, chemical and oil spills, forest fires, floods, and other sudden-onset emergencies that damage the environment and human health and welfare. It acts a switchboard for disaster notification and alert issuing regular information and situation reports disseminated worldwide. Demands from affected countries are matched with offers from donors ready and willing to assist. It is also prepared to channel available data, maps, satellite images and other useful information, from sources to relevant end-users, and to act as a focal point mobilising urgent multilateral assistance. The unit can arrange for professional, impartial and independent initial assessments and post-emergency analyses to help countries in the response phase. It also provides guidelines for assessments, contingency and emergency response planning, improving emergency reporting, procedures and mechanisms and supplying relevant contact points. OCHA can make emergency cash grants of up to $50,000 for immediate needs.

Special Resources for Emergencies

If there is a call after a natural disaster for international interventions to assist the victims, OCHA provides the following resource mobilisation and co-ordination services at international and field levels:

Disaster-Response System: round-the-clock readiness for disasters—OCHA operates a 24-hour a day disaster response system to help co-ordinate the actions of the international community in response to disasters. It monitors the possible occurrence of natural disasters in close contact with UN Resident Coordinators world-wide. The response system is triggered when OCHA is alerted that a disaster had occurred. The OCHA situation report is a main co-ordination tool. It provides detailed information on damage caused, actions taken, relief needs, national response capacity, international aid required and assistance being provided. These reports are disseminated to emergency relief services of donor government, the UN system and inter-governmental and nongovernmental organisations. They are also posted on OCHA's Internet site "ReliefWeb". Additional co-ordination measures at international level include donor information and inter-agency meetings.

Field Co-ordination: Providing On-site Assessment and Co-ordination Support: OCHA can field a United Nations Disaster Assessment and Co-ordination (UNDAC) team to assist the Government of the affected country, the UN Resident Co-ordinator and the UN DMT in on-site assessment and field-level co-ordination during the initial emergency phase. It can establish an On-Site Operations Co-ordination Centre (OSOCC) to support the local emergency management authority in co-ordinating the activities of international relief providers.

International Appeals: Mobilising the International Community to Provide Help: At the request of the Government of an affected country, OCHA launches an appeal for international assistance. When the situation warrants, OCHA provides cash grants and acts as a channel for donor contributions. If appropriate, OCHA also facilitates the preparation and launch of UN Inter-Agency

Appeals for immediate relief assistance and with a view to ensuring the country's smooth transition from relief to rehabilitation and reconstruction.

Activation a/International Emergency Response Networks to Mobilise Assets: Based on stand-by arrangements and agreed emergency procedures within the established networks, OCHA facilitates the mobilisation of specific assets—including human, technical, logistics and material resources—from the international community. These may include international Urban Search and Rescue (SAR) teams, military and civil defence (protection) assets required for co-ordination, logistics, telecommunications and other support. Such resources are frequently provided as self-sustained service packages and on a bilateral basis.

Other Support: OCHA in co-operation with WHO, WFP and four governments, maintains stocks of various relief items in its warehouse in Pisa, Italy. Supplies can be dispatched to the field either as a bilateral donation, or through the UN, on behalf of WHO or WFP, or at the request of the UNDMT concerned to help fill critical relief gaps. Standing co-operation agreements with other governments enable access to field co-ordination support resources such as specially equipped field vehicles, telecommunications equipment and administrative support. Although these standby resources are primarily for use by UNDAC teams in natural disasters, they may be accessed on an informal basis by OCHA in the event of large-scale emergencies.

CANADIAN CENTRE FOR EMERGENCY PREPAREDNESS

Mission Statement

The Canadian Centre for Emergency Preparedness (CCEP) is a not-for-profit organization based in Burlington, Ontario devoted to the promotion of emergency risk management to individuals, communities and organizations, in both government and the private sector, with the aim of reducing the risk, impact and cost of natural, human-induced and technological disasters.

CCEP's objectives are to raise awareness of the increasing risks of disasters, promote the need for sound disaster management practices and disseminate information on the availability of professional expertise and resources, including technology.

CCEP will achieve its mission through the promotion of the following:

Disaster Management Principles & Practices

- Methodologies (e.g. Incident Command System, Ten Professional Practices for Business Continuity)
- Standards (e.g. NFPA 1600)
- Programmes (e.g. Partnerships for Safer Communities, Community Emergency Response Volunteer programmes).

Education & Training

- Recognized public and private institutions that provide post secondary and post graduate courses in emergency risk management and business continuity (e.g. Universities/Colleges, public, NGO and private sector training institutions).

Career Development

- Advice to those interested in pursuing a career in disaster management
- Promotion of professional certification bodies (e.g. IAEM, CEPA, DRII/DRIC, BCI, DRIE).

Research Results

- Participating in disaster management research

- Disseminating results of research
- Providing opportunities for disaster researchers and disaster management practitioners to come together

Services & Products

- Annual World Conference on Disaster Management (http://www.wcdm.org/)
- Official publication—Emergency Management Canada
- Disaster Management Career Site (http://www.disastermanagementjobs.com/)

About CCEP

Background

In the late 1980's, increasing pressure from citizens' action groups and a growing body of regulatory legislation encouraged Canadian industry to adopt a proactive approach to disaster planning. In 1991, the Major Industrial Accidents Council of Canada released a national standard on emergency planning for Canadian industry.

Federal and provincial government training programmes directed to employees were limited, and subsequent fiscal restraint and down-sizing caused these to stall. It became apparent that there was a substantial deficiency in available training for emergency responders and business continuity planners in Canada, and those alternative training options were required.

In 1992, the Regional Government approached Hamilton's Mohawk College of Applied Arts and Technology with the objective of forming a partnership to further enhance this training. Mohawk College had the expertise and infrastructure to help develop and deliver formal programmes of instruction. Out of this initiative came the proposal to establish the Canadian Centre for Emergency Preparedness.

World Conference on Disaster Management:

The first forerunner of the **World Conference on Disaster Management (WCDM)** was organized in October, 1989. This programme originally began as an initiative of the Regional Municipality of Hamilton-Wentworth and its success confirmed the need for emergency preparedness training, not only in Canada but worldwide. Further conferences were held in 1991 and 1992 to bring together disaster managers from around the world and provide an opportunity for delegates to learn the critical skills of disaster response and recovery. These were comprehensive events which addressed the skills, practices and procedures essential to planning and preparing for emergency or disaster situations, incorporating all of the disciplines involved in disaster response and post-incident relief. Since 1994 the Conference has been an annual event and is now held at the Metro Toronto Convention Centre every summer.

The conference and trade show now attracts over 1500 delegates from five continents to attend presentations and workshops in business continuity, emergency planning and emergency management. The WCDM has become the premier North American event for training and networking among Emergency Response, Emergency Management, Emergency Health Care, Business Continuity Planning, Risk Management, and Security professionals world-wide, and for the organizations which supply and service these professions.

Templates/Documents

Everyone is constantly looking for help in the form of templates and examples. Why re-invent the wheel if there is something out there that works for you? We will attempt to help you find what you are looking for by providing some free CCEP templates for downloading and links to other free and paying template/example sites.

CCEP Templates

- Assessment Checklist

- Risk Assessment Spreadsheet
- Business Impact Analysis
- Strategy Worksheets
- Emergency Plan
- Business Continuity Plan
- Crisis Communications Plan
- Exercise Evaluation Form
- Emergency Management Team Set Up

Other Sites Offering Templates, Samples & Actual Documents

Free Templates/Documents/Forms

- Action Front Data Recovery Labs—Data Emergency Guide (PDF File-380KB)
- BCI Good Practice Guidelines
- British Columbia—Provincial Emergency Plans
- Business Contingency Preparedness—Business Continuity Checklists
- Crisis Communications—Readiness Checklist
- Crisis Management Checklist—Fineman PR
- DRJ—Sample Disaster Recovery Plans
- DRJ's Toolbox
- Emergency Management Guide Template for Schools (Kentucky)
- Emergency Management Institute—Word Documents/PowerPoint Visuals
- FFIEC—Business Continuity Planning Booklet for Examiners
- Floodmaps.Net—Statement of Work Templates
- General Security Checklist—Computer Security Resource Center (CSRC)
- Guide to Data Protection Auditing—UK Information Commissioner
- Hazardous Materials Emergency Response Guidebook
- ICS Forms—FIRESCOPE
- ICS Forms—National Wildfire Coordinating Group (NWCG)

- Incident Management Checklist—Sun Guard
- Interpol—IT Security Checklist
- Interpol—Disaster Victim Identification Forms
- National Academy Press—Terrorism and Security Document Collection
- National Education Association (Crisis Communications Templates for Educators)
- National Institute for Chemical Studies—Shelter in Place Plan
- Office of Hazardous Materials Safety—Forms/ Documents
- Praxiom Research Group Limited—Human Security Plan
- Project Scope Solutions Group—Privacy Compliance Assessment Forms
- Radio Communications Plans, Message Forms—PERCS (BC)
- Region of Halton (Ontario)—Emergency Plan
- Strategic Plan Workbook for Risk Programmes—DelCreo Inc.
- Western New York Disaster Preparedness and Recovery Manual for Libraries and Archives
- Virtual Corporation—The Business Continuity Management (BCM) Maturity Model

Templates/Documents You Can Purchase

- Bankpolicies.com
- Disaster Survival Planning Network
- Emergency Management Toolkit—The Emergency Preparedness and Emergency Management Center
- ITBusinessEdge—IT Security Manual Template
- Janco Associates, Inc—Disaster Recovery, Security, Safety
- PLAN-IT-CONTROL-IT
- Project Scope Solutions Group—Privacy Compliance and Information Risk Management Policies, Forms, Analysis Toolkits, and Guidebooks

- Security Policy World
- Sentryx—Business Continuity Planning Methodology

GUJARAT STATE DISASTER MANAGEMENT AUTHORITY

Creation of Authority

The GSDMA has been constituted by the Government of Gujarat by the GAD's Resolution dated 8 February, 2001. The Authority has been created as a permanent arrangement to handle the natural calamities. The objectives for constitution of this authority have been clearly spelt out and precisely defined in para (2) of the said Resolution.

These are as follows:

1. To provide relief to the people for the loss incurred due to natural calamity and to under take rehabilitation and reconstruction as also social and economic activities or restoration of the situation
2. To make efforts to minimize the impact of natural calamities through precautionary programmes and schemes.
3. To analyze and study the reasons of natural calamities and to suggest the remedies to avoid or minimize the effects of such natural calamites.
4. To make the best use of the funds, grants, donations, assistance received from Government of India and other foreign countries or from any other institutions/ persons for prevention of such natural calamities or for handling the after-effects; to obtain loans and make proper use of the funds received by the Authority.

The headquarters of this authority is at Gandhinagar and its jurisdiction is throughout the entire state of Gujarat. It is supposed to function as an autonomous body. Its activities are non-profitable and are duly registered as a charitable institution under the Societies Registration Act, 1860, with the competent Authorities. The Authority works under the aegis of the Rehabilitation and Reconstruction Division, a separate cell created under the GAD.

In the year 2002 the Government of Gujarat declared, "Disaster Management Policy" for the state. Following this policy the Government passed "Gujarat State Disaster Management Act, 2003". The bill was passed by the state assembly on 28 March, 2003 and the Act has come into force from 13 May, 2003. The State of Gujarat become the first state in India to have enacted an Act to provide legal and regulatory framework for disaster management.

With the effect of the Gujarat State Disaster Management Act 2003, the Society constituted earlier as GSDMA, stands dissolved under Section 49 of the Act, and the Authority under sub-section 1 of the Section (6) came to an existence.

The Government of Gujarat vide Notification No. DMA-1003-1488-B dated 29th August, 2003 in the Official Gazette established an Authority in the name of Gujarat State Disaster Management Authority with effect from 1 September, 2003 and specified Gandhinagar as the headquarters of the said Authority under the sub section (1) & (3) of the Section 6 of the Act.

Constitution of the Authority

Section 7 of the GSDM Act 2003 provides the constitution of the Authority. Accordingly the Authority shall consist of chairperson and not more than fourteen other members as follow s, namely.

(a) The Chief Minister of the State, ex-officio, who shall be the Chairperson;
(b) Two Ministers nominated by the Chief Minister by virtue of their office from amongst the Council of Ministers of the State;
(c) The Chief Secretary of the State, ex-officio;
(d) The Secretary to the Government of Gujarat, Revenue Department, ex officio;
(e) The Chief Executive Officer of the Authority, ex-officio;

(f) The State Relief Commissioner, ex-officio; and
(g) The Director General of Police of the State, ex-officio;
(h) Such other officers of the State Government as may be appointed by the State Government by virtue of their office:

Provided that when a proclamation made under Article 356 of the Constitution is in force in the State, the Central Government may appoint three persons, in place of the Chief Minister and other two Ministers, to be the Chairperson and members of the Authority and the persons so appointed shall vacate their office upon the revocation or cesser of operation of such proclamation.

The members of the Authority shall hold office during the pleasure of the State Government and shall receive such remuneration as may be prescribed.

Vision

To go beyond reconstruction and make Gujarat economically vibrant, agriculturally and industrially competitive with improved standards of living and with a capacity to mitigate and manage future disasters

Objective

The Government of Gujarat (GOG) established the Gujarat State Disaster Management Authority (GSDMA) on 8 February, 2001 to co-ordinate the comprehensive earthquake recovery programme. The GSDMA is registered as a society under the Societies Registeration Act. The objectives of GSDMA are:

- To undertake social and economical activities for rehabilitation & resettlement of the affected people that would include new Housing, Infrastructure, Economics Rehabilitation, social Rehabilitation and other related programme.
- To prepare programmes and plans to mitigate the

losses on account of disasters as a strategy for long terms disaster preparedness.

- To undertake research and study regarding causes for losses on account of natural disaster and to suggest remedial measures for minimizing the same.
- To obtain funds for rehabilitation and resettlement and to ensure optimum utilization of these funds obtained in the form of grant, aid, assistance or loan from Government of Gujarat, Government of India, World Bank and ADB, USAID, DFID, IFRC, and donors, NGOs, and from financial institutions, Public and private trusts or any other organisations.
- To manage Gujarat Earthquake Rehabilitation and Reconstruction Fund.
- To act as a nodal agency and to co-ordinate various issues relating to the deserving victims out of the funds, either directly or through a common fund created for these purpose in any other feasible mode.
- To provide to arrange financial assistance so as to achieve the objects of the society.
- To raise money through financial instruments, bonds, deposits or such other manner may be permissible under the provision of Societies Registration Act, 180 and the Bombay Public Trust Act 1950
- To develop approach, philosophy, policy guidelines and action plan and other relevance aspects for meeting out disaster of any kind; Management, Administration, Investment & Reinvestment of funds out of sale proceeds received from the sale of land, buildings, Equipments, furniture, fixtures, debris or any other things or articles or infrastructure.
- To act as a nodal agency and to coordinate various issuers related to the maintenance of hygienic living conditions, welfare of victims, environmental maintenance and such other welfare measures, as may be assigned to the deserving authority.
- To do all the acts and things conducive for the attainment of the above objects in the most possible

manner, which are relevant to fulfil the objects of SOCIETY?

GUJARAT INSTITUTE OF DISASTER MANAGEMENT

About GIDM

The Gujarat Institute of Disaster Management (GIDM) was established on 26 January, 2004 by the GoG with the aim of human resource development (HRD) for disaster management in the state. GIDM was conceived as a state level autonomous institution/which was to work in close collaboration with the GSDMA. GIDM is expected to become a premier state level institute for training/education and research in disaster management/with state of the art facilities. The main thrust of the institute is to provide proper insight/knowledge and skills to stakeholders at various levels in the state/so that they can accomplish appropriate disaster management tasks.

Although GIDM is currently functioning in the premises of SPIPA (Sardar Patel Institute of Public Administration) at Ahmedabad/will finally be located at Gandhinagar. The erstwhile NDM Cell of SPIPA/which was providing disaster management training only to government officers in the state/ has been merged with GIDM since 1 April, 2004.

Objectives

The salient objectives of the institute are to:

- Impart training on all stages of disaster management/ for disasters/which are likely to occur in the state. In order to achieve this/the institute will:
- Identify training needs of different target groups and conduct their training programmes.
- Design and develop appropriate training courses and training materials. Conduct "Training of Trainers" programmes. Increase awareness and education of

stakeholders on disaster management through mass media/audio-visual aids and extension machinery. Offer open and distance education courses on various aspects of disaster management for different target groups.

- Act as an information/resource center for disaster management by building up of a resource base through seminars/conferences/research studies and networking with knowledge based Institutions/Agencies and make such resources available to the stakeholders whenever needed. Conduct and support research in disaster management for improving the quality of training/ education and for systems development. Provide consultancy services in the field of disaster management research/education and training and in allied sciences.

GUJARAT STATE DISASTER MANAGEMENT POLICY (GSDMP)

Overview

Need for a Policy

The state of Gujarat ('the state') has been prone to disasters. Over the years, these disasters have caused extensive damage to life and property and have adversely impacted economic development. The Government of Gujarat ('GoG') recognises the need to have a proactive, comprehensive, and sustained approach to disaster management to reduce the detrimental effects of disasters on overall socio-economic development of the state. GoG believes that there is a need for a policy that articulates its vision and strategy for disaster management in the state. In this context the Gujarat State Disaster Management Authority (GSDMA) provides guidelines to various entitle involved in disaster management in the state to discharge their responsibilities more effectively. With this in view, the GSDMA has formulated the Gujarat State Disaster Management Policy ('GSDMP' or 'the Policy').

Training Calendar for the Year 2006—07

Sr. No.	Month	Date	Course Title	Duration (Days)
1.	May	01-03	Basic of Disaster Management	3
2.		04-06	Basic of Disaster Management	3
3.		08-10	Basic of Disaster Management	3
4.		15-17	Basic of Disaster Management	3
5.		18-20	Basic of Disaster Management	3
6.		22-26	Drought Mitigation and Management	5
7.	June	05-09	Drought Mitigation and Management	5
8.		12-16	Flood Mitigation and Management	5
9.	July	10-12	EOC Management and Incident Command System	3
10.		13-15	EOC Management and Incident Command System	3
11.		19-21	Preparation of Disaster Management Plan	3
12.		24-28	Flood Mitigation and Management	5
13.	August	01-05	Cyclone Mitigation and Management	5
14.		21-25	Cyclone Mitigation and Management	5
15.	September	04-05	Role of Media and Disaster Management	2
16.		06-07	Role of Media and Disaster Management	2
17.		11-12	Emergency Medical Response	2
18.		13-14	Emergency Medical Response	2
19.		15-16	Emergency Medical Response	2
20.		18-20	Preparation of Disaster Management Plan	3
21.	October	09-10	Disaster Management-Indus trial/Chemical Accident	2
22.		11-12	Disaster Management-Indus trial/Chemical Accident	2

(Contd.)

(Contd.)

Sr. No.	*Month*	*Date*	*Course Title*	*Duration (Days)*
23..	November	06-10	Tsunami Mitigation and Management	5
24.		13-17	Tsunami Mitigation and Management	5
25.		20-21	Damage and Loss Assessment	2
26.		22-23	Damage and Loss Assessment	2
27.	December	04-08	Earthquake Mitigation and Management	5
28.		11-15	Earthquake Mitigation and Management	5
29.	January	03-04	Disaster Management-Major Building Collapse	2
30.		05-06	Disaster Management-Major Building Collapse	2
31.		11-12	School Safety	2
32.		17-18	School Safety	2
33.		19-20	Cattle Management in Disaster	2
34.		24-25	Cattle Management in Disaster	2
35.		29-31	Relief Management in Disaster	3
36.	February	05-07	Relief Management in Disaster	3
37.		14-15	Community Preparedness	2
38.		16-17	Community Preparedness	2
39.		19-20	Disaster Management-Major Transportation Accident	2
40.		21-22	Disaster Management-Major Transportation Accident	2
41.		26-27	Disaster Management—Major Fire	2
42.		28-01	Disaster Management—Major Fire	2

Aim

The aim of the Gujarat State Disaster Management Policy is establishing necessary systems, structures, programmes, resources, capabilities and guiding principles for reducing disaster risks and preparing for and responding to disasters and threats of disasters in the state of Gujarat in order to save lives and property, avoid disruption of economic activity and damage to environment and to ensure the continuity and sustainability of development.

Objectives

- To assess the risks and vulnerabilities associated with various disasters,
- To develop appropriate disaster prevention and mitigation strategies,
- To provide clarity on roles and responsibilities for all stakeholders concerned with disaster management so that disasters can be managed more effectively,
- To develop and maintain arrangements for accessing resources, equipment, supplies and funding in preparation for disasters that might occur,
- To ensure that arrangements are in place to mobilize the resources and capability for relief, rehabilitation, reconstruction and recovery from disasters,
- To create awareness and preparedness and provide advice and training to the agencies involved in disaster management and to the community,
- To strengthen the capacities of the community and establish and maintain effective systems for responding to disasters,
- To ensure co-ordination with agencies related to disaster management in other Indian states and those at the national and international level,
- To ensure relief/assistance to the affected without any discrimination of caste, creed, community or sex.
- To establish and maintain a proactive programme of

risk reduction, this programme being Implemented through existing sectoral and inter-sectoral development programmes and being part of the overall development process in the state,

- To develop and Implement programmes for risk sharing and risk transfer for all types of disasters.
- To address gender issues in disaster management with special thrust on empowerment of women towards long term disaster mitigation.
- To develop disaster management as a distinct management discipline and creation of a systematic and streamlined disaster management cadre.

Key Elements of the Gujarat State Disaster Management Policy

- GoG will have the prerogative to define the occurrence of a disaster and define the boundaries of the disaster-affected site by issuing a 'disaster declaration". The declaration can be made on the recommendation of SRC or DC.
- GoG views disaster management as a long-term process that involves the creation of disaster management and mitigation capacity in thc state. In addition to developing systcms and processes designed to providc relief and rehabilitation.
- The establishment of the Gujarat State Disaster Management Authority ('GSDMA' or the Authority') as a nodal agency is an important element in the overall framework for disaster management in the state. GSDMA will facilitate, co-ordinate and monitor work for mitigation and preparedness for disasters. It will also coordinate and monitor emergency relief measures, relief, reconstruction and rehabilitation. The Authority would be provided with statutory powers in its role, as per the proposed Gujarat State Disaster Management Act, 2002.
- The Revenue Department, through the offices of the

State Relief Commissioner and the District Collectors along with relevant Government departments will be responsible for Implementing emergency relief measures and relief after a disaster. GSDMA will facilitate, co-ordinate and monitor the activities related to disaster management of the Revenue Department and other relevant Government Departments, where necessary.

- State Relief Commissioner and District Collectors will be provided special powers to deal with emergency situations created by disasters. When a disaster Impacts an area covering several towns and cities within a district, the Government personnel and their facilities shall be placed under the operational control of the respective District Collector for the duration of the emergency. Government departments will simplify procedures to mobilize resources in these emergency situations.
- Development planning will incorporate disaster management principles as an integral part of the overall planning process.
- GoG will look at all aspects of risk sharing and risk transfer to ensure that the costs associated with managing disasters are distributed across a wider population.
- Links will be established between the nodal agency (GSDMA), Government departments, local authorities, NGOs, research agencies, public sector, private sector, community groups and other stakeholders to share knowledge, establish coordination mechanisms and augment capacity of all the stakeholders.
- A mechanism of continuous feedback shall be instituted so that learning can be translated into more effective relief, rehabilitation and reconstruction efforts and the process of capacity creation and relief, rehabilitation and reconstruction feed into each other.
- Self-reliance shall be developed by promoting and encouraging the spirit of self-help and mutual

assistance among local authorities and constituents.

- All administrative subdivisions of the state will develop and maintain documented plans of their disaster management functions and activities.
- To ensure that all responsible agencies, their staff and the public are familiar with policy, plans and procedures related to disaster management, periodic exercises and drills shall be conducted at all levels, with specific emphasis at the district and local levels.

Key Responsibilities

- Responsibility for the declaration of a disaster at any level in the state rests with State Government the declaration can be made on the recommendation of the State Relief Commissioner ('SRC') or a District Collector ('DC').
- Responsibility for initiation and execution of emergency relief measures and relief in times of disasters rests with state Revenue Department, in conjunction with other relevant Government departments. The state Revenue Department shall act through its functionaries at the state level (the State Relief Commissioner) and the district level (the District Collector).
- Responsibility for facilitation, coordination and monitoring of the development and Implementation of reconstruction and rehabilitation activity following disasters rests with GSDMA, utilizing the resources and expertise of relevant Government departments, district administration, local authorities, non-governmental organizations ('NGOs'), the public sector, the private sector, international development agencies, donors and the community.
- Responsibility for coordinating the development, Implementation, review and maintenance of disaster management plans and programmes rests with GSDMA, utilising the resources and expertise of

relevant Government departments, district administration, local authorities, NGOs, the public sector, the private sector, international development agencies, donors and the community Responsibility for coordination and monitoring of the programmes of risk reduction rests with GSDMA. Responsibility for initiation and Implementation of the risk reduction programme rests with the relevant Government departments, NGOs the private sector and the community.

Introduction

The state of Gujarat has been prone to disasters. These disasters have caused extensive damage to life and property and have adversely impacted economic development. Examples include the persistent droughts in the state and the devastating earthquake that hit Gujarat on 26 January, 2001. In response to this, the Government of Gujarat has decided to formulate a policy that addresses various aspects of management of these disasters in a systematic and sustained manner.

The Government of Gujarat has envisaged the development of a holistic approach designed to manage disasters on a more proactive basis. The approach involves formulating a comprehensive policy on all phases of disaster management, and addresses the entire gamut of disasters arising from natural (droughts, floods, earthquakes, clones etc.) and manmade (oil spills, forest fires, chemical catastrophes etc.) causes. This policy takes full cognizance of other related policies and initiatives at both the national and state level. In particular, this policy is intended to be consistent with the disaster management policy at the national level.

In order to achieve its objective of institutionalizing a disaster management ('DM') framework in the state, the GoG has established a nodal agency, namely the Gujarat State Disaster Management Authority, to facilitate, coordinate and monitor disaster management activities and promote good disaster management and mitigation practices in the state. The establishment of the GSDMA is a key element in the overall disaster management policy of the State Government The GoG also proposes to introduce legislation in the form of a Gujarat State Disaster Management Act to provide a legal framework for disaster management in the state.

GoG acknowledges its responsibility to proactively manage disasters. Hence, this policy document articulates GoG' vision and strategy for managing disasters proactively, systematically and in a sustainable manner. The document also provides guidelines to various entitles involved in disaster management in the state for discharging their responsibilities more effectively.

Principles for Disaster Management

Principles of Gujarat State Disaster Management Policy

('GSDMP') Disaster management is not a separate sector or discipline but an approach to solving problems relating to disasters Impacting any sector-agricultural. Industrial, environmental, social etc. Ultimately, disaster management is the responsibility of all sectors, all organizations and all agencies that may be potentially affected by a disaster. Utilizing existing resources ensures efficiency in resource utilization and lower costs.

With this background in mind, GoG has outlined a set of key principles that will guide the development and implementation of the DM policy in Gujarat. These principles are designed to provide guidance during all phases of disaster management and are consistent with internationally accepted best practices.

Integrating Disaster Management into Development Planning

The objectives of the DM policy or any sectoral policy should sub-serve the overall goals of the state relating to economic and social development. Hence, policies on sustainable development should seek to reduce possible losses from disasters, as a matter of course. In other words, disaster prevention and preparedness should be an integral part of every development policy. Therefore, the state's development strategy shall explicitly address disaster management as an integral part of medium and long-term planning, especially for disaster prone districts in the state.

Multi-hazard Approach to Disasters

The GoG recognises that disasters can either be man-made, natural or even arising out of technological causes. Although the preparedness for long-gestation disasters such as droughts is fairly adequate in the state, the existing DM framework needs to be augmented to meet the needs in the aftermath of unexpected and large-scale disasters such as cyclone and earthquake. A robust DM policy must therefore provide, plan and prepare for all types of hazards and disasters that may be reasonably expected to occur in a region.

Sustainable and Continuous Approach

One of the objectives of sustainable development is to increase the inherent strength of all agencies. Including the community to deal with disaster situations. Achieving this objective requires sustained initiatives encompassing social, economic and infrastructure issues. Further, once capacity is built, it must be sustained and this would be an ongoing and continuous activity. The Government of Gujarat alms to improve on a continuous and sustainable basis, the infrastructure and processes for relief, rehabilitation and reconstruction and institutionalise capacity building at all levels within the state in order to be able to mitigate the Impact of disasters.

Leverage Existing Government Machinery

The GoG shall strive to ensure that the long-term approach to disaster management utilises the existing administrative machinery of the State Government at all levels within the state in order to undertake communication, capacity creation, relief, rehabilitation and reconstruction. Information collection and dissemination and sharing of disaster management best practices. All Government departments, bureaus, corporations, authorities and agencies are encouraged to utilise all available resources within their respective areas for disaster management before seeking assistance from entitles in other areas or higher authorities. New institutions may be established where the existing mechanisms are found inadequate.

Effective Inter-agency Co-operation and Co-ordination

Successful disaster response requires a quick and organised response. The active participation of affected communities, NGOs, private sector and various Government departments like Fire Brigade, Police, Health etc. is thus critical to any response activity. Therefore, the DM policy in Gujarat shall focus on establishing response mechanisms that are quick, co-ordinated and participative.

Capacity Building

Managing disasters using only a handful of stakeholders would be inefficient. The Government of Gujarat therefore recognises that the DM policy will need to strengthen the resilience and capacity of NGOs, private sector and the local community to cope with disasters while simultaneously building the capacity of the Government machinery to manage disasters. Effective disaster management requires that the community especially vulnerable groups like women, landless labour etc. be fully aware of the extent of their vulnerability to disasters to reduce its Impact, prior to its actual occurrence. Further, NGOs, private sector and the community must understand and be familiar with DM principles and practices, what their own responsibilities are, how they can help prevent disasters, how they must react during a disaster and what they can do to support themselves and relief workers, when necessary. Training is an integral component of capacity building.

Development of Disaster Management as a distinct managerial discipline will be taken up to create a systematic and streamlined disaster management cadre. Gender issues in disaster management will be addressed and the empowerment of women towards long term disaster mitigation will be focused upon.

Autonomy and Equity

Disasters are catastrophic events whose Impact is felt across socio-economic boundaries. Consequently, any DM effort should be neutral and non-discriminatory. To that extent, it is necessary that the DM institutions possess the autonomy to make decisions in a fair, scientific and systematic manner. Disaster assistance and relief must also be provided in an equitable and consistent manner without regard to economic or social status of beneficiaries. Relief/assistance must be provided without any discrimination of caste, creed, religion, community or sex

Legal Sanction

The institutions individuals responsible for Implementing disaster-management activities must have the necessary legal sanction and validity with requisite powers for managing emergency situations. This is necessary to ensure that they are recognised by all stakeholders as the legitimate policy making and/or Implementation authorities. The GoG alms to create a legal framework that incorporates the roles of all relevant institutions responsible for managing disasters through the proposed Gujarat State Disaster Management Act, 2002.

Accommodating Aspirations of People

The objective of any effort relating to disaster management is to benefit the community. People are central to the decision-making process for disaster management and their priorities should be reflected in the programmes undertaken.

Accommodating Social Conditions

Disaster management efforts should be sensitive to local customs, beliefs, and practices and be adapted to local conditions. In addition, changes in the community and evolving social and economic relationships must be borne in mind to avoid confrontation and bottlenecks. This will ensure participation of the local community and foster a culture of joint responsibility for disaster management at all levels.

Financial Sustainability

GoG is committed to allocating funds in the long term to ensure the sustain ability of disaster management effort. One of the key elements in ensuring the long-term sustenance and permanency of the organisation is the manner in which funds would be generated and deployed on an ongoing basis. This is necessary in view of Gig's focus on disaster mitigation.

Cost Sharing and Cost Recovery

The GoG encourages citizens and Government agencies to proactively enhance their capacity to deal with disasters. It is not possible for the GoG to bear all the costs of disasters on a sustainable basis, or provide rehabilitation on a long-term basis. The long-term approach is to move towards spreading the risks through various risk transfer mechanisms and in centivising individuals and other entitles to protect their interests through insurance. However, in doing so, GoG would seek to protect the interests of poorer sections of the society through appropriate mechanisms.

Develop, Share and Disseminate Knowledge

No single organisation can claim to possess all the capabilities required to provide effective disaster management. The disaster management entitles within Gujarat will typically network with a number of other entities to augment their capabilities. In addition, an institute dedicated to conducting research, development and training activities related to disaster management, shall be set up in the state. This institute would aid in the sharing and dissemination of specialised knowledge related to disaster management among various Implementation agencies, NGOs, private sector and the community in the state. Also, basic concepts related to disaster management and the role of the community therein shall be included in the curriculum of schools. This shall serve to sensitise people to the participative approach needed for effective disaster management. Information and knowledge embracing all facets of disaster-from mitigation to amelioration—shall be infused in schools, colleges and teacher's training syllabi.

Gujarat State Disaster Management Policy—Approach and Strategy

The Gujarat State Disaster Management Policy considers the understanding of hazards and disasters, their behavior, and the risks they pose to the community as fundamental to achieving successful disaster management. Thus, the strategy for implementing the GSDMP emphasises an integrated approach to disaster management, covering the following phases of managing disasters as essential components of any disaster management programme:

- Pre-disaster Phase
- Disaster/Impact Phase
- Post-disaster Phase

In order to carryout the prescribed activities contained within this policy, the GoG has defined a framework of operation for a set of agencies that play a key role in disaster management. The GSDMP envisages a DM framework where the following entitles play significant roles:

- Gujarat State Disaster Management Authority;

- State Relief Commissioner
- Government Departments,
- District Administration, headed by the District Collector,
- Local Authorities, including Municipal Corporations, District, Talukas, Gram Panchayats etc.
- Voluntary agencies, including NGOs,
- Public sector,
- Private sector,
- Community

The Implementation framework is based on the premise that disaster management is not a separate sector or discipline but an approach to solving problems that facilitates disaster management, harnessing the skills and resources across stakeholders. Therefore, a key element of the policy framework is to leverage the resources and capability of existing entitles and builds new capabilities, wherever necessary. While for most activities, the Implementation agencies remain the local authorities and Government functionaries, at the state level, GSDMA provides the overall direction and guidance that keeps the focus of various entitles on disaster management

Approach and Strategy for Implementation

Phase I: Pre-Disaster Phase-Prevention, Mitigation & Preparedness

The pre-disaster phase includes prevention, mitigation, and preparedness activities. These activities involve extensive data collection, maintaining directories of resources, developing action plans, capacity building, training and community awareness activities, among others. Government departments, district administration, local authorities and other relevant agencies will develop plans for prevention and mitigation of disasters and will build capacity and ensure preparedness in the event of a disaster actually taking place. The private sector, NGOs and the community would actively co-operate with the relevant agencies and would participate in training and other activities, conducted to augment their disaster management capabilities. in this context, GSDMA will act as the nodal agency for mitigation, preparedness and capacity creation and would facilitate and monitor the same. GSDMA will develop linkages with other stakeholders such as lending agencies. Government departments, local authorities, NGOs, private sector and community groups, national and international agencies in order to share knowledge and augment capacity on a holistic basis. The capabilities developed in this phase will play a critical role in all subsequent phases.

Key Activities in Pre-Disaster Phase

The following are the primary activities that will be carried out in this phase:

- *Planned Development*: There is a significant relationship in the way disasters and development affect each other. A long-term disaster management approach requires that planning activities for development should include robust mitigation practices. GoG would ensure that the planning activities of the state administration and local authorities take into account disaster risks and provide for suitable preventive and mitigating measures.
- *Development of Policies and Guidelines*: Effective disaster management requires the formulation of clear guidelines and subsequent compliance by all Government authorities, private sector entitles and the public at large. GoG would develop appropriate guidelines that would include:
    - Civil/architectural/structural/land use planning specifications,
    - Other guidelines specific to disaster type, like quarantine (epidemic), cropping Patterns (flood), evacuation (flood/cyclone) etc.
    - Development of laws/by laws that assist the Implementation of a framework for disaster management.

- *Establishing a Proper Chain of Command*: It is Imperative that a clear chain of command is established for effectively managing activities that immediately follow a disaster. The GoG will establish a clear chain of command with GSDMA as the nodal agency for all disaster management activities and coordination mechanisms across all entitles responsible for Implementation in the state.
- *Risk Assessment*: Before commencing preventive and preparedness activities, it is Important to identify and assess different types of risks for the state or parts of the state. Relevant departments would co-ordinate with GSDMA for a thorough assessment of:
  - *Hazards*: Classification of the region into zones based on hazard potential, and
  - *Vulnerability*: Assessment of degree of vulnerability of any given structure/people/region to the Impact of the hazard. The assessment will be used for developing detailed contingency plans and mitigation measures.
- *Develop Disaster Management Plans*: Detailed disaster management plans that are tailored to local needs would enable the relevant authorities and the community to respond systematically and effectively to disasters. The guidelines for such plans will be prepared by stakeholders like Government departments, district administration, local authorities and expert agencies etc. In consultation with GSDMA. The relevant authorities will prepare plans using these guidelines and ensure that these are constantly reviewed and updated. Existing procedure manuals viz. Relief Manuals and Flood Memorandum etc. would be reviewed and updated by the relevant Government department, under the overall guidance of the Authority. In addition, GSDMA and the relevant Government departments will prepare, and constantly update, a master contingency plan for the state based on the local plans. All District Collectors shall. In

advance, designate evacuation areas for use in emergencies and define plans for providing essential services to those areas, when in use.

- *Develop Repositories of Information*: It is critical that the relevant authorities should be in a position to quickly establish contact with people and resources in the aftermath of a disaster. GSDMA and the relevant Government departments will ensure that a comprehensive repository of information such as names, contact details, etc. is created, maintained and made easily accessible to the relevant authorities at all times.
- *Establish Communication and Technology Networks*: A robust state-wide information network is critical not only for managing disasters but also for effective functioning of the state government. Hence, the GoG will ensure that a comprehensive information network is available. This network must enable timely collection of hazard-related information and rapid dissemination of relevant information and warnings. GoG, in conjunction with GSDMA, will ensure that appropriate levels of redundancies are built info the network from a disaster perspective.
- *Developing Early Warning Mechanisms*: Early warning mechanisms help the relevant authorities in taking timely preventive measures and thereby, reduce the damage caused by disasters. Wherever possible, the relevant authorities. in conjunction with Government departments, shall set up early warning mechanisms to give advance warning for hazards like clones, floods etc. This shall include the setting up of Regional Response Centres, If necessary, for providing key early warning information and preparing for a response. In the event of occurrence of disaster. GSDMA shall ensure that these mechanisms are aligned with the overall disaster management plan for the state.
- *Establish Flexible Procedures*: Emergency situations may warrant simplified procedures for decisions relating

to evacuation, procurement of essentials, deployment of resources and such other activities. The relevant Government departments shall accordingly define flexible procedures for emergency situations.

- *Building Capabilities and Expertise*: It is necessary to build strong capabilities and expertise for handling various aspects of disasters. GSDMA shall network with a number of entitles such as disaster management agencies, research institutions, disaster management specialists, NGOs, community groups, line departments, local Government authorities and other stakeholders to augment the capabilities of all relevant entitles. In addition, GoG would set up an institute dedicated to conducting research, development and training activities related to disaster management in the state. This institute would aid in the sharing and dissemination of specialised knowledge related to disaster management among various Implementation agencies, NGOs, private sector and the community in the state. This institute will develop disaster management as a distinct management discipline for streamlined disaster management cadre.
- *Capacity Building*: The capacity of a community to withstand disasters is a function of:
  - awareness of the risks associated with disasters,
  - understanding of appropriate responses to disasters,
  - possessing the capacity to respond (training, research, availability of resources, skilled cadres),
  - setting up emergency response mechanisms that mobilize and deploy these trained resources in a quick, efficient and systematic manner.

  Hence, GSDMA and the relevant authorities shall ensure that the required awareness, resources and training are provided to the community. The community will also be urged to develop self-reliance by promoting and encouraging the spirit of self-help and mutual assistance. GSDMA shall support these initiatives by providing necessary resources and expertise from time to time. Also, basic concepts related to disaster management and the role of the community therein shall be included in the curriculum of schools. This shall serve to sensitise people to the participative approach needed for effective disaster management. GSDMA and the relevant Government departments shall ensure that personnel in specialised areas (medical care, rescue etc.) are adequately trained and available for deployment in emergency situations. Disaster management capacity building will have special thrust on empowering women towards long-term disaster mitigation.

- *Health and Medical Care*: Health and medical care is one of the most critical and Immediate response component in any disaster response situation. The capacity for providing medical assistance in disaster situation including the emergency response quality will be developed through trained personnel and appropriate infrastructure.
- *Knowledge Management*: The experience from previous disaster situations can provide valuable insights in managing disasters. It is vital that these learning's be captured in a systematic manner and utilised through knowledge management systems, feedback mechanisms etc. GSDMA and relevant authorities shall develop systems and processes that enable knowledge management by capturing, storing and effectively utilising information related to previous experience in disaster management. Information and knowledge embracing all facets of disasters from prevention to amelioration shall be disseminated in schools and colleges.
- *Funds Generation*: Disasters can cause extensive strain on financial resources because of relief, reconstruction and rehabilitation activities. In addition, activities relating to mitigation of and preparedness for disaster situation require funds. GoG intends to have a

budgetary allocation for disaster management. Further, funds would be made available through the Calamity Relief Fund. In addition, GSDMA, as nodal agency, would also identify alternative sources of funds for activities related to disaster management in the state.

- *Identifying Avenues for Risk Sharing and Transfer*: Risk sharing or risk transfer is a means of transferring a part of the disaster risk to a third party, which is willing to indemnify the beneficiary against the disaster for a specified premium. GoG would expire innovative means of sharing the costs associated with disasters through risk sharing, risk transfer and other measures since this would alleviate the burden on the state exchequer. This could be done through tax surcharge levies. Imposition of local taxes, beneficiary funding, disaster insurance, micro finance and bans, bonds, tax saving schemes linked to disaster relief investments etc.

Pre-disaster Phase—Roles of Relevant Agencies

The Gujarat State Disaster Management Authority

The Authority, in close co-ordination and with assistance of relevant Government departments would:

- Develop, maintain and update the Gujarat State Disaster Management Policy;
- Develop risk assessment programme and emergency plans that focus on disaster preparedness and mitigation,
- Establish an effective disaster management structure that can compile, Implement and monitor plans, as per the state policy;
- Incorporate disaster reduction, prevention and mitigation in socio-economic development planning,
- Give recognition to and ensure that district administration and local authorities are able to enforce

safety standards and rules, and strengthen their institutional capacity to deal with disasters and Implement disaster management plans,

- Streamline the development. Implementation and maintenance of contingency plans, and ensure that lifeline support systems are in place or enhanced,
- Enhance the existing capacity to limit damage by Improving surveillance and early warning systems,
- Facilitate in establishment of an enabling legislative and financial framework for disaster management, with due attention to the role of the different tiers of Government, the private sector and individuals,
- Develop and Implement educational and information programmes to raise public awareness with special emphasis on risk reduction and preparation,
- Stimulate the active involvement of the community, local groups, women, and disabled people in disaster management programmes with a view to facilitating the capacity of the community to deal with disasters,
- Promote and support research, development of new technologies and the use of local knowledge in measures that are aimed at supporting risk reduction and relate to disaster management activities,
- Ensure that regional and international experience, knowledge and resources are made available to support efforts in risk reduction and disaster management in the state.

Government Departments

Government departments must ensure adequate assistance to GSDMA, the district administration and local authorities for activities in this phase. These departments should ensure their active co-operation in setting up communication centers, drawing up contingency plans, assisting in capacity building, developing plans, gathering data, and Identifying and training appropriate personnel, under the overall direction of GSDMA.

District Collectors

The DC plays a co-ordinating role at the district level to ensure that the various Government functionaries in the district effectively carry out the DM activities in this phase. Working in close co-operation with Government departments and local bodies, the roles of DCs in this phase include:

- Ensuring that prevention, mitigation and preparedness activities are carried out in accordance with the appropriate guidelines,
- Providing inputs to GSDMA relating to various aspects of disaster management. Including early warnings, status of preparedness etc.
- Ensuring that relevant officials in the district possess the knowledge to deal with disaster management issues,
- Developing an appropriate relief Implementation strategy for the district, taking into account the unique circumstances of the district and prevailing gaps in institutional capacity and resources of the district,
- Facilitating and co-ordinating with local Government bodies to ensure that pre-disaster DM activities in the district are carried out optimally
- Facilitating community training, awareness programmes and the installation of emergency facilities with the support of local administration, NGOs, and the private sector,
- Establishing adequate inter-department coordination on issues related to disaster management,
- Reviewing emergency plans and guidelines,
- Involving the community in the planning and development process,
- Ensuring that local authorities. Including Municipal Corporations, Gram Panchayats etc. in the district, are involved in developing their own mitigation strategies,
- Ensuring appropriate linkage between DM activities and planning activities,
- Revisiting/reassessing contingency plans related to disaster management,

- Ensuring that proper communications systems are in place, and contingency plans maximize the involvement of local agencies,
- Ensuring that DM related equipment, especially fire-fighting equipment are well-maintained and ready to use.

Local Authorities

Local authorities should work in close co-ordination with and provide all assistance to relevant Government departments, under the overall guidance of DC or GSDMA. They should ensure that staff is adequately trained and all necessary resources are in a ready-to-use state. They would also be responsible for ensuring compliance to all specifications, as may be stipulated by Government departments or GSDMA, for structures under their jurisdiction.

Private Sector

The private sector should ensure their active participation in the pre-disaster activities in alignment with the overall plan developed by the GSDMA or the DC. They should also adhere to the relevant building codes and other specifications, as may be stipulated by relevant local authorities.

Community Groups and Voluntary Agencies

Local community groups and voluntary agencies including NGOs should actively assist in prevention and mitigation activities under the overall direction and supervision of the GSDMA or the DC. They should actively participate in all training activities as may be organised and should familiarise themselves with their role in disaster management.

Phase II: Impact Phase-Emergency Relief Measures and Relief

This phase includes all measures that are taken immediately in the aftermath of a disaster. The speed and efficiency of the response in this phase will crucially determine the loss to life and property. The ability of the state to respond to a disaster will be developed during the pre-disaster phase and the capabilities and institutions developed therein will be brought into play in this phase. Equally important will be the deployment of trained personnel, proper flow of information and speed of decision making.

The Revenue Department, in conjunction with other relevant Government departments would carry out activities in this phase. GSDMA will facilitate, co-ordinate and monitor the activities in this phase, wherever required. In case GSDMA believes that adequate relief is not being provided, it will be entitled to direct the SRC or the DC in taking requisite measures. The district administration headed by the DC, in conjunction with local authorities, shall be responsible for carrying out relief activities when the Impact of a disaster is restricted within the geographical boundaries of a district. The SRC shall coordinate and support relief activities of district administrations, where a disaster has affected more than one district recognizing the Importance of a clear chain of command in emergencies; the GoG will provide the SRC and DCs special powers to coordinate the activities of all Government authorities within their jurisdiction.

Key Activities in Impact Phase

The following are the primary activities that need to be carried out as part of emergency relief measures and in the relief phase to implement the policy guidelines:

Search and Rescue: The first priority in the aftermath of a disaster is to minimize loss of lives by undertaking rescue efforts for the affected people and providing medical treatment People who are trapped under destroyed buildings or are isolated due to floods or cyclones need immediate assistance. The District Collector, in conjunction with local authorities will be responsible for the search and rescue operations in an affected region. In doing so, the DC will be guided by relevant disaster management plans and will be supported by Government departments and local authorities.

Subsistence, Shelter, Health and Sanitation: Disasters can disrupt food supply, water supply and sanitation mechanisms. They may also force people to abandon their houses, either temporarily or permanently. Such situations typically result in an immediate need for shelter and protection against an incidence of epidemic. The relevant Government departments and local authorities would provide temporary shelter, health and sanitation services to rescued victims in order to prevent an outbreak of disease.

Infrastructure and Essential Services: Disasters can cripple the infrastructure of the state in terms of roads, public buildings, airfields, ports, communication network etc. An Immediate priority after a disaster is to bring the basic infrastructure into operating condition and deal with fires and other hazardous conditions that may exist in the aftermath of the disaster. The local authorities would work in close coordination with relevant Government departments like R&B, Police etc. to restore infrastructure to normal operating conditions.

Security: Usually, in a disaster situation, the police and security personnel are preoccupied with conducting search and rescue missions. Some people could take advantage of the situation and resort to looting and other anti-social activities. Consequently, it is necessary that security agencies functioning under the administrative control of the district authorities be geared to prevent this and provide a sense of security to citizens. SRC and DCs may invoke special powers vested in him/her by GoG, if existing powers regarding the same are inadequate.

Communication: The SRC, the district administration and local authorities would communicate to the larger community the Impact of the disaster and specific activities that are being or need to be undertaken to minimize the Impact. Some of these activities could include:

Media Management/PR: To ensure precise communication of the Impact of disaster and relief measures being taken and generate goodwill among community and other stakeholders,

Community Management: This includes communicating to

the affected communities with a view to preventing panic reactions, while providing relevant information and handling welfare enquiries,

Feedback Mechanisms: Using various mechanisms. Including the communication network to get feedback on relief measures and urgent needs of various agencies involved in emergency relief measures and relief.

Preliminary Damage Assessment: In the aftermath of a disaster, the district administration and local authorities receive simultaneous requests for assistance from scores of people and the resources at the disposal of the local administration are over-stretched. Hence, It is necessary to utilize and deploy the resources in the most efficient manner. Such deployment is not possible without undertaking a preliminary damage assessment. Once a disaster strikes, the Government departments and the local authorities shall carry out a preliminary need and loss assessment' and the district administration shall mobilize resources accordingly.

Funds Generation: The GoG allocates funds in the state Budget for relief activities. In addition, funds may be available through the Calamity Relief Fund. However, these funds may not be adequate to meet disaster management requirements in the aftermath of large-scale disasters like the January, 2001 earthquake in the state. In such circumstances, the GoG shall explore additional sources of funding through aid, grants, bans etc., as identified in the pre-disaster phase.

Finalizing Relief Payouts and Packages: Relief packages shall be customized, if required, to the specifics of the disaster by the GoG. Relief packages would include details relating to collection, allocation and disbursal of funds to the affected people. Relief would be provided all the affected families without any discrimination of caste, creed, religion, community or sex whatsoever.

Post-relief Assessment: GSDMA, with assistance from Government departments, district administration and local authorities will document learning from the relief experience, which can be inputs into further mitigation, relief or rehabilitation and reconstruction plans.

Impact Phase—Roles of Relevant Agencies

Emergency relief measures and relief in the immediate aftermath of a disaster is primarily carried out under the supervision of the Revenue Department. As far as possible, the relevant Government departments and district administration shall carry out their functions in accordance with the appropriate action plan developed under the guidance of GSDMA.

The Gujarat State Disaster Management Authority

The Authority shall develop policies and principles that guide and govern the emergency relief measures and relief in this phase. The Authority would also facilitate, co-ordinate and monitor emergency relief measures and relief being carried out by relevant agencies, if required, h this phase, GSDMA would:

- Recommend provision of additional powers to the Implementation agencies to coordinate and handle emergency relief measures and relief, if existing powers are inadequate,
- Facilitate, co-ordinate and monitor emergency relief measures and relief efforts of Implementation agencies,
- Co-ordinate with agencies of other states and other national and international agencies, if necessary, to augment the relief being provided,
- Ensure effective Implementation of policy guidelines by providing guidance to Implementing agencies from time to time.

The State Reset Commissioner

The SRC plays a direct and active role in relief. For a disaster that Impacts more than one district in the state, the SRC leads the relief efforts using the appropriate action plan. The SRC, either directly or through the respective District Collectors, co-ordinates and monitors the relief efforts using all the resources available with the State Government. In this phase, the SRC would:

- Recommend to the State Government when disaster needs to be declared,
- Supervise and undertake relief, if necessary, where disaster is declared,
- Support the DC in carrying out emergency relief measures in respective districts.

Government Departments

Functionaries of various Government departments will carry out relief operations as per disaster management plans developed, under the overall supervision of the SRC and the DCs. The respective district heads from the various Government departments shall report to the District Collector for the activities in this phase.

District Collectors

In this phase, the DC is responsible for all activities related to disaster management for his/her district including the flowing:

- Recommend to the State Government, declaration of disaster,
- Undertake and supervise emergency relief measures and relief operations in the district, with assistance of other relevant Government departments, local authorities, voluntary agencies, community groups etc.
- Assess need for additional resources and coordinate with the SRC and GSDMA for accessing statewide resources, if required.

Local Authorities

Local Authorities, including Municipal Corporations, Municipalities, District, Talk, and Gram Panchayats etc. would follow appropriate guidelines and procedures in undertaking emergency relief measures and relief activities, under the overall supervision and direction of the SRC or the DC.

Private Sector

The private sector would participate in the emergency relief measures and relief activities under the overall supervision and direction of the SRC or the DC. Based on the training and other capacity-building inputs received from GSDMA and other authorities, they should be able to mobilize resources immediately and commence emergency relief measures and relief at the earliest, if required. They should also actively provide relevant information regarding magnitude of effect of disaster, need for additional resources etc. They should also co-operate with relevant authorities in the conduct of a preliminary damage assessment etc.

Community Groups and Voluntary Agencies

Local community and voluntary agencies including NGOs are usually the first-responders in the aftermath of a disaster. The community and voluntary agencies should undertake rescue and relief measures immediately, to the extent possible on their own, before the district or the state administration steps-in. After the intervention of the district or state administration they should continue the works of rescue and relief under the overall direction and supervision of the SRC or the DC. They should work in close coordination with DC/SRC to avoid duplication and ensure equity. They should take a pro-active role in assisting the victims of disaster and should provide inputs to relevant authorities as to the magnitude of effect of disaster, need for additional resources etc. They should also co-operate with relevant authorities in the conduct of a preliminary damage assessment etc.

Phase III: Post-Disaster Phase—Reconstruction & Rehabilitation

The thrust of Government policy in this phase will be to ensure a speedy return to normalcy and mitigation of long-term consequences of the disaster. The policy objective of the Government in this phase will be to focus on economic and social consequences of the disaster and directing efforts to improve the same. The policy objectives will be carried out through the machinery of the state as well as with the aid of other stakeholders with whom long-term relationships have been developed in the pre-disaster phase.

Key Activities in Post-Disaster Phase

The following activities would be carried out in this phase to achieve policy objectives:

- *Detailed Damage Assessment*: While a preliminary damage assessment is carried out during the impact phase, a detailed assessment must be conducted before commencing reconstruction and rehabilitation activities. The relevant Government departments and local authorities shall initiate detailed assessment at their respective level for damages sustained in housing. Industry/services, infrastructure, agriculture, health/ education assets in the affected regions.
- *Assistance to Restore Houses and Dwelling Units*: GoG may. If needed, will formulate a policy of assistance to help the affected to restore damaged houses and dwellings. This should neither be treated as compensation for damage nor as an automatic entitlement.
- *Relocation* (*need based*): The GoG believes that need-based considerations and not extraneous factors drive relocation of people. The local authorities. In consultation with the people affected and under the guidance of GSDMA, shall determine relocation needs taking into account criteria relevant to the nature of the calamity and the extent of damage. Relocation efforts will include activities like:
  - Gaining consent of the affected population,

- Land acquisition,
- Urban/rural land use planning,
- Customizing relocation packages,
- Obtaining due legal clearances for relocation,
- Getting the necessary authorization for rehabilitation.
- Livelihood rehabilitation measures for reheated communities, wherever necessary.

■ *Finalizing Reconstruction & Rehabilitation Plan*: The effectiveness of any reconstruction and rehabilitation is based on detailed planning and careful monitoring of the relevant projects. GSDMA will oversee reconstruction and rehabilitation work and ensure that it takes info account the overall development plans for the state. GSDMA will approve reconstruction and rehabilitation projects based on:

- Identification of suitable projects by relevant departments,
- Project detailing and approval by the relevant technical authority.

■ *Funds Generation*: Reconstruction & rehabilitation projects are fairly resource intensive. These projects have been financed in the past primarily through the state exchequer. in the recent past, funds have also been raised from international agencies. GoG shall finalize the fund generation mechanism. Including the covenants and measures that govern fund inflow and disbursement and usage. This includes:

- Estimation of funds required based on detailed damage assessment reports and consolidation of the same under sect oral and regional heads,
- Contracting with funding agencies and evolving detailed operating procedures for fund flow and corresponding covenants.

■ *Funds Disbursement and Audit*: The funds raised from funding agencies are usually accompanied by stringent disbursement and usage restrictions. It is therefore important to monitor the disbursement of such funds to ensure that none of the covenants are breached. GSDMA, in conjunction with relevant agencies, shall monitor disbursal of funds by:

- Prioritizing resource allocation across approved projects,
- Establishing mechanisms (like a chain of banks, collection centres, nature of accounts, spread etc) for collection of funds,
- Ongoing monitoring and control of fund usage throughout actual project Implementation.

- *Project Management*: Since rehabilitation and reconstruction effort typically involves the co-ordinated efforts of several entitles, the GoG shall encourage the respective entities to strengthen programme management capabilities to ensure that synergies across and within entitles are managed efficiently. In addition. It is also necessary to constantly monitor the activity to ensure that the project is executed on time. in accordance with the technical specifications and to the satisfaction of the beneficiaries. GSDMA, in conjunction with relevant Government departments, will monitor the reconstruction activity that is carried out by various Implementation agencies. Typical Implementation activities would include:
  - Disaster proofing and retrofitting of houses,
  - Creation/Retrofitting of structures—including roads, bridges, dams, canals etc that may have been destroyed/damaged due to the disaster
  - Restoration of basic infrastructure facilities, for example, ports, airports, power stations etc.
  - Creation of health centres, first aid centres, hospitals, groups of doctors and surgeons etc.
  - Restoration of the industrial viability of the affected area.
  - Restoration of livelihood.
- *Communication*: Communication activities are necessary to convey to the larger community the scope and nature of the proposed reconstruction and rehabilitation effort

so as to increase the stakeholder awareness and buy-in for the ongoing activities. Hence, GSDMA and relevant Government departments, district administration and local authorities shall undertake:

- *Ongoing media management/Public Relations*: To ensure accurate communication of the reconstruction and rehabilitation measures being taken to various stakeholders,
- *Community Management*: This includes communicating to the affected communities with a view to appraising them of efforts being made for their relocation/rehabilitation/reconstruction,
- *Feedback Mechanisms*: Using the communication network to get feedback on reconstruction and rehabilitation measures.

- *Dispute Resolution Mechanisms*: GSDMA, in conjunction with relevant agencies, shall institutionalize mechanisms to address beneficiary grievances at various levels, as well as explore innovative ways of dispute minimization like involving the community in reconstruction initiatives. Appropriate mechanism with penalties for dealing with false claims will be evolved to prevent misuse of assistance.
- *Implementing Initiatives for Recovery of Reconstruction Costs*: The GoG shall finalize and Implement select recovery measures such as:
  - Imposing tax surcharge levies (central),
  - Imposing local taxes,
  - Facilitation of funding responsibility sharing by beneficiaries etc.

Post-Disaster Phase—Roles of Relevant Agencies

The post-disaster phase will mainly comprise reconstruction and rehabilitation activities. Currently, the activities in this phase are primarily carried out by the local bodies (Gram Panchayats, District, Talk, Municipal Corporations and Municipalities etc.) and various Government departments and boards. However, their activities in this phase shall be in accordance with the reconstruction and rehabilitation plans framed by GSDMA, in conjunction with implementing authorities.

The Gujarat State Disaster Management Authority

The Authority shall through the line departments/local bodies conduct a detailed assessment of damage, formulate estimates of financial support required and raising the required funds from various Governments, national and international funding agencies etc. The Authority would be responsible for the deployment of funds, as per identified priorities. The Authority would facilitate, co-ordinate and monitor reconstruction and rehabllltatbn efforts of various Government departments and other Implementation agencies in terms of project timelines, processes, funds deployment and benefits accruing to the affected community. As part of the same, the Authority would also be responsible for meeting the guidelines and providing feedback on various parameters related to the progress and outcome of the reconstruction and rehabilitation efforts to the various funding agencies and other stakeholders.

Government Departments and Local Authorities

Government departments and local authorities will conduct detailed damage assessment and will carry out the reconstruction and rehabilitation activities. in accordance with the policies and guidelines specified by the Authority. They would also be responsible for reporting various parameters, as may be required by GSDMA, related to the progress and outcome of the various projects undertaken by them.

District Collectors

The DC plays a co-ordinating role at the district level to ensure that the various Government departments effectively carry out the rehabilitation and reconstruction activities in this phase. The primary responsibilities of the DC in this phase are:

- Coordinating the reconstruction and rehabilitation

efforts in the district or a part of the district,

- Assisting GSDMA in monitoring the progress and outcome of reconstruction and rehabilitation efforts on the basis of the mechanisms established by GSDMA.

Private Sector

The private sector should provide fair estimates of damage assessment to relevant authorities and provide feedback in terms of their priorities and concerns for work related to rehabilitation and reconstruction. They should participate in the post-disaster activities. In co-ordination with GSDMA or the DC and in alignment with the overall policies and guidelines developed by the Authority. They should co-operate in providing feedback regarding progress and outcome of rehabilitation and reconstruction projects undertaken in their vicinity.

Community Groups and Voluntary Agencies

Community groups and voluntary agencies. Including NGOs should provide fair estimates of damage assessment to relevant authorities and provide feedback In terms of their priorities and concerns for work related to rehabilitation and reconstruction. They should participate in the post-disaster activities. In co-ordination with GSDMA or the DC and in alignment with the overall policies and guidelines developed by the Authority They should co-operate in providing feedback regarding progress and outcome of rehabilitation and reconstruction projects undertaken in their vicinity.

ANNEXURE 3
UNDMTS IN ACTION:
CASE STUDIES AND BEST PRACTICES

GEORGIA DMT CONTINGENCY PLANNING PROCESS

Background

The establishment of a Disaster Management Team in Georgia

resulted from the evolution of activities starting in 1996 when the DMTP started its activities in Georgia with a training needs assessment mission. In May, 1997 a sub-regional consultation was organised with the participation of the UN System, Government Officials and Scientists from Armenia, Azerbaijan, Georgia. In October, 1998 a sub-regional DMTP Workshop was conducted for high/mid level Armenian, Azure and Georgian Officials along with the UN System and national/international NGO representatives. DMTP initiated in 1999 a national disaster-management capacity-building project in Georgia financed by UNDP, (currently under implementation). At the suggestion of DMTP Member Agencies/Organisation workshop for the UN and National country teams with the key objective to improve co-ordination in emergency and disaster management was included in the 2001 DMTP Work Plan. Upon the arrival of the current UN Resident/ Humanitarian Co-ordinator to Georgia in September, 2001, the UN Country Team confirmed the need to finalise preparatory activities for the DMTP Workshop and the DMTP Secretariat fielded a programming mission in Georgia.

The programming mission for a DMTP workshop was held in October, 2001. The findings of this mission concluded that the UN Agencies and other international organisations, as well as representatives of the GoG Department of Extreme Situations and Civil Defence, Ministry of Interior, agreed there was a need for the promotion of a joint strategy for emergency and crisis management in the country. In particular, the experience in responding to droughts in 2000 and 2001 confirmed the lack of preparedness in the Country Team and that the early warning underestimated the risk. It was also confirmed that there was a need for and interest in establishing a Disaster Management Team. Many DMTP partners underlined the need for a sub-regional approach in regard to natural disaster preparedness and prevention.

DMTP Workshop

The DMTP workshop was held in Georgia from 3-7 December,

2001 with the overall objective to obtain the commitment for establishing a collaborative platform and partnership for improved disaster and emergency co-ordination by creating a DMT. The workshop's immediate objectives were aimed at explaining the UN DMTP concept and seeking ways to adjust the concept to the Georgia-specific realities begin clarifying roles and responsibilities of its members and setting the stage for collaborative action on contingency planning for potential emergency scenarios in Georgia.

It was found that guidelines for inter-action needed to be elaborated and UN and international preparedness should be systematised. As part of the future DMT action plan, contingency arrangements need to be made jointly to ensure that the team will be able to rapidly perform the functions required in case of an emergency.

A system of regular DMT meetings needed to be established, the DMT and its facilities needed to be organised in order to provide effective and efficient support to the emergency assistance operations in the country. It was felt that office organisation and responsibilities, available resources and means for information management should be agreed at the inter-agency level. The country team would have to also consider linkages between emergency response and disaster reduction and recovery in the context of the DMT activities in the future. A particular task would be to mainstream disaster risk considerations into all new development projects in the country.

Lessons learned, with particular focus on how emergencies were dealt with in past years by the international and national response teams needed to be shared. The workshop devoted sessions to the roles and responsibilities of the DMT, to identifying possible actions for the DMT, and presentations of relevant GoG entities regarding their roles, responsibilities and assets. Working groups focused on the topics of assessment and information management, sectoral response and overall GoG and international community co-ordination.

There were many outcomes from the workshop. The following summarises the key points:

1. **Regarding specific actions to increase preparedness, the DMT should:**
   (a) have contingency plans updated regularly by in-country international organisations
   (b) monitor early warning indicators
   (c) train staff
   (d) conduct baseline assessments
   (e) maintain a resource inventory of implementing agencies
2. **Regarding co-ordination and disaster management activities in Georgia, the workshop agreed on the outline of response co-ordination mechanisms:**
   (a) initial information on disaster is sent from disaster site and from international disaster monitoring centres to the Department of Extreme Situations and Civil Defence Government Co-ordination Centre
   (b) rapid Response/Assessment Teams are deployed to Disaster Site (Government is to determine if DMT should join initial assessment)
   (c) government establishes On-site Crisis Centre to oversee rescue/response. This may be a joint Crisis Centre with DMT if the scale of the crisis so requires.
   (d) the inter-Ministerial Standing Commission on Emergency and Civil Defence receives ongoing assessment information from disaster site (On-site Crisis Centre) and arranges in-country mobilisation of resources, normally with assistance from the DMT regarding aid from international organisations, including DMT resources
   (e) standing Commission request DMT assistance according to standard operational procedures (to be developed); DMT issues appeal, if necessary
   (f) joint GoG/DMT Co-ordination Team oversees distribution/allocation of received assistance including any administrative problems

3. **The agreed next steps to be taken by the Georgia DMT included the following:**
   (a) finalise and disseminate workshop report
   (b) elaborate the Roles and Responsibilities of the DMT in Georgia
   (c) heads of Agencies to confirm to the UN Resident Co-ordinator the names of DMT Focal Points
   (d) agree on the Work Plan for year 2002
   (e) elaborate an inter-agency contingency plan—interface with national preparedness plans—promote its elaboration (with DESCD, Ministry of Defence & other key ministries)
   (f) decide on creation of working groups, such as for contingency planning, sectoral coordination, information management, capacity analysis (jointly between international organisations and national partner agencies/ministries)
   (g) synthesise and integrate various hazard mapping initiatives
   (h) in collaboration with DESCD, Ministry of Defence and other key ministries and the DMT Members, draft an agreement for co-ordination in disaster and emergency management
   (i) define additional training needs (joint for international agencies and national partners, such as training on needs assessment, co-ordination, conflict prevention, etc.)
   (j) Create a library and electronic database comprising all disaster, emergency, and crisis management guides, projects, training materials and make those available to all DMT members (UNDP-DMTP Project)

The first seven of these action steps were completed by mid 2002, including the elaboration of contingency plan outlines which was facilitated by holding a contingency planning workshop.

Following the decision to have a DMT, the first official DMT meeting was held in February, 2002, with many of the participants from the December workshop and some new additions. The DMT considered and approved the following summary description of its composition, objectives and major roles and responsibilities.

Summary
Disaster Management Team in Georgia

Composition

An expanded Disaster Management Team in Georgia was established in December, 2001 following a Disaster Management Training Programme (DMTP) workshop. It consists of UN agencies as well as interested international NGOs and donors.

Objective

The DMT is a mechanism for emergency preparedness and response co-ordination, providing a forum for information exchange, discussion, and seeking consensus. It supports and assists the UN Resident Coordinator in the exercise of his system-wide functions, as UN Resident Co-ordinator and also as Humanitarian Co-ordinator. The DMT recognises and in no way supersedes the mandates and specific functions of the various organisations.

Major Roles and Responsibilities

The primary purpose of the DMT is to prepare for and facilitate a prompt, effective and concerted country-level response by the UN system and other major actors in the event of a disaster/emergency. The Team should ensure co-ordination of international assistance to the receiving government in respect to emergency response, rehabilitation, reconstruction, and disaster mitigation. The team should co-ordinate all disaster-related activities, technical advice and material assistance provided by the participating organisations, as well as take steps to avoid wasteful duplication or competition for resources by agencies.

The Disaster Management Team will:

- define the functional responsibilities of each member of the DMT in the event of a disaster or emergency as part of the country contingency plan;
- compile, evaluate, and keep up-to-date information about disaster risks and preparedness arrangements in the country, the resources likely to be available for use in an emergency, and the kinds of international assistance likely to be required in particular situations;
- establish, in advance, the systems and procedures that will be needed to manage the DMT response to potential disasters, including arrangements for assessments, information management, communications and co-ordination; draw up and regularly review an action/preparedness plan for the UN system at the country level so that all members know in an emergency what to do, when and how, in order to complement each other and provide concerted assistance to the Government and affected populations which is timely, coherent and effective;

(Contd.)

(Contd.)

- establish the DMT co-ordination mechanisms for preparedness and response for likely scenarios; if needed, designate suitable offices and earmark computing, communications and other necessary equipment;
- document all operating procedures fully and clearly, and make this documentation readily available to all concerned;
- send OCHA/DMTP copies of government and agency-specific preparedness plans and other relevant documents.
- review the implications of known and potential hazards for the development process in the country and co-ordinate the assistance of the various UN and international organisations in relation to risk reduction measures and national disaster preparedness arrangements, identify opportunities for collaboration in joint and/or parallel projects in various sectors that may directly or indirectly contribute to risk reduction and preparedness, particularly at the local level

In the event of an emergency or disaster that does not fall within the mandate and overall competence of given UN organisations, the DMT seeks to:

- arrange assistance to the Government, mobilising and co-ordinating international assistance and in assessing the situation and the practical possibilities for meeting the priority needs;
- establish a consolidated DMT assessment of the requirements for international assistance, incorporating the conclusions of any expert assessment missions organised by the headquarters of the competent agencies;
- develop an integrated plan and consolidated appeal for the provision of concerted assistance by the UN system, taking account of the resources expected to be mobilised from national and other sources;
- co-ordinate the communication of the DMT assessment, plan and appeal to OCHA, the headquarters of other agencies and local representatives of potential donors and operational organisations;
- co-ordinate the delivery of assistance by DMT agencies and facilitate their resource mobilisation efforts at country level, including approaches to the local representatives of potential donors;
- arrange the provision of consistent and coherent operational support and technical assistance to the Government, where required, possibly including the establishment and operation of an Emergency information and Co-ordination Support Unit or through assistance to OCHA's UN Disaster Assessment and Co-ordination Team (UNDAC);
- anticipate the time when the international emergency response should be scaled down or end, and in particular when "external" international aid staff are present, when and how an "exit" strategy should be conducted

Contingency Planning Workshop

A three-day contingency planning workshop was held at UN House, Tbilisi from 20-22 February, 2002. At the workshop, two scenarios were identified: "renewed conflict in Abkhazia" and "major earthquake in Tbilisi." These scenarios were considered from the sectoral perspective by four workgroups formed at the workshop (food and nutrition; health and water/sanitation; shelter/nonfood items and information management/co-ordination). In addition, lead agencies for each of the four workgroups were identified.

Development of Contingency Plans

At the contingency planning workshop, work was initiated on the development of contingency plans for the DMT. The following information for contingency planning was summarised or outlined for both scenarios:

1. a description of the humanitarian scenario with an estimate of the main humanitarian consequences
2. an estimate of the main humanitarian needs, expressed as a percentage of sectoral categories
3. identification of local coping mechanisms, which included a description of local resources available to meet potential needs
4. identification of the main actors in the response
5. constraints and gaps in meeting the needs generated by the scenario were identified, such as lack of funds and lack of institutional capacity
6. the main planning assumptions were articulated, such as a "free corridor" for displaced people and availability of resources for food and shelter
7. the issue of the need for early warning indicators elaboration was raised
8. sectoral coordination was arranged with a lead organisation identified
9. the workgroups agreed to develop sectoral response plans, which would include within each sector the sectoral objectives, the basic elements of response, how needs assessment and coordination would be achieved, as well as an identification of preparedness actions and follow-up required within each sector

Subsequent to the initial work on these contingency plans, the UN Humanitarian Co-ordinator in Georgia received a letter from the GoG Head of standing commission on Emergencies and Civil Defence of the National Security Council, Minister of Interior, General-Mayor of Police. The letter asserted that the GoG will co-operate with the DMT at all stages of disaster management and that they plan to jointly elaborate a memorandum that would describe the relationship modality between the DMT and the GoG at all stages of disaster management and would define the functions and responsibilities of these parties.

The work of the DMT has continued to meet its work plan objectives, elaborated at the DMTP workshop. For example, on 26 April, 2002 an other workshop was held, this time to increase DMT members' awareness of national disaster preparedness planning and response capacities, and possible gaps in these areas, in order for the DMT to best make its own preparedness plans, and to support the Government and related institutions in this regard. The Head of the Department of Extreme Situations and Civil Defence was invited to present the mechanism of national disaster response plans. Lessons learned from the 1988 Spitak, Armenia earthquake were also shared by an invited earthquake specialist from Armenia.

Ironically an earthquake occurred in Tbilisi the day before the workshop was held. Fortunately, its severity did not come close to the Contingency Plan scenario of a magnitude 8 earthquake, affecting 400,000 of Tbilisi's population. Nevertheless, five people were killed, 52 were injured and severe damage was inflicted on Tbilisi housing and public infrastructure. In the 1 May, 2002 OCHA Situation Report No. 4, it was reported that the GoG requested assistance from the international community. However, of the remaining emergency needs that were identified on 1 May, it was estimated that resources already in-country could meet them. The Georgia DMT assessed the four field sites where approximately 362 families had been located in order to identify any remaining gaps in assistance. The DMT then decided which agencies among them would take lead responsibility for addressing the gaps discovered in their assessment.

The DMT has tested its capacity while responding to the 25 April earthquake consequences. The DMT was mobilized immediately and emergency relief assistance was provided to the victims of the earthquake. Fortunately the scale of the emergency was relatively low, thus DMT member agencies were able to cope with locally available resources. The DMT also worked closely with the Special State Commission chaired by the State Minister and assisted Government in developing the emergency appeal covering immediate relief and more long-term rehabilitation programmes. By the end of May, UNDP also initiated a mission of an expert who worked closely with the Government in elaborating a rehabilitation programme.

On 3-6 June, a special mission was fielded from OCHA Geneva to provide the DMT and the Government with the information regarding the various international coordination mechanisms and support available in times of disasters or emergencies. Among the types of international support discussed included: UNDAC, INSARAG, MCDU, telecommunications teams, and other OCHA-specific support, as well as support by other key UN agencies (e.g., logistics coordination by WFP). The mission also reviewed with OCHA, the Government and the DMT how these support functions would be provided and how they will be linked and coordinated with the relevant in-country entities.

On 4-15 July, the DMT hosted another mission from SDC (that is a member of the DMT) that fielded an expert in Georgia to undertake lessons learned study from the 25 April earthquake. A draft lessons learned paper was developed by the DMT by the end of May that was also used for this SDC study. The findings and recommendations of this study will be incorporated in the draft contingency plan.

CHINA FLOODS 1998: UNDMT RESPONSIVENESS

Introduction

The relentless rains suffered by China in summer 1998, caused vast flooding that affected around 180 million people or one seventh of China's population. The floods caused major devastation in central, southeast, north and northeast China, mainly along the Yangtze River and its tributaries. The Songhuajiang and Nenjiang Rivers also flooded much of the northeastern provinces.

Devastation ranged from human tragedy to massive infrastructure damage. Up to 28 January, 1999, the Government reported 4,150 deaths. Eighteen million people were evacuated from the flooded areas. More than 23 million hectares of crops were affected, of which 5.3 million hectares were completely lost. A total of 13 million houses were affected with 6.9 million of these being destroyed. Damages to houses, health clinics, schools, factories, water supply facilities, roads, bridges, and irrigation systems are estimated at US$ 31 billion.

The disaster was caused by extremely heavy rainfall, along with the melting of long-present and deep snow that had accumulated on the Qinghai-Tibet plateau. According to Chinese Government officials, the rampant deforestation on the upper-reaches of the Yangtze, was a cause of soil erosion and silting in the river, and therefore constituted a major contributing factor. In addition, many areas surrounding the river, including former flood plains, have become overpopulated and are exploited for agricultural production.

Although China's rivers flood annually, the extent of the floods in 1998 has been unparalleled. Unparalleled not only in the magnitude of the geographic areas affected, but also in the huge numbers of people affected and the duration of time they spent on dykes. In the south, along the Yangtze River basin, more than 2.9 million people sought refuge on dykes. In previous floods, people remained on the dykes for up to two weeks. As a result of the deluge in 1998, people were forced to live on the dykes for up to five months. All these survivors rendered homeless and with no remaining source of income, existed in overcrowded conditions, with insufficient shelter and under deteriorating sanitary and health environment. When weather conditions abruptly worsened, their situation became yet more critical. This was particularly true in mid-November in the north, when bitterly frigid Siberian winds began to whip the landscape. The temporary shelters were not built to withstand such an onslaught, and people in the north had once again to be relocated, this time to existing buildings in other areas of the province.

Chinese Government Response

China's advanced prevention policy, based on timely predictions, forecasting and early warning, significantly limited the scope of damage inflicted by the floods. These early warning systems continued into the autumn, when the water receded.

The rescue relief operations mounted by the Chinese Government have been impressive at every level of implementation and the Chinese people exhibited exemplary attitudes both in country and abroad, in coping with the effects of the floods. The massive mobilisation of farmers, villagers, police and the Army to shore up the dykes and provide relief to the affected populace precluded much greater suffering and loss of human life. The Chinese fund-raising campaigns ensured much-needed supplies for the victims during the first weeks of the disaster. The Chinese Red Cross, the international Federation of Red Cross and Red Crescent Societies (IFRC) and those non-governmental organisations involved provided substantial and essential relief assistance, which complemented and enhanced the Government's efforts and those of international organisations.

United Nations Response

In view of the devastating scale of the disaster, the Government of the People's Republic of China decided to appeal for international support to complement its own massive efforts. On 27 August, 1998, the Government approached the United Nations (UN) through the Chinese permanent mission in New York, with a plea for help in mobilising and coordinating international assistance. In early September, a joint United Nations Disaster Assessment and Co-ordination (UNDAC) and a UN inter-agency Mission were fielded to determine the immediate disaster relief needs. Such UNDAC teams are established by the Office for the Co-ordination of Humanitarian Affairs (OCHA) to assist in meeting international needs for early and qualified information during the first phase of a sudden-onset emergency. The United Nations Development Programme (UNDP), the World Health Organisation (WHO), the World Food Programme (WFP), and the Food and Agriculture Organisation of the United Nations (FAO) participated in the joint inter-agency assessment team. In light of the mission's findings and under the guidance of the UN Resident Co-ordinator, the UN system in China launched the *International Appeal/or Flood Emergency Relief and Immediate Rehabilitation* on 23 September, 1998.

Based on international experience in disaster management, the US$ 139 million appeal was designed to complement Government's efforts. The appeal was designed to last for four months and aimed to provide emergency relief to the most vulnerable flood victims in the form of food, shelter, water supply and sanitation facilities, disease control services, seed and fertiliser, and the construction of new schools. These funds could be channelled either through the United Nations system or through concerned international, bilateral or NGO organisations and agencies.

Donor Response

More than 110 million US dollars were provided by the international community of which 80 million (73%) were channelled through the UN system. Donors included twenty-one governments, eighteen national Red Cross societies, two Hong Kong NGOs, seven UN agencies and seven international private contributors.

Summary of the UN Emergency Relief Programme

United Nations Development Programme (UNDP)

Through the Ministry of Civil Affáirs, UNDP delivered US$

3,609,765 of assistance for emergency shelters provided by the Governments of Austria, Belgium, Italy, Norway, Sweden, and the United Kingdom. The main objective of this assistance was to provide temporary shelters in the south and construction materials in the north to the most vulnerable victims of the 1998 floods. Close to 50,000 people benefited from this assistance. By the end of December, 1998, the project had delivered a total of 6,693 tents in 104 townships in four provinces. These tents will be returned to the Ministry of Civil Affairs, refurbished and kept in regional emergency relief storage for use in future emergencies.

In addition, about 16,000 people benefited from the provision of construction materials in the north. The Government matched the contribution provided by the international community for the construction materials. The combined assistance covered between 25 to 33 per cent of the total reconstruction costs for each house. Flood victims were also eligible for a Government loan to meet the balance. Some houses were completed before the ground froze at the beginning of the winter. Because of the harsh winter conditions, the construction of other houses had to be postponed until springtime. Houses will be rebuilt on the highest ground of the village. Through UNDP and the China International Centre for Economic and Technical Exchanges (CICETE) at the Ministry of Foreign Trade and Economic Co-operation (MOFTEC), the British Government provided UNDP with £ 500,000 for school rehabilitation. The contribution is being used to procure construction materials with which to rebuild 34 primary schools and 1 middle school in 20 counties of Jiangxi Province. The work should be completed during the summer of 1999.

In addition, UNDP organised a workshop to train 30 frontline relief operation managers in 14 flood-prone provinces and municipalities in Northern China. This took place from on 13-16 January, 1999. The initiative was a follow-up to the UNDP disaster management workshop held for 13 flood-prone provinces in Southern China in June, 1998, just before the catastrophic floods.

World Food Programme (WFP)

The four hardest hit provinces of Anhui, Hubei, Hunan and Jiangxi, were targeted in the Chinese Government's request to the UN World Food Programme (WFP) for food aid. A beneficiary caseload of 5.8 million villagers received 107 days' rations of rice between October, 1998 and March, 1999; equivalent to 310,000 metric tones.

Austria, Canada, Denmark, Sweden, Switzerland, the United Kingdom and the United States contributed 285,000 metric tons of wheat worth some $70 million. The wheat was swapped for rice by the Chinese Government, on a "no loss, no gain" basis. The Government of China also contributed 100,000 metric tons of rice to the operation.

In November 1998, rice was distributed amongst 5.8 million people, many living in temporary shelters on dykes. Then as water levels dropped, flood victims returned to their home areas and participated in *Food-for-Work* projects including house building the restoration of drinking water wells, land clearance, the de-silting of irrigation channels and farm road repair.

During the *Food-for-Work* phase from December, 1998 to February, 1999, people in the central and southern provinces repaired or rebuilt over 79,000 houses and renovated 2,000 km (1,250 miles) of farm and village roads. A total of 55,130 hectares (136,000 acres) of farmland were cleared of silt, 247,000 water wells or tanks and 7,600 km (4,750 miles) of irrigation canals were refurbished.

World Health Organisation (WHO)

In response to the request for medical emergency relief assistance the Government of Japan (through a bilateral agreement with China) and the Government of Sweden (through WHO) pledged 11 million and 1 million US dollars respectively. The relief activities minimised the adverse health effects to the flood victims by providing water purification tablets, medicines, vaccines, cold chain equipment, syringes, sterilising equipment, diagnostic tests, pesticides, blankets and tents for emergency relief posts, vehicles and also training in the surveillance of infectious diseases.

The 12 million US dollars were expanded in the purchase of health relief items on the international and local market. The Ministry of Civil Affairs and the Ministry of Health distributed the purchased medicines, vaccines and equipment to the counties with the greatest needs in the eight provinces most adversely affected by the floods. Great efforts were made to provide transport of medical personnel and equipment during the Sub-National Poliomyelitis Eradication Immunisation Days in December, 1998 and January, 1999, ensuring delivery of a high level of service. Disaster surveillance training courses were given to health care providers in the first quarter of 1999. The Government of Japan, the Government of Sweden and WHO conducted field investigations in September, November, December, 1998 and in January, 1999, in order to evaluate the effectiveness of the project.

The response to the health section of the UN inter-agency appeal has been significant and the projects were successful in preventing serious outbreaks of disease and unnecessary illness and death. The health care situation will, however, remain critical until the end of summer 1999. The co-operation of the Governments of Japan and Sweden and the WHO with the Government of China has led to effective relief health programmes for Chinese flood victims.

United Nations Children's Fund (UNICEF)

A UNICEF assessment mission carried out in early September, 1998 identified serious risks of post-flood disease outbreak in Hunan, Hubeis, and Jiangxi provinces. Proposals were made for emergency activities to rapidly restore safe water and environmental sanitation conditions for displaced families as they returned to their homes in 18 of the most severely affected counties. This effort included tools to develop and implement management and supervision protocols designed to ensure environmental clean-up and intensive health education.

Project activities covering 205 townships and 2,453 villages in the three provinces were completed. Villagers were contacted and mobilised to clean away silt, rubbish and polluted water, and they sterilised the environment with chemicals. Health education activities were carried out directly for the benefit of nearly all the families and schoolchildren. These included distribution of simple posters and pamphlets.

Access to safe water was re-established for most areas by the end of 1998. This included the restoration of 192 water stations and placement of 55,920 hand-pumps. The project aimed to provide safe water for a population of over two million persons.

Evaluation and field audit visits found that the project had been fully implemented in all target areas. The United States, United Kingdom, Greece, Sweden and Hong Kong Committee supported this effort for UNICEF.

Food and Agricultural Organisation of the United Nations (FAO)

FAO joined the OCHA/UNDAC mission to the field in September, 1998. The report of the mission formed the first inter-agency appeal, which was launched in September, 1998.

In response to the Government request for emergency assistance, FAO has integrated two TCP emergency assistance projects into its regular 1998 programme in order to assist the farmers affected by the unprecedented floods in the seven most severely flood-affected provinces of Anhui, Jiangxi, Hunan, Hubei, Heilongjiang, Jilin and Inner Mongolia. The assistance was designed to rehabilitate agriculture by providing farmers with seeds (1,540 tons) and fertilisers (536 tons). This assistance was very well received by the Government and by the farmers themselves.

FAO's multidisciplinary mission was funded by the Government of Sweden in response to FAO's request in the first UN Inter-Agency Appeal launched in September, 1998. The mission was fielded in November/December, 1998 and assessed damage and rehabilitation needs for the agriculture, livestock, forestry and fisheries sectors in the seven most severely flood-affected provinces of Anhui, Jiangxi, Hunan and Hubei along the Yangtze River and Heilongjiang, Jilin and Inner Mongolia in the northeast region. On the basis of the mission's findings, FAO participated in the second UN Inter-Agency Appeal launched in February, 1999 for an amount of US$ 18.5 million, envisaged for restocking the crop, livestock, forestry and fisheries sectors and for co-ordinating activities.

It is considered that emergency assistance is still needed to provide timely support to the Government and affected farmers. Higher agricultural production must be sustained in order to feed the population in the short-term.

United Nations Educational, Scientific and Cultural Organisation (UNESCO)

UNESCO's educational assistance to China has included the construction of schools, the provision of chairs, desks, blackboards, library books and teaching equipment as well as scholarships for the neediest students enabling them to purchase school textbooks and to pay basic school fees. UNESCO's assistance is in conformity with the Ministry of Education's new standards for school construction, which aim to improve amenities and provide greater resistance to flooding. Construction was carried out with a view to long-term self-sustainability.

UNESCO is currently constructing many schools in Heilongjiang Province. These projects will be completed by September, 1999, in time for the new school year. Further construction of urgently needed schools is subject to availability of funds. Continuous efforts will be made to mobilise additional funding from the private and public sectors to fulfil the need for schools in the hardest hit and the most underdeveloped areas affected by the floods.

The United Nations Office for the Co-ordination of Humanitarian Affairs (OCHA)

In response to the UN Inter-Agency Appeal for Emergency Relief and Initial Rehabilitation, some donors made their contribution to the Chinese Government directly, while others channelled their contributions through the different UN agencies. US$ 1,738,985.39 of the total relief funds were channelled through OCHA. After deduction of the standard programme support costs of 3 per cent, a net amount of US$ 1,688,335.33 remained. An OCHA Emergency Grant of US$ 50,000 along with a balance of US$ 16,210 from previous contributions for China was added to this figure. Therefore a total of US$ 1,754,545.33 was available for programme implementation. From this contribution, US$ 1,633,953 were used for temporary shelter and US$ 120,269.31 for the coordination of UN agency relief services in Beijing, China. The breakdown of the funds channelled through OCHA is shown in the Certified Financial Statement of Accounts, which accompanies this narrative report to the OCHA donors.

On the basis of the findings of the UNDAC mission, and following consultations with the Ministry of Civil Affairs, UNDP developed a temporary shelter project whereby tents would be provided for the south and construction materials for the north. The shelter project was supported by the Ministry of Civil Affairs and approved by each donor. 4,690 simple and padded tents were purchased in the interests of this project with contributions channelled through OCHA. In total four provinces benefited from this project.

OCHA recruited a consultant to assist the UN Resident Co-ordinator in providing co-ordination services. Five assessment and monitoring missions were carried out in co-ordination with the UN agencies and the Chinese government. An inter-agency relief programme-monitoring mission was then carried out, in December, 1998, together with donor representatives. The objectives of the mission were to give donors direct access to information on the impact of their contributions, and to help potential donors to better understand how emergency relief funds channelled through the UN system were used. Having participated in this mission, Canada made emergency food contributions through one of the UN agencies, to a value of US$ 8 million.

The OCHA disaster management consultant also

conducted a mission in the north of the country, to the Inner-Mongolia Autonomous Region. The findings were shared with UNDMT members. The findings increased the level of attention paid by the UN agencies to the affected provinces and the autonomous region in the north. A week later, UNICEF acted on the mission results by fielding an in-depth mission to one of the three counties in the Inner-Mongolia Autonomous Region, and formulating a post-flood relief programme for the North that has received US$ 1.3 million from the Australian Government. The programme is benefiting three flood-affected provinces in the north. UNDP also allocated US$ 50,000 to support the government rehabilitation and reconstruction efforts in the Inner-Mongolia Autonomous Region.

The OCHA consultant attended UNDMT weekly meetings and co-ordinated disaster relief and initial rehabilitation activities with the Chinese Government. The consultant also contributed to the preparation of periodic progress reports on the first inter-agency appeal and assisted in the preparation of the United Nations Inter-agency Appeal for Disaster Mitigation and Post-flood Relief in China which was issued on 10 February, 1999. Furthermore, the OCHA consultant was instrumental in preparations for and the implementation of the International Workshop on Natural Disaster Management, held from 10 to 12 June, 1999 in Beijing. This task included the coordination of presentations with all international participants as well as the preparation of an outline, a workshop brochure, invitations, presentations and the development of the final report.

Programme Impact

On the strength of the financial contributions, the Government of China and UN Agencies together provided emergency relief in the form of shelter, food, water supplies, sanitation facilities, disease control services, seeds, fertilisers and construction of new schools (see Table 1). The Government's co-operation was essential for implementation of all of these programmes.

Table 1: Flood Emergency Relief and Immediate Rehabilitation Needs as Delineated in the Appeal Launched by the UN System in China

Relief Activity	*Amount of Appeal (US$)*	*Amount Pledged (US$)*	*Amount Channeled Through UN (US$)*
Shelter	$ 28,800,000	$4,122,765	$ 3,609,765
Food	$ 87,700,000	$ 70,636,053	$ 70,636,053
Medicine	$ 7,000,000	$ 12,000,000	$ 1,000,000
Water and Sanitation	$ 5,400,000	$ 2,820,000	$ 2,820,000
Agriculture	$ 90,000	$590,000	$ 590,000
Education and Initial Rehabilitation	$ 9,600,000	$ 16,465,656	$ 1,035,656
Associated relief assistance	$ 0	$3,900,000	$ 0
Co-ordination	$ 450,000	$ 345,847	$ 345,847
Total	$ 139,040,000 (100%)	$110,880,321 (79.75%)	$ 80,037,321 (57.56%)

Total amounts provided by donors, and the amounts channeled through the UN system, September, 1998. In addition to the above amounts, FAO provided 2 TCP emergency projects valued at US$ 800,000 for provision of seeds and fertilisers under its regular programme to flood affected farmers in 7 provinces.

The international response to the appeal had a positive impact on millions of the most vulnerable flood victims, including the young, old, disabled and sick, during a period of more than 4 months. The relief activities reached flood victims in all 7 of the most affected provinces (See Table 2).

Table 2: Number of Flood-Victims and Flood Affected Provinces that Benefited from Emergency Relief and Immediate Rehabilitation Assistance

Relief Activity	*Number of Beneficiaries*	*Number of Affected Provinces Reached*
Shelter	50,0000	7 of 7
Food	5,800,000	4 of 7
Medicine	3,000,000	7 of 7
Water and Sanitation	2,800,000	6 of 7
Agriculture	160,000	6 of 7
Education and Initial Rehabilitation	57,000	2 of 7

Rehabilitation activities implemented by UN agencies in collaboration with the Chinese Government, September, 1998 to May, 1999.

The World Bank Group and the Asian Development Bank simultaneously launched emergency recovery loans. Although these activities were not included in the Joint Appeal, they were coordinated with the UN System relief response. The emergency rehabilitation programmes received US$ 380 million to finance the rehabilitation and reconstruction work on flood damaged facilities and infrastructures. A total of 50 million flood-affected persons in 6 affected provinces will benefit from the programmes.

Field-level Co-ordination and Follow-up on the United Nations Inter-Agency Appeal

During the disaster response, the United Nations Disaster Management Team (UNDMT), under the leadership of the UN Resident Co-ordinator, played an important role in effectively coordinating and programming UN and international resources in China. The UNDMT was activated in June, 1998. It includes representatives from all UN agencies present in China, as well as representatives from the World Bank and IFRC. UNDP chaired the meetings. OCHA detailed a disaster management consultant to assist in co-ordinating UNDMT activities.

From August onward, the team met weekly to co-ordinate and monitor agency activities. In recognition of the need for centralised co-ordination, the team established itself as a focal point for the UN agencies and donors. Speakers from Government, UN agencies, and other relief agencies briefed on their findings and activities. As the skills of each team member strengthened over time, the team as a whole achieved higher levels of co-ordination, planning, and decision making. Monthly progress reports on all UN projects were jointly prepared and distributed to all donors, embassies and UN agencies. UNDMT briefings were arranged for UN agencies. Government, the press, embassies and donors.

From October, 1998 to January, 1999, separate individual assessments were conducted by FAO, UNDP, the United Nations Educational, Scientific and Cultural Organisation (UNESCO), the United Nations Children's Fund (UNICEF), the United Nations Industrial Development Organisation (UNIDO), the World Bank, and IFRC. Missions either focused on monitoring implementation of the activities of the September appeal or assessing the remaining needs. A joint visit in December, 1998 was organised by UNDP/OCHA, UNICEF and WFP to provide opportunities for donor representatives to monitor the progress of donor-funded programmes. Missions were carried out in the seven worst affected provinces: Hubei, Hunan, Jiangxi, Anhui, Jilin, Heilongjiang and the Inner Mongolia Autonomous Region.

Several of the most pressing relief and rehabilitation needs did not feature in the September appeal, as they could neither be assessed nor met in many of the most badly damaged provinces until floodwaters had receded. For example, FAO were unable to assess the full extent of damages and rehabilitation needs for livestock, fisheries, and agriculture during their first joint mission in September. FAO returned to the affected areas in November to determine the assistance required for rehabilitation of agriculture and production facilities. Similarly, flood relief efforts could not be completed before the winters freeze in the remote northern regions and provinces; relief efforts had to resume with the spring thaw. Therefore, under the guidance of the UN Co-ordinator, the UNDMT also took the lead in preparing and launching a Second Appeal on 10 February, 1999.

The objectives of February's appeal were to reinforce flood relief efforts; to rehabilitate essential human settlements, education and production facilities; and to set in motion integrated flood management and information systems in order to mitigate flood risk in the future. This appeal was not limited to a specific time period. UNDMT will provide an assessment of the response by early 2000.

Capacity Building

Capacity building is one of the major achievements of the UN flood relief programmes. Overtime the capacity of the UNDMT improved considerably. While external help from UNDAC was essential to drawing up the first appeal, the members of UNDMT prepared and launched the second appeal on their own. One member of the UNDMT received specialised international assessment training from OCHA.

Emphasis was placed on training Government counterparts at every level of administration, whether at village or national capacity. WHO conducted 9 national and provincial level workshops for training Epidemic Prevention Station staff in disaster surveillance. UNDP trained disaster managers at county and provincial level in disaster management and preparedness and 27 provinces benefited from the training. UNICEF trained 24,982 relief personnel through the *Training-For-Trainers* programme for disease prevention and environmental disinfection. The training proved to be cost-effective at provincial, county, township, and village levels. In addition, WFP trained national volunteers and short-term international staff in monitoring food distribution.

Lessons Learned

Lesson 1: UNDMT proved to be an efficient mechanism/or the co-ordination of the emergency relief

UNDMT developed into a UN inter-agency co-ordination focal point. Programmes and activities were co-ordinated to avoid duplication. UNDMT members shared information on the disaster situation, discussed further relief needs as identified by field missions, and took action to adjust the programme to maximise the impact of the programmes. For example, OCHA conducted an assessment mission to Inner Mongolia on the basis of discussions at UNDMT meetings and identified continued needs for medicines, construction materials, and water and sanitation in the province in December, 1998. This led UNICEF to field a follow-up mission to further assess the needs and to confirm the findings. After the evaluation, WHO, UNICEF and UNDP reallocated some of their disaster funds to address these needs. The quality progress reports, the two appeals and the development of a knowledge body were

a result of teamwork. Articles were accepted for publication in international journals, such as the Humanitarian Affairs Review. The press and donors themselves were regularly informed as to progress and any hindrance to the programme activities.

Lesson 2: Early assessment of relief needs is essential if the quality of emergency relief assistance is to be improved, and unnecessary delays avoided.

By the time the UNDAC/Inter-UN agency teams were able to visit the affected areas, 2 whole months had elapsed since the floods had occurred. The Chinese Government should be encouraged to facilitate timely assessments by international agencies and UN organisations. Immediate needs assessment following a disaster paves the way to an earlier release of international disaster funding than is otherwise possible, and also promotes effective planning of relief assistance programmes.

Lesson 3: Cost sharing with the Government speeds up the process and increases the extent of the emergency relief

Cost sharing with the Government enabled UN relief assistance to reach flood victims in a timely manner. The collaboration significantly strengthened the ties between UN agencies and their Government counterparts. The WFP relief and *Food-For-Work* programme, the UNESCO education programme, and the UNDP construction materials programme were matched with a contribution by Chinese Government. WFP started its *Food-For-Work* programme with the Government's share of funds. Without this cost sharing, the programmes would have started several months later, greatly hindering the effectiveness and the output of the programme.

The UNICEF programme proved to be comprehensive and cost-effective, and became a model for the implementation of water and sanitation programmes. The model included training in safe water delivery, public health education and rehabilitation of damaged water supply systems. The central Government initiative to allocate an additional CNY 45 million (US$5.5 million) for new projects to tackle water and sanitation problems in other flood-affected counties was modelled on UNICEF's successful programme.

Lesson 4: Rapid transfer of funds is essential for timely implementation of emergency relief

Most agencies were able to develop and implement new and timely disaster emergency funds transfer systems during 1998. However, in one case, it took several months for the appropriate UN agency in China to receive the funds that had been pledged by the donors. Emergency relief funding mechanisms throughout the UN system need to be in place for timely emergency relief response so that valuable time is not lost. Administrative procedures, designed for regular development activities, are not always adequate.

Lesson 5: UN Appeals were less efficient in mobilising funds for rehabilitation and mitigation, but highly effective for immediate emergency relief

Despite the importance and usefulness of rehabilitation and mitigation, it is easier to mobilise funds for emotionally driven relief responses that are strongly associated with the immediate event than for longer-term disaster reduction needs. The UNDMT experience confirmed that donors responded spontaneously to the first appeal and less enthusiastically to the second, which focused on essential capacity development needs for flood rehabilitation, disaster prevention and mitigation.

Follow Up

The aftermath of the devastating floods in China has been

marked by exceptional co-operation between the Government of China and the UN system. New professional relationships between UNDMT and the Chinese Government Disaster Management Team have been created while information and ideas have been shared. This process is important and has created strong foundations for times when the Chinese Government and the UN system may be faced with new emerging disasters.

Appendix

International Initiatives at Modelling Risk

This Appendix presents a review of international indicator projects dealing with risk and development—These projects are presented under four headings: Disaster Risk Reduction, Disaster Risk Reduction and Environmental Management, Environmental Management and Sustainable Development, and Sustainable Human Development—Every effort was made to ensure this list was a complete at the time of publication—apologies to any groups or individuals working on projects that have not been included:

A.1 DISASTER RISK REDUCTION

Identification of Global Natural Disaster Hotspots

The Hotspots project aims to generate a global natural disaster risk assessment-Risks of human and economic losses will be estimated through spatial analysis by assessing the exposure of a global set of dement at risk—people, infrastructure and economic activities—to all major natural hazards—droughts, floods, storms, earthquakes, volcanoes and landslides—The analysis will be based on the actual geographic distributions of these phenomena rather than on national level statistics—Risks of losses among the dements at risk posed by each hazard individually, will be aggregated across varying time scales to arrive at the aggregate, multi-hazard risk—A series of case studies will be undertaken as the second component of the Hotspots project to complement the global-scale analysis.

For more information please see the websites:

www.preventionconsortium.org files/hotspots2002/dilley.pdf and
http://Doherty.ldgo.Columbia.edu/CHHR/Hotspot/hotspotmain.html

HAZUS

Undertaken by the United States Federal Emergency Management Agency (FEMA), Hazards U.S. (HAZUS) uses Geographic Information Systems (GIS) technology to compute estimates of damage and losses that could result from earthquake events. To support FEMAs mitigation and emergency preparedness efforts, HAZUS is being expanded into HAZUS.MH, a multi-hazard methodology with new modules for estimating potential losses from wind and flood (coastal and riverine) hazards.

For additional information regarding HAZUS please visit the following websites:

www.nibs.org/hazusweb/and
www.fema.gov/hazus/index.shtm

Tyndall Climate Change/Disaster Risk Index

The UK based Tyndall Centre for Climate Change Research uses data relating to natural disasters for the assessment of recent historical and current risk associated with climatic variability. Current risk associated with extreme climate events is used as a proxy for risk associated with climate change in the future—The data used is derived from EM-DAT with population data from the World Bank. The results of the risk study will be examined within the context of considerations of vulnerability. Once high-risk countries have been identified it will be necessary to examine the vulnerability of different population groups at a sub-national scale in order to target resources for capacity building; adaptation funds will be useless if they are not employed in a process driven fashion that takes into account the particular geographical, political, economic and social circumstance of the vulnerable groups in question.

For more information please see:

www.tyndall.ac.uk/publications/working_papers/working_papers.shtml

A.2 DISASTER RISK REDUCTION AND ENVIRONMENTAL MANAGEMENT

Environmental Vulnerabilities Index

The South Pacific Applied Geoscience Commission (SOPAC) Environmental Vulnerability Index (EVI) is among the first tools being developed to focus environmental management at the same scale that environmentally significant decisions are made, and to focus these on outcomes—The method uses 54 indicators to assess the vulnerability of the environment at the national scale. The EVI has been designed to reflect the status of a country's environmental vulnerability the extent that the natural environment is prone to damage and degradation—It does not address the vulnerability of the social, cultural, or economic environment, nor the environment that has become dominated by these same human systems.

For more information regarding the EVI please visit the following web site: www.sopac.org

Small Islands Developing States Index

Paragraphs 113 and 114 of the Programme of Action for the Sustainable Development of Small Island Developing States that was endorsed by the General Assembly in 1994 by resolution 49/122 call for the development of a vulnerability index for Small Island Developing States (SIDS). Accordingly, the UN Department of Economic and Social Affairs (UNDESA) undertook initial studies in 1996 in order to provide a conceptual framework for the development of a vulnerability index. This index is still in the development stage. In the

Caribbean, ECHO has developed a Composite Vulnerability index to compare losses to natural disaster events in the region. During 2002-2003, the Economic Commission for Latin America and the Caribbean/Caribbean Development and Cooperation Committee (ECLAC/CDCC) has explored potential methodologies for a social vulnerability index for Caribbean SIDS.

For further information regarding the Small Island Developing States index, please visit the website:

www.un.org/esa/sustdev/aboutsids.htm

For the ECHO Composite Vulnerability index please see:

www.disaster.info.desastres.net/dipecho/

The Water Poverty Index

The Water Poverty index assesses communities and countries by water scarcity, examining both physical and socio-economic factors. The index is based on the formulation of a framework that incorporates six variables: resources, access, capacity, use, environmental and geospatial. Of 147 countries with relatively complete data, most in the top half are either developed or richer developing countries.

For further information please visit the website:

www.nerc.wallingford.ac.uk/research/WPI/

A.3 ENVIRONMENTAL MANAGEMENT AND SUSTAINABLE DEVELOPMENT

Bellagio Principles: Guidelines for the Practical Assessment of Progress toward Sustainable Development

These principles deal with four aspects of assessing progress toward sustain ability. Principle 1 establishes a vision of sustain able development. Principles 2 through 5 deals with the content of any assessment and the need to merge a sense of the overall system with a practical focus on current priority issues. Principles 6 through 8 deal with key issues of the process of assessment, while Principles 9 and 10 deal with the necessity for establishing a continuing capacity for assessment.

For additional information please visit the following website:

http://iisd.ca/measure/bellagiol.htm

Dashboard of Sustain ability indicators

The Dashboard of Sustainability was presented at the World Summit on Sustainable Development (WSSD) in Johannesburg. It is based on the UN Commission on Sustainable Development (CSD) indicator set and contains 19 social, 20 environmental, 14 economic and 8 institutional indicators. It includes data for over 200 countries. The latest version, RioJo, allows a comparison of the global situation at the time of the Rio Summit in 1992 with the current state of the world.

For more information please visit the USD homepage:

www.iisd.org

Ecological Footprint Accounts

Ecological Footprint Accounts document humanity's demands on nature—A population's Ecological Footprint is the biologically productive area needed to produce the resources used and absorb the waste generated by that population—Ecological Footprint Accounts calculate the combined size of these areas—The average world citizen has an Ecological Footprint of 2-3 global hectares (5-6 acres), the average German's is 4-7 global hectares (12 acres), and the average American's is 9-6 global hectares (24 acres).

For more information please see the website:

www.redefiningprogress.org/programmes/sustainability/ef/

Environmental Sustainability Index

The Environmental Sustainability Index (ESI) works towards

the development of a measure of overall progress of global environmental sustainability. Currently incorporating 142 countries, the 2002 ESI scores are based upon a set of 20 core indicators. The ESI tracks the relative success of each country in the five core components of environmental systems: reducing stress, reducing human vulnerability, social and institutional capacity, and global stewardship.

For more information please see the following websites:

www.weforum.org, www.ciesin.Columbia.edu, www.yale.edu/envirocenter

Millennium Ecosystem Assessment

The Millennium Ecosystem Assessment undertakes an analysis of the capacity of an ecosystem to provide goods and services important for human development. The fundamental unit of interest is the ecosystem itself—The approach taken is to assess the capacity of the system to provide various goods and services and then to evaluate the trade-offs among those goods and services.

For more information regarding the Millennium Ecosystem Assessment please visit the following website:

www.millenniumassessment.org/en/about/index.htm

Pilot Environmental Performance Index

The Environmental Performance Index (EPI), launched in 2002, permits national comparisons on efforts to manage a narrow set of common policy objectives concerning air and water quality, climate change and ecosystem well-being—The EPI enables benchmarking of progress towards meeting immediate national policy objectives, facilitates Judgements about environmental performance, and can be used to identify important differences in performance that may warrant intervention and investigation.

For more information please see the following websites:

www.weforum.org, www.ciesin.Columbia.edu, www.yale.edu/envirocenter

A-4 SUSTAINABLE HUMAN DEVELOPMENT

The Human Development Index

UNDP's Human Development Index (HDI) measures a country's achievements in three aspects of human development: longevity, knowledge and a decent standard of living—Although the HDI is a useful tool it is not enough to measure a country's level of development. A fuller picture of a country's level of human development requires analysis of other human development indicators and information.

For further information please visit the following UNDP website: http://hdr.undp.org

The Human Poverty Index

UNDP's Human Poverty Index for developing countries (HPI-1) measures deprivations in the same three aspects of human development as the HDI (longevity knowledge and a decent standard of living). The Human Poverty Index for industrialised countries (HPI-2) includes social exclusion—Many National Human Development Reports now break down the HPI by district level or language group to identify the areas or social groups within the country most deprived in terms of human poverty. The results can be dramatic, creating national debate and helping to reshape policies.

For more information please visit the following web page: http://hdr.undp.org/statistics/faq.cfm

The Human Insecurity Index

The Index of Human Insecurity is a classification system that distinguishes countries based on how vulnerable or insecure they are the index uses indicators of sustainable development, although parallels with indicators of human well-being and social indicators are evident.

For more information please visit the following website: www.gechs.org/aviso/avisoenglish/sixlg.shtml

Freedom House Index

Freedom in the World is an institutional effort by Freedom House to monitor the progress and decline of political rights and civil liberties in 192 nations and in major related or disputed territories. The Survey rates each country on a seven-point scale for political rights and civil liberties and divides the world into three broad categories: "Free", "Partly Free", and "Not Free". For more information please visit the Freedom House homepage: www.freedomhouse.org

Transition Index

This index offers analysis of the transition to market economies and macroeconomic performance in Central and Eastern Europe and the Commonwealth of Independent States (CIS), drawing on the European Bank for Reconstruction and Development's (EBRD) experience as an investor in the region. Country-by-country assessments include macroeconomic tables, output and expenditure, and foreign direct investment. They also provide key data on liberalisation, stabilisation, privatisation, enterprise reform, infrastructure, financial institutions and social reform.

For more information please visit the EBRD homepage: www.ebrd.corn

Human Rights Indicators

This project measures the commitment of governments to respect and fulfil human rights—Four factors are part of their assessment of commitment: an index measuring commitment to international and regional human rights standards by governments, an index of civil and political human rights violations by governments, an index approximating commitment to fulfilment of economic, social and cultural rights, and an index measuring in a preliminary way, commitment to gender equality by governments.

For more information regarding the Human Rights

Indicators please visit the Danish Centre for Human Rights web page: www.humanrights.dk/departments/PP/PA/Concept/Indicato/

AIDS Programme Effort Index

The AIDS Programme Effort Index (API) measures the amount of effort put into national AIDS programmes by both domestic and international organizations. The API was implemented in 40 countries in 2000.

For more information regarding the API please visit the following website: www.tfgi.com/Api_final.doc

Bibliography

A review process regarding the institutional arrangements within the United Nations pertaining to disaster reduction is currently being carried out and will be completed, following the World Conference on Disaster Reduction, with an evaluation of the role and performance of the International Strategy for Disaster Reduction.

A/CONF. 172/9

A/CONF. 191/11.

A/CONF. 199/20, paragraph 37e.

A/CONF. 199/20.

According to the principles contained in *General Assembly Resolution* 46/182.

ActionAid. 2002. 'Halfway There' www.actionaid.org/ourpriorities/downloads/halfwaythere.pdf

Adger, W.N. (1999). Institutional Adaptation to Environmental Risk under the Transition in Vietnam. *Annals of the Association of American Geographers* 90: 738-58.

Adger, W.N. (1999). Social Vulnerability to Climate Change and Extremes in Coastal Vietnam. *World Development* 27: 249-69.

Albala-Bertrand, J.M. (1993). *Political Economy of Large Natural Disasters: with Special Reference to Developing Countries.* Oxford: Clarendon Press.

Alexander, D. (1993). *Natural Disasters.* London: UCL Press.

Alexander, D. (2000). *Confronting Catastrophe: New Perspectives on Natural Disasters.* New York: Oxford University Press.

Allen, E. (1994). Political Responses to Flood Disaster: The Case of Rio De Janeiro, 1988. In A. Varley (Ed.) *Disasters, Development and the Environment.* London: Belhaven.

Amjad Bhatti, Madhavi Malalgoda Ariyabandu (2002). *Disaster Communication: A Resource Kit for the Media.* Colombo, Sri Lanka: Duryog Nivaran.

Anand, S. and Sen, Amartya. 2000. 'The Income Component of the Human Development Index', *Journal of Human Development*, Vol. 1, No. 1.

Anderson, E., Brakenridge, G.R., 2001. NASA-supported Dartmouth Flood Observatory.

Anderson, M. (1990).Which Costs More: Prevention or Recovery? In A. Kreimer and M. Munasinghe (Eds.) *Managing Natural Disasters and the Environment*: 17-27. Washington, DC: World Bank.

Anderson, M. and Woodrow, P. (1989). *Rising from the Ashes: Development Strategies in Times of Disaster.* Boulder, CO: Westview (reprinted, 1999, by IT Publications, London).

Anderson, M. and Woodrow, P. 1989, *Rising from the Ashes: Development Strategies in Times of Disaster.*Westview Press, Boulder, CO, U.S.

Ariyabandu, M. (1999). *Defeating Disasters: Ideas for Action.* Colombo, Sri Lanka: Duryog Nivaran and Intermediate Technology Development Group.

As identified in *General Assembly Resolution* 57/270B.

As per *General Assembly resolution* 58/214 of 23 December, 2003.

As reaffirmed at the twenty-third special session of the General Assembly on the topic "Women 2000: gender equality, development and peace for the twenty-first century".

Asian Disaster Preparedness Center. 2003. www.adpc.net/audmp/audmp.html, www.adpc.net/audmp/India.html

Baas, S., Batjargal, E. and Swift, J. (2001). From Wisner, B. (2002). Background Paper, Invited Contribution.

Babin, S. and Sterner, R., 2001. Atlantic Hurricane Track Maps & Images, http://fermi.jhuapl.edu/hurr/index.html

Bankoff, G. (2001). Rendering the World Safe: Vulnerability as Western Discourse. *Disasters* 25 (10): 19-35.

Barnett, A. and Whiteside, A. (2001). *AIDS in the Twenty-First Century: Disease and Globalization.* Basingstoke, U.K.: Palgrave/Macmillan.

Bebbington, A. and Perrault, T. (1999). Social Capital and Political Ecological Change in Highland Ecuador: Resource Access and Livelihoods. *Economic Geography* 75 (4): 395-419.

Benjamin, S. (2000). Governance, Economic Settings and Poverty in Bangalore. *Environment and Urbanisation* 12 (1): 35-56.

Benson, C. (2003). Macroeconomic Concepts of Vulnerability:

Dynamics, Complexity and Public Policy. In Bankoff, G., Frerks, G. and Hilhorst, T. (Eds.) *Vulnerability: Disasters, Development and People.* London: Earthscan.

Benson, C. and Clay, E. (1998). *The Impact of Drought on Sub-Saharan African Economies.* World Bank Technical Paper No. 401. Washington, DC: World Bank.

Berke, P., Kartez, J. and Wenger, D. (1993). Recovery after Disaster: Achieving Sustainable Development, Mitigation and Equity. *Disasters* 17 (2): 93-109.

Birdwell K.R. and Daniels, R.C., 1991. A Global Geographic Information System Data Base of Storm Occurrences and Other Climatic Phenomena Affecting Coastal Zones, 1991. http://cdiac.esd.ornl.gov/ndps/ndp035.html

Birdwell, K.R. and Daniels, R.C. (1991). A Storm Climatology Database with Applications in Regional and Global Change Studies. *Bulletin of the American Meteorological Society,* Vol. 72, No. 7.

Birdwell, K.R., and Daniels, R.C. 1991. A Global Geographic Information System Data Base of Storm Occurrences and Other Climatic Phenomena Affecting Coastal Zones (1991). http://cdiac.esd.ornl.gov/ndps/ndp035.html

Black, R. (1998). *Refugees, Environment and Development.* Harlow. Essex: Longman.

Blaikie, P. *et al.* 1996. *At Risk: Natural Hazards, Peoples Vulnerability and Disasters.* Routledge.

Blaikie, P.M. and Brookfield, H.C. (1987). *Land Degradation and Society.* London: Methuen.

Blaikie, P.M. and Brookfield, H.C., Cannon, T., Davis, I. and Wisner, B. (1994). *At Risk: Natural Hazards, People's Vulnerability, and Disasters.* London: Routledge.

Blong, R.J. 1984. *Volcanic Hazards, A Sourcebook on the Effects of Eruptions.* Academic Press Australia.

Bolt, B.A., Horn, W.L., Macdonald, G.A., and Scott, R.F. 1975. *Geological Hazard.* Berlin/Heidelberg/New York: Springer-Verlag.

Bosnia and Herzegovina, Council of Ministers, Law on Ministries and Other Bodies of Administration of Bosnia and Herzegovina, *Sarajevo,* January, 2003.

Brosnam, D. (2000). *The Montserrat Volcano: Sustainable Development in Montserrat.* Portland, or: Sustainable Ecosystems Institute. www.sei.org/sustainable_development.html

Brown, H.A. (1994). *Economics of Disasters with Special Reference to the Jamaican Experience.* Working paper 2, Jamaica: Centre for Environment and Development, University of the West Indies.

Bull-Kamanga, Liseli *et al.* (2003). From Everyday Hazards to Disasters, the Accumulation of Risk in Urban Areas. *Environment and Urbanisation,* Vol. 15, No. 1, April, 2003. London: IIED.

Burton, I., Kates, R.W. and White, G.F. 1993: *The Environment as Hazard, Second Edition.* New York/London: Guilford Press, p. 290 pp. [pp. 31-47]

Caballeros, R. and R. Zapata (1999). *America Latina: el impacto de los desastres naturales en el desarrollo, 1972-1999.* México, CEPAL.

Cannon, T. (1994). Vulnerability Analysis and the Explanation of 'Natural' Disasters. In Varley, A. (Ed.) *Disasters, Development and the Environment:* 13-30. London: Belhaven Press.

Cannon, T. (2000). Vulnerability Analysis and Disasters. In Parker, D. (Ed.) *Floods:* 43-55. London: Routledge.

Cannon, T. (2002). Gender and Climate Hazards in Bangladesh. In Masika, R. (Ed.) *Gender, Development and Climate Change:* 45-50. Oxford: Oxfam.

Cannon, T., Twigg, J., Rowell, J. (2003). *Social Vulnerability, Sustainable Livelihoods and Disasters.* London: DFID.

Cardona, O.D. (2003). The Need for Rethinking the Concepts of Vulnerability and Risk from a Holistic Perspective: a Necessary Review and Criticism for Effective Risk Management. In Bankoff, G., Frerks, G. and Hilhorst D. (Eds.) *Mapping Vulnerability: Disasters, Development and People.* London: Earthscan.

Cardona, O.D. 2003. 'The Notion of Disaster Risk: Conceptual Framework for Integrated Management'. In *Indicators for Disaster Risk Management,* Operation ATN/JF-7907-RG, Report Phase I, IADB-IDEA/Universidad Nacional de Colombia, Manizales, Colombia.

Cardona, O.D., Yamín, L.E., Arámbula, S. and Molina, L.F. (2002). Retención y Transferencia del Riesgo Sísmico en Colombia: Evaluación Preliminar de una Posible Estrategia Financiera y del Mercado Potencial, Universidad de los Andes, CEDERI, Departamento Nacional de Planeación de Colombia—World Bank.

Caribbean Disaster Emergency Response Agency, www.cdera.org/doccenter/publications/CDM%20Strategy%20FDF.pdf

Carter, N. 1991. *Disaster Management, a Disaster Manager's Handbook.* Manila: Asian Development Bank.

Castells, M. (1996). *The Information Age: Economy, Society and Culture Volume 1, The Rise of the Network Society.* Oxford: Blackwell Publishers.

Challenger, B. (2002). Linking Adaptation to Climate Change and Disaster Mitigation in the Eastern Caribbean: Experiences and Opportunities. Paper presented at the UNEP Expert Group Meeting on Integrating Disaster Reduction and Adaptation to Climate Change. Havana, Cuba.

Chambers, R. (1989). Editorial Introduction: Vulnerability, Coping and Policy. *IDS Bulletin* 20 (2): 1-7.

CIESIN, IFPRI, WRI, 2000. Gridded Population of the World (GPW), Version 2, http://sedac.ciesin.org/plue/gpw/

Coburn, A.W., Spence, R.J.S. and Pomonis, A. 1991: *Vulnerability and Risk Assessment.* UNDP Disaster Management Training Programme, p. 57.

Colletta, N.J. and Cullen, M.L. (2000). *Violent Conflict and Transformation of Social Capital: Lessons from Cambodia, Rwanda, Guatemala and Somalia.* Washington DC: World Bank.

Comfort, L., Wisner, B., Cutter, S., Pulwarty, R., Hewitt, K., Oliver-Smith, A., Weiner, J., Fordham, M., Peacock, W. and Krimgold, F. (1999). Reframing Disaster Policy: The Global Evolution of Vulnerable Communities. *Environmental Hazards* 1 (1): 39-44.

Coordination Center for the Prevention of Natural Disasters in Central America. 2003. www.cepredenac.org/11_engl/11_index.htm

Council of the National Seismic System, 2002. *Earthquake Catalog,* http://quake.geo.berkeley.edu/cnss/

Cuny, F. and Hill, R. (1999). *Famine, Conflict and Response: A Basic Guide.* West Hartford, CT: Kumarian Press.

de Haan, Arjan (2000). Migrants, Livelihoods and Rights: The Relevance of Migration in Development Policies, *DFID Social Development Working Paper Number 4.*

de Waal, A. (2000). Democratic Political Process and the Fight against Famine. IDS Working Paper No. 107. Brighton: Institute of Development Studies.

DEC (Disasters Emergency Committee) (2001). Independent Evaluation of Expenditure of DEC India Earthquake Appeal Funds January, 2001-October, 2001. London: DEC.

—— (2002). The Gujarat Earthquake: Monitoring *Visit Report to DEC*. www.dec.org.uk

Defined by *General Assembly Resolution* 46/182.

Deichmann, Uwe, 1996. *GNV197—Human Population and Administrative Boundaries Database for Asia*, UNEP/GRID-Geneva, www.grid.unep.ch/data/grid/gnv197.php

Demuth, S. and Stahl, K. 2001. *Assessment of the Regional Impact of Droughts in Europe (ARIDE), Final Report*, Institute of Hydrology, University of Freiburg, Freiburg, Germany.

Devereux, S. (2001). Famine in Africa. In S. Devereux and S. Maxwell (Eds.) *Food Security in Sub-Saharan Africa*, Ch. 5. London: ITDG Publishing.

DFID Bangladesh (2003). Poverty, Disasters and the Environment in Bangladesh: A Quantitative and Qualitative Assessment of Causal Linkages. Paper prepared by C. Kelly and M.H. Khan Chowdhary with the collaboration of Concern, Disaster Forum and Helen Keller International Bangladesh, December, 2003 for DFID, U.K.

DHI Water and Environment. 2002. 'Environmental Improvement and Flood Mitigation Project for the Klang River, Malaysia (2001-2002)' www.dhi.dk/dhiproj/Country/Malaysia/Klang/

Disaster Mitigation for Sustainable Livlihoods Programme. 2003. www.egs.uct.ac.za/dimp/

Donlin C. and Fitzgibbon, T., 2001. Geopubs—Online Geologic Publications of the Western United States, USGS: http://geopubs.wr.usgs.gov/docs/wrgis/fact

Dovers, S. and Handmer, J. (1993). Contradictions in Sustainability. *Environmental Conservation* 20: 217-22.

Drèze, J. and Sen, A. (1989). *Hunger and Public Policy*. Oxford: Clarendon Press.

Economic Commission for Latin America and the Caribbean, www.eclac.cl/analisis/TIN53.htm#6

EM-DAT: The OFDA/CRED International Disaster Database, Université Catholique de Louvain, Brussels, Belgium. www.cred.be/emdat

Emel, J. and Peet, R. (1989). Resource Management and Natural Hazards. In Peet, R. and Thrift, N. (Eds.) *New Models in Geography*, Vol. 1: 49-76. London: Unwin Hyman.

Enarson, E. (2001). *We Want Work: Rural Women in the Gujarat Drought and Earthquake*. http://online.northumbria.ac.uk/geography_research/radix/resources/surendranagar.doc

Enarson, E. and Morrow, B. (Eds.) (1997). *Gendered Terrains of Disaster: Through Women's Eyes.* New York: Praeger.

Escobar, A. (1995). *Encountering Development: The Making and Unmaking of the Third World.* Princeton: Princeton University Press.

FAO (Food and Agriculture Organisation) (1999). Adverse effect of the drought on domestic food production during 1998/1999 in Iraq. www.casi.org.uk/info/fao_dr.html

FAO (Food and Agriculture Organisation) 1998. 'The State of Food and Agriculture 1998' www.fao.org/docrep/W9500E/w9500e07.htm

FCCC/CP/1997/7/Add.l, decision 1/CP.3, annex.

Fernandez, Maria Augusta (1999). *Cities at Risk: Environmental Degradation, Urban Risk and Disasters.* Quito, Ecuador: LA RED/USAID.

Fernando, Priyanthi and Fernando, Vijitha. (1997). *South Asian Women: Facing Disasters, Securing Life.* Colombo, Sri Lanka: Duryog Nivaran.

For a more comprehensive listing of relevant frameworks and declarations, see information document: Extracts Relevant to Disaster Risk Reduction from International Policy Initiatives 1994-2003, Inter-Agency Task Force on Disaster Reduction, ninth meeting 4-5 May, 2004.

Fordham, M. (2003). Gender, Development and Disaster: The Necessity for Integration. In Pelling, M. (Ed.) *Natural Disasters and Development in a Globalizing World:* 57-74. London: Routledge.

Fothergill, A. (1996). Gender, Risk and Disaster. *International Journal of Mass Emergencies and Disasters* 14 (1): 33-56.

Frances, C. and Hanlon, J. (2001). *Mozambique and the Great Flood of 2000.* Oxford: Indiana and James Currey.

Francois, Jean and Rufin, Jean-Christophe (1996). *Economie des guerres civiles.* Paris: Hachette.

Freeman, P., Martin, L., Mechler, R. and Warner, K. (2002). Catastrophes and Development: Integrating Natural Catastrophes into Development Planning. Disaster Risk Management Working Paper 4. Disaster Management Facility.Washington, DC: The World Bank www.worldbank.org/dmf/files/catastrophes_complete.pdf

Gass, V. (2002). *Democratizing Development: Lessons from Hurricane*

Mitch Reconstruction. Washington, DC: Washington Office on Latin America (WOLA).

Gaye M. and Diallo, F. (1997). Community Participation in the Management of the Urban Environment in Rufisque, Senegal. *Environment and Urbanisation* 9 (1): 9-29.

General Assembly Resolution 55/2.

General Assembly Resolution 57/270B, follow-up to United Nations conferences, and the General Assembly resolutions on Implementation of the International Strategy for Disaster Reduction, which request the Secretary-General to report to the second committee of the General Assembly under-Sustainable development (54/219, 56/195, 57/256 58/214, 58/215, 59/231).

General Assembly Resolution 58/213. Further implementation of the Programme of Action for the Sustainable Development of Small Island Developing States.

General Assembly Resolution 58/214.

General Assembly Resolution 58/291.

General Assembly Resolutions 59/231, 58/214, 57/256, 56/195, 54/219.

General Assembly Resolutions on natural disasters and vulnerability (59/233, and 58/215)

General Assembly resolutions on natural disasters and vulnerability (59/233, and 58/215)

Giardini, D. 1999. *Annali di Geofisica, the global seismic hazard assessment programme (GSHAP) 1992-1999,* Instituto Nazionale di Geofisica, Vol. 42, No. 6, December, 1999, Rome, Italy.

Giardini, D., Grünthal, G., Shedlock K. and Zhang, P. 2000. Global Seismic Hazard Assessment Programme, www.seismo.ethz.ch/GSHAP/

Gibson, J.L. (1998). Social Networks and Civil Society in Processes of Democratisation. *Studies in Public Policy* No. 301, Centre for the Study of Public Policy (CSPP), University of Strathclyde, Glasgow.

Gibson, J.L. 1998. *Social Networks and Civil Society in Processes of Democratisation.* Studies in Public Policy # 301, Centre for the Study of Public Policy, University of Strathclyde.

Gilbert, R. and Kreimer, A. (1999). Learning from the World Bank's Experience of Natural Disaster Related Assistance. Disaster Management Facility, Working Paper Series 2.Washington, DC: The World Bank. www.worldbank.org/dmf/files/learningfromwb.pdf

Glantz, M. (2001). *Once Burned, Twice Shy? Lessons Learned from the 1997-98 El Niño.* Tokyo: United Nations University Press.

Global Identifier Number (GLIDE) 2001. www.glidenumber.net/

Global Volcanism Programme, National Museum of Natural History, E-421, Smithsonian Institution, Washington DC 20560-0119, www.nmnh.si.edu/gvp/index.htm

— —.Volcanic Activity Reports, Pinatubo, Index and All Reports, National Museum of Natural History, Smithsonian Institution, Washington, DC: www.nmnh.si.edu/gvp/volcano/region07/luzon/pinatubo/var.htm#1605

Goodhand, J., Hulme, D. and Lewer, N. (2000). Social Capital and the Political Economy of Violence: A Case Study of Sri Lanka. *Disasters* 24 (4): 390-406.

Government of Algeria (2003). Bilan officiel du gouvernement après le seisme 21 mai 2003, Ministere del Interireur et des Collectivite Locales, in El Moudjahid.

Government of Haiti (2003). Rapport de suivi du Plan National de Gestion de Risques et de Disastres, mimeo.

— —(2001). Enquete Budget-Consommation des Menages (EBCM 1999-2000) Volume II (Institut Haitien des Statistique *et al* informatique). www.ht.undp.org/pnud-hai/projets/Bestpract.htm

Grameen Bank. 2003. www.grameen-info.org

Haas, E., Kates, R. and Bowden, M. (1977). *Reconstruction Following Disaster.* Cambridge, MA: MIT Press.

Hamza, M. and Zetter, R. 1998. Structural Adjustment, Urban Systems and Disaster Vulnerability in Developing Countries. *Cities* 15 (4): 291-99.

Haq, K. and Kirdar, U. (Eds.) (1987). *Human Development, Adjustment and Growth.* Islamabad: North South Roundtable.

Hardoy, J.E., Mitlin, D. and Satterthwaite, D. (2001). *Environmental Problems in an Urbanizing World.* London: Earthscan.

Hazard is defined as: "A potentially damaging physical event, phenomenon or human activity that may cause the loss of life or injury, property damage, social and economic disruption or environmental degradation. Hazards can include latent conditions that may represent future threats and can have different origins: natural (geological, hydro-meteorological and biological) or induced by human processes (environmental degradation and technological hazards)" UN/ISDR. Geneva 2004.

Heijmans, A. and Victoria, L. (2001). *Citizen-Based and Development-Oriented Disaster Response.* Quezon City, Philippines: Center for Disaster Preparedness. cdp@info.com.ph

Herd, D.G. 1982. *Glacial and Volcanic Geology of the Ruiz-Tolima Volcanic Complex,* Cordillera Central, Colombia: Publicaciones Geológicas Especiales del INGEOMINAS, no. 8, p. 48.

Hewitt, K. (Ed.) (1983). *Interpretations of Calamity.* Boston: Allen and Unwin.

— —. 1995. Sustainable Disasters? Perspectives and Powers in the Discourse of Calamity, in Crush, J. (Ed.) *Power of Development,* pp. 115-28. London: Routledge.

— —(1997). *Regions of Risk: A Geographical Introduction to Disasters.* Harlow: Longman.

— —(1998). Excluded Perspectives in the Social Conception of Disaster. In Quarantelli, E. (Ed.) *What is a Disaster:* 75-91. London: Routledge.

Hill, A. and Cutter, S. (2001). Methods for Determining Disaster Proneness. In Cutter, S. (Ed.) *American Hazardscapes: The Regionalization of Hazards and Disasters,* Washington, DC: Joseph Henry Press.

Holland, G.J. 1980. An Analytic Model of the Wind and Pressure Profiles in Hurricanes. *Monthly Weather Review* (108): 1212-18.

Holloway, A. (2003). Background paper, invited contribution for *Reducing Disaster Risk.*

Hossain, Hameeda, Dodge, Cole P. and Abed, F.H. 1992. *From Crisis to Development: Coping with Disasters in Bangladesh.* Dhaka, Bangladesh: University Press.

Houghton, J. *et al.* (Eds.) (2001). *Climate Change 2001: The Scientific Basis.* Cambridge: Cambridge University Press.

IASC (Inter-Agency Standing Committee) (2002). *Growing the Sheltering Tree: Protecting Human Rights through Humanitarian Action.*

IDNDR (International Decade for Natural Disaster Reduction) (1999). *Proceedings: Programme Forum.* Geneva: IDNDR.

IFRC (International Federation of Red Cross and Red Crescent Societies) (1998). *World Disasters Report 1998.* Geneva: IFRC.

— —(1999). *Vulnerability and Capacity Assessment: An International Federation Guide.* Geneva: IFRC.

——(1999). *World Disasters Report 1999*. Geneva: IFRC.

—— (2000). *World Disasters Report 2000*. Geneva: IFRC.

——(2001). *World Disasters Report 2001*. Geneva: IFRC.

——(2002). *World Disasters Report 2002: Focus on Reducing Risk*. Geneva: IFRC.

——(2003). *World Disasters Report 2003*. Geneva: IFRC.

IISD (International Institute for Sustainable Development), IUCN (World Conservation Union) and SEI (Stockholm Environment Institute) 2003. Livelihoods and Climate Change: Combining Disaster Risk Reduction, Natural Resource Management and Climate Change. A conceptual paper prepared by the Task Force on Climate Change, Vulnerable Communities and Adaptation. Winnipeg, Canada: IISD

In compliance with General Assembly resolution 58/118 and OAS *General Assembly Resolution* 2018 (xxxiv-0/04).

International Decade for Natural Disaster Reduction, www.unisdr.org/unisdr/indexidndr.html, www.unisdr.org/dialogue/basicdocument.htm#framework

International Institute for Environment and Development, www.iied.org/human/eandu/eandu_details.html

IPCC (Intergovernmental Panel on Climate Change) 2001. Climate Change: impacts, adaptation and vulnerability, summary for policy makers and technical summary for Working Group II Report. Geneva: IPCC.

IRI/Columbia University, National Centers for Environmental Prediction, Climate Prediction Center. 2002.

ISDR (United Nations International Strategy for Disaster Reduction) 2001. Report of Working Group 3 to the ISDR Inter Agency Task Force for Disaster Reduction 2001.

——. 2002. *Living with Risk: A Global Review of Disaster Reduction Initiatives* Preliminary edition. Geneva: ISDR.

ISDR (United Nations International Strategy for Disaster Reduction)/RADIUS. 2001. *United Nations Initiative Towards Earthquake Safe Cities*. Geneva: ISDR.

ISRIC, UNEP. 1990. Global Assessment of Human Induced Soil Degradation (GLASOD), www.grid.unep.ch/data/grid/gnv18.php

Jabry, A. 2003. *Children in Disasters*. London: PLAN International. www.plan-uk.org/action/childrenindisasters

Johnson, L.T. 2003. Housing, Sanitation and Drinking Water:

Strengthening Lives and Livelihoods, in Palakudiyil, T. and Todd, M. (Eds.) *Facing up to the Strom: How Communities can Cope with Disaster: Lessons from Orissa and Gujarat.* London: Christian Aid.

Kasperson, R. and Kasperson, J. (Eds.) 2000. *Global Environmental Risk.* London: Earthscan.

Kelman, I. 2003. Beyond Disaster, Beyond Diplomacy. In Pelling, M. (Ed.) *Natural Disasters and Development in a Globalizing World:* 110-123. London: Routledge.

Khondker, H.H. 1992. Floods and Politics in Bangladesh. *Natural Hazards Observer* 16 (4): 4-6.

Kirby, A. (Ed.) 1990. *Nothing to Fear: Risks and Hazards in American Life.* Tucson: University of Arizona Press.

Kreimer, A. and Munasinghe, M. (Eds.) 1991. *Managing Natural Disasters and the Environment.*Washington, DC: World Bank.

Kropac, Michael. 2002. *Urban Development and Disaster Mitigation: DMI's Bhuj Reconstruction Project.* Ahmedabad, India: Disaster Mitigation Institute.

Krüger, Fred. 1999. Drought Hazards and Threatened Livelihoods—Environmental Perceptions in Botswana. In Lohnert, B. and Geist, H. (Eds.) *Coping with Changing Environments:* 175-190.

La Red. 1998. *Revista Desastres y Sociedad 9. Especial El Niño.* Lima: La Red. www.desenred ando.org/public/revistas/dys/rdys09/ index.html

Landsea, Christopher W. 2000. NOAA/AOML, FAQ: Hurricanes, Typhoons, and Tropical Cyclones.www.aoml.noaa.gov/hrd/ tcfaq/tcfaqA.html#A1

Landsea, Christopher W. 2000. NOAA/AOML, FAQ: Hurricanes, Typhoons, and Tropical Cyclones. www.aoml.noaa.gov/hrd/ tcfaq/tcfaqA.html#A1

Lavell, Allan (Ed.) 1994. *Viviendo en Riesgo: Comunidades Vulnerables y Prevencion de Desastres en America Latina.* Bogota, Colombia: CEPREDENAC/FLACSO/La Red.

Lavell, Allan 1994. Prevention and Mitigation of Disasters in Central America: Vulnerability to disasters at the local level. In Varley, A. (Ed.) *Disasters, Development and Environment:* 49-63. Chichester, UK: Wiley.

Lavell, Allan and Franco, Eduardo. 1996. *Estado, Sociedad y Gestion de los Desastres en America Latina: En Busqueda del Paradigma Perdida.* Bogota, Colombia: La Red/FLACSO.

Le Marechal, A. 1975. *Carte geologique de l'ouest du Cameroun et de l'Adamaoua,* 1:1,000,000; ORSTOM.

Leeman, W.P. 1999. Volcanism & Volcanic Hazards Summary of basic terms and concepts, Rice University, www.ruf.rice.edu/~leeman/volcanic_hazards.html

Lewis, J. 1984. A Multi-Hazard History of Antigua. *Disasters* 8 (3): 190-7.

— —. 1990. The Vulnerability of Small Island-States to Sea Level Rise: the Need for Holistic Strategies. *Disasters,* 14 (3): 241-248.

— —. 1999. *Development in Disaster-prone Places.* London: IT Books.

Livelihoods Connect (DFID) 2003. 'Livelihoods Security in an Emergency Project' www.livelihoods.org/post/Docs/emergency.doc

Lungo, Mario and Baires, Sonia. 1996. *De Terremotos, Derrumbes e Inundados: Los Riesgos Ambientales y el Desarrollo Urbano Sostenible en El Salvador.* San Salvador: FUNDE/La Red.

Macrae, J. and Zwi, A. (Eds.) 1994. *War and Hunger: Rethinking International Responses to Complex Emergencies.* London: Zed Press.

Madeley, J. 1999. *Big Business, Poor Peoples: the Impact of Transnational Corporations on the World.* London: Zed Books.

Maskrey, A. 1989. *Disaster Mitigation: A Community Based Approach.* Development Guidelines No.3 Oxford: Oxfam.

— —. 1996. *Terremotos en el Tropico Humedo: la Gestion de los Desastres del Alto Mayo, Peru (1990-1991), Limon, Costa Rica (1991) y Atrato Medio, Colombia (1992).* Bogota, Colombia: La Red.

— —. 1998. *Navegando entre Brumas: La Aplicacion de los Sistemas de Informacion Geografica al Analisis de Riesgo en America Latina.* Bogota, Colombia: La Red.

— —. 1999. Reducing Global Disasters. In: J. Ingelton (Ed.) *Natural Disaster Management:* 84-6. Leicester: Tudor Rose.

Maskrey, A. and Romero, Gilberto. 1986. *Urbanizacion y Vulnerabilidad Sismica en Lima Metropolitana.* Lima, Peru: PREDES.

McGranahan, G., Jacobi, P., Songsore, J., Surjadi, C. and Kjellén, M. 2001. *The Citizens at Risk: From Urban Sanitation to Sustainable Cities.* London: Earthscan.

McIntire, J. 1987. Would Better Information from an Early Warning System Improve African Food Security? In Wilhite, D. and Easterling, W. (Eds.) *Planning for Drought:* 283-93. Boulder, CO: Westview.

Merged Analysis of Precipitation (CMAP) monthly gridded precipitation, http://iridl.ldeo.columbia.edu

Middleton, N. and O'Keefe, P. 1998. *Disasters and Development: The Politics of Humanitarian Aid.* London: Pluto Press.

Mitchell, J. (Ed.) 1999. *Crucibles of Hazard: Mega-Cities and Disasters in Transition.* Tokyo: United Nations University Press.

Morrissey, Oliver. 2001. Research Paper: Pro Poor Conditionality for Aid and Debt Relief in East Africa. Nottingham University, www.nottingham.ac.uk/economics/credit/research/papers/ CP.01.15.PDF

Moser, C. 1998. The asset Vulnerability Framework: Re-assessing Ultra Poverty Reduction Strategies. *World Development* 26 (1): 1-19.

Munich RE. 2002. *Topics: Annual Review, Natural Catastrophes 2002.* Munich, Germany.

Narayan, D. and Petesch, P. (Eds.) 2002. *Voices of the Poor.* New York: Oxford University Press/World Bank ODI (Overseas Development Insititute) 2002. *Understanding Livelihoods in Rural India: Diversity, Change and Exclusion.* Personal communication, Status report on Orissa disaster mitigation programme. Indian Red Cross Society 2001.

Newhall, C.G. and Self, S. 1982. The volcanic Explosivity Index (VEI): An Estimate of Explosive Magnitude for Historical Volcanism. *Jour. Geophys. Res.* (Oceans & Atmospheres), 87: 1231-8.

Nomdo, Christina and Coetzee, Erika. 2002. *Urban Vulnerability: Perspectives from Southern Africa.* Capetown, South Africa: PeriPeri Publications.

OAS (Organisation of American States) 2001. 'The Caribbean Disaster Mitigation Project in the Dominican Republic' www.oas.org/cdmp/document/papers/tiems.htm, www.oas.org/cdmp/document/papers/tiems.htm

OECD (Organisation for Economic Cooperation and Development)/Development Assistance Committee. 2002. Development Cooperation Report.

OECD and UNDP (United Nations Development Programme). 2002. *Sustainable Development Strategies: A Resource Handbook.* Compiled by Barry Dalal, Clayton and Stephen Bass of the International Institute for Environment and Development. Earthscan Publications Ltd.

OECS (Organisation of Eastern Caribbean States). *Human Development Report 2002.* The OESC Secretariat.

OFDA/CRED. 2001. EM-DAT: The OFDA/CRED International Disaster Database, www.cred.be/emdat

Oliver, Smith, A. 1999. Peru's Five Hundred-Year Earthquake: Vulnerability in Historical Context. In Oliver, Smith, A. and Hoffman, S. (Eds.) *The Angry Earth:* 74-88. New York: Routledge.

Overseas Development Institute for DFID, 'Keysheets' www.keysheets.org/ppip/purple_2_disasters.pdf

Özerdem, A. 2003. Disaster as Manifestation of Unresolved Development Challenges: The Marmara Earthquake in Turkey. In Pelling, M., (Ed.) *Natural Disasters and Development in a Globalising World.* London: Routledge.

Pacific Islands Development Programme n.d. Agricultural Development and Disaster Preparedness. Honolulu: East-West Center.

PAHO (Pan American Health Organization). 1982. *Epidemiologic Surveillance after Natural Disaster.* Washington, DC: Pan American Health Organization.

——. 1994. Empowering Local Communities to Reduce the Effects of Disasters. *Disasters: Preparedness in the Americas* 60 (October): 1, 7.

——. 2000. *Natural Disasters: Protecting the Public's Health.* Washington, DC: PAHO.

Parker, D. (Ed.) 2000. *Floods.* 2 Vols., London: Routledge.

Peduzzi, P. 2000. Insight of Common Key Indicators for Global Vulnerability Mapping. Presentation for the expert meeting on Vulnerability and Risk Analysis and Indexing, Geneva 11-12 September, 2000, UNEP/DEWA/GRID-Geneva, www.grid.unep.ch/activities/earlywarning/preview/appl/reports/reports.htm

——. 2001. Project of Risk Evaluation, Vulnerability Indexing and Early Warning (PREVIEW), UNEP/DEWA/GRID-Geneva, www.grid.unep.ch/activities/earlywarning/preview/index.htm

Peduzzi, P., Dao H., Herold, C., Mouton, Frédéric. 2003. *Global Risk and Vulnerability Index Trends per Year (GRAVITY), Phase IIIa: Drought analysis,* scientific report UNDP/BCPR, Geneva, Switzerland.

— —. 2002. *Global Risk and Vulnerability Index Trends per Year (GRAVITY), Phase II: Development, analysis and results,* scientific report UNDP/BCPR, Geneva, Switzerland.

— — and Rochette, D. 2001. *Feasibility Study Report on Global Risk and Vulnerability Index Trends per Year (GRAVITY).* Scientific Report UNDP/BCPR, Geneva, Switzerland.

Pelling, M. 1999. Participation, Social Capital and Vulnerability to Urban Flooding in Guyana. *International Journal of Development* 10: 469-86.

— —. 2002. Assessing Urban Vulnerability and Social Adaptation to Risk: A Case Study from Santo Domingo. *International Development Planning Review* 24 (1): 59-76.

— —. 2003a. (Ed.) *Natural Disasters and Development in a Globalizing World.* London: Routledge.

— —. 2003b. *The Vulnerability of Cities: Natural Disasters and Social Resilience.* London: Earthscan.

Pelling, M. and Uitto, J. 2002. Small Island Developing States: Natural Disaster Vulnerability and Global Change. *Environmental Hazards* 3: 49-62.

Pelling, M., Özerdem A. and Barakat, S. 2002. The Macro-economic Impact of Disasters, *Progress in Development Studies* 2 (4).

Peri Peri (Ed.) 1999. *Risk, Sustainable Development and Disasters: Southern Perspectives. Cape Town, South Africa: Peri* Peri Publications/Disaster Mitigation for Sustainable Livelihoods, Department of Environmental and Geographical Sciences, University of Cape Town.

Plan Puebla-Panama. 2003. Iniciativa Mesoamericana de Prevencion y Mitigacion de Desastres, 2003. Document Estrategico.Mineo.

PRSP Monitoring and Synthesis Project, www.prspsynthesis.org/connections9.pdf

ReliefWeb. 2002. UN declares 6 November: International Day for preventing the exploitation of the environment in war and armed conflict. UNEP 5, November 2002.

Republique d'Haiti, Ministere de l'economie et des finances. 2001. *Enquête Budget-Consommation des ménages* (EBCM 1999-2000). Volume: II. Revenue. Depenses et consommation des menages.

Resilience: "The capacity of a system, community or society potentially exposed to hazards to adapt, by resisting or changing in order to reach and maintain an acceptable level of functioning and structure This is determined by the degree to which the social system is capable of organising itself to increase this capacity for learning from past disasters for better future protection and to improve risk reduction measures." UN/ISDR. Geneva 2004.

Review of the Yokohama Strategy and Plan of Action for a Safer World (A/CONF.206/L.1).

Roy, B.C., Mruthyunjaya and Selvarajan, S. 2002. Vulnerability to Induced Natural Disasters with Special Emphasis on Coping Strategies of the Rural Poor in Coastal Orissa, India. Paper prepared by the UNFCC COP8 Conference, October-November, 2002.

Sachs, Jeffrey *et al.* 2001. Macroeconomics and Health: Investing in Health for Economic Development. Report of the Commission on Macroeconomics and Health to the Director-General of the World Health Organization. 20 December, 2001.

Salazar, A. 2002. *Normal Life after Disasters? 8 Years of Housing Lessons, from Marathwada to Gujarat, Architecture + Design.* New Delhi. January/Febuary.

Sanderson, D. 2000. Cities, Disasters and Livelihoods. *Environment and Urbanization* 12 (2): 93-102.

Schiff, Maurice and Walters, L. Alan. 2003. Regional Integration and Development. World Bank Working Paper. Washington DC: Oxford University Press.

Schloemer, R.W. 1954. *Analysis and Synthesis of Hurricane Wind Patterns over Lake Okehoee,* Fl. Hydromet Rep. 31, p. 49. [Govt. Printing Office, No. C30.70:31].

Seaman, J., Leivesley, S. and Hogg, C. 1984. *Epidemiology of Natural Disasters.* Basel: Karger.

Sen, Amartya. 2000. *Development as Freedom.* New York: Random House.

Sharma, A. and Gupta, M. 1998. Reducing Urban Risk, India, TDR project progress report. Delhi, India: SEEDS Smith, K. 2001. *Environmental Disasters.* 3rd edition. London: Routledge.

Simkin, T. and Siebert, L. 1994. *Volcanoes of the World.* Washington, DC: Geoscience Press.

Smith, K. 1996. *Environmental Hazards, Assessing Risk and Reducing Disaster.* London, New York: Routldlege.

SNPMAD—PNUD. 2002. *Gestion del riesgo es igual a desarollo—lecciones de la experiencia.*

Some of these frameworks and declarations are listed in the annex to this document.

Stephen, Linda. 2002. From Wisner, B. 2002, background paper, invited contribution.

Stewart, Frances, Fitzgerald, Valpy and Associates. 2001. *War and Underdevelopment: Volume 1: The Economic and Social Consequences of Conflict.* Queen Elizabeth House Series in Development Studies.

Strand H., Wilhelmsen, L. and Gleditsch, N.P. 2003. *Armed Conflict Dataset Codebook.* Oslo: PRIO.

Structural measures refer to any physical construction to reduce or avoid possible impacts of hazards, which include engineering measures and construction of hazard-resistant and protective structures and infrastructure. Non-structural measures refer to policies, awareness, knowledge development, public commitment, and methods and operating practices, including participatory mechanisms and the provision of information, which can reduce risk and related impacts". UN/ISDR. Geneva, 2004.

Such as the Tampered Convention on the Provision of Telecommunication Resources for Disaster Mitigation and Relief Operations (1998), which entered into force 8 January, 2005.

The establishment of national platforms for disaster reduction was requested in Economic and Social Council resolution 1999/63 and in *General Assembly resolutions* 56/195, 58/214, and 58/215. The expression "national platform" is a generic term used for national mechanisms for coordination and policy guidance on disaster risk reduction that need to be multi-sectoral and inter-disciplinary in nature, with public, private and civil society participation involving all concerned entities within a country (including United Nations agencies present at the national level, as appropriate). National platforms represent the national mechanism for the International Strategy for Disaster Reduction.

The Johannesburg Plan of Implementation of the World Summit on Sustainable Development, Johannesburg, South Africa, 26 August-4 September, 2002, paragraphs 37 and 65.

The scope of this Framework for Action encompasses disasters caused by hazards of natural origin and related environmental and technological hazards and risks. It thus reflects a holistic and multi-hazard approach to disaster risk management and the relationship, between them which can have a significant impact on social, economic, cultural and environmental systems, as stressed in the Yokohama Strategy (section I, part B, letter I, p. 8).

The United Nations Advisory Board on Water and Sanitation established by the Secretary-General made an urgent appeal to halve loss of human life caused by major water related disasters, including tsunami, by 2015.

Third World Network. 'Caribbean: Plan needed to mitigate impact of natural disasters' www.twnside.org.sg/title/mitigate.htm

To serve as a tool for sharing experience and methodologies on disaster reduction efforts. States and relevant organizations are invited to actively contribute to the knowledge-building process by registering their own effort on a voluntary basis in consideration of the global progress of the Conference outcomes.

Tobin, G. and Montz, B. 1997. *Natural Hazards: Explanation and Integration.* New York: Guilford.

Tobin, G.A. and Montz, B.E. 1997.*Natural Hazards, Explanation and Integration.* New York, London: Guildford Press.

Topinka, L. 2001. Cascades Volcano Observatory, USGS, Vancouver, Washington, U.S., http://vulcan.wr.usgs.gov/Volcanoes/

Transparency international, 2001. Global Corruption Report 2001, www.transparency.org U.S. Geological Survey. 1997.HYDRO1k, an Elevation Derivative Database, http://edcdaac.usgs.gov/gtopo30/hydro

Twigg, J. 2001. *Corporate Social Responsibility and Disaster Reduction: A Global Overview.* London: Benfield Greig Hazard Research Centre, University College London.

— —. 2002. The Human Factor in Early Warnings: Risk Perception and Appropriate Communications. In Zschau, J. and Kueppers, A. (Eds.) *Early Warning Systems for Natural Disaster Reduction:* 19-26. Berlin: Springer-Verlag.

— — and Bhatt, M. 1998. *Understanding Vulnerability: South Asian Perspectives.* London and Colombo: IT Publications.

U.S. Agency for International Development (USAID) 2002. Mozambique 1999-2000 Floods Impact Evaluation: Resettlement Grant Activity, July, 2002. Emergency Recovery:

Agriculture and Commercial Trade, Abt Asscs. Inc. (with Afrisurvey and Caresoft Lda.), Agricultural Policy Development Project (APD). Washington DC: USAID

UN (United Nations) 2000. United Nations Millennium Declaration, General Assembly Resolution A/RES/55/2, September, 2000: 6.

——. 2002. *Documents Related to Disaster Reduction, Volume 2, 2000-2002.* www.unisdr.org/unisdr/UNseries2.htm

——. 2003. Millennium Declaration: Report of the Secretary-General, UN General Assembly, 2 September, 2003. UNDP *Human Development Report 2003.* www.actionaid.org/ourpriorities/downloads/halfwaythere.pdf

——. 2003. Millennium Development Goals, March, 2003. New York: UN. www.un.org/millenniumgoals

UNCRD (United Nations Centre for Regional Development) 2003. *Sustainability in Grass Roots Initiatives: Focus on Community Based Disaster Management,* Kobe, Japan.

UNCTAD (United Nations Conference on Trade and Development). 2002. *The Least Developed Countries Report 2002, Escaping the Poverty Trap.* New York and Geneva: UNCTAD.

UNDESA (Department of Economic and Social Affairs) Population Division. 2002. *World Urbanization Prospects.*

UNDESA and United Nations Centre for Human Settlements (HABITAT). 2001. *Compendium of Human Settlements Statistics 2001, Sixth Issue.* New York: UN.

UNDP (United Nations Development Programme) 1997. *Governance for Sustainable Human Development.*

——. 2002a. Expert Group Meeting on the Role of Regional Organizations in Strengthening National Capacities for Disaster Reduction, Geneva.

——. 2002b. *Conceptual Shifts in Sound Planning: Towards an Integrated Approach to HIV/AIDS and Poverty.*

——. 2003a. *Disease, HIV/AIDS and Capacity Limitations: A Case of the Public Agriculture Sector in Zambia.*

——. 2003b. Bureau for Crisis Prevention and Recovery (BCPR) Mission Report to Bolivia 2003.

——. 2003c. National Human Development Report, UNDP Colombia, El Conflicto, callejón con salida.

——. 2003d. *Hũman Development Report 2003.* New York: UNDP.

UNDP. 2002. A Climate Risk Management Approach to Disaster

Reduction and Adaptation to Climate Change, UNDP Expert Group Meeting, Havana, Cuba, 19-21 June, 2002.

UNDP. 2003a. Human Development Indicators, www.undp.org/hdr2003

— —. 2003b.Millennium Development Goals, www.undp.org/mdg/countryreports.html

— —. 2003c. Bureau for Crisis Prevention and Recovery, Disaster Reduction and Recovery Unit, www.undp.org/erd/disred/index.htm

UNDRO (United Nations Disaster Relief Coordinator) 1979. Natural Disasters and Vulnerability Analysis in *Report of Expert Group Meeting* (9-12 July, 1979). Geneva: UNDRO. p. 49.

UNEP, CGIAR, NCGIA. 1996. Human Population and Administrative Boundaries Database for Asia, www.grid.unep.ch/data/grid/human.php

UNEP. 2002. Division of Technology, Industry and Economics, Awareness and Preparedness for Emergencies on Local Level (APELL), APELL in Korea, www.uneptie.org/pc/apell/programme/casestudies/casestud.html

UNEP. 2002. GEO: Global Environment Outlook 3. Past, present and future perspectives, UNEP.

UNEP/GRID, 2002. GEO-3 Data portal, http://geodata.grid.unep.ch/

UNHABITAT (United Nations Centre for Human Settlements) *Cities in a Globalizing World 2001.*

UNHABITAT (United Nations Centre for Human Settlements) www.unhabitat.org/habrdd/global.html, www.unchs.org/istanbul+5/14.pdf

United Nations, *Treaty Sense,* Vol. 1760, No. 30619

United Nations, *Treaty Sense,* Vol. 1771, No. 30822.

United Nations, *Treaty Sense,* Vol. 1954, No. 33480

Varley, A. (Ed.) 1994. *Disasters, Development and Environment.* Chichester: Wiley.

Vasta, Krishna. 2002. Microfinance for Disaster Risk Management, background note.

Vermieren, January, 2000. Risk Transfer and Finance Experience in the Caribbean. In *Managing Disaster Risk in Emerging Economies.* Washington, DC: World Bank.

VHP (Volcano Hazards Programme) 2000. Strategy for reducing volcanic risk, U.S. Department of the Interior, U.S. Geological

Survey, Menlo Park, CA. U.S.: http://volcanoes.usgs.gov/About/What/Assess/

Vulnerability is defined as: "The conditions determined by physical, social, economic, and environmental factors or processes, which increase the susceptibility of a community to the impact of hazards". UN/ISDR. Geneva 2004.

WHO (World Health Organization) 1990. *Health for All When a Disaster Strikes.* Vol. 2. Geneva: WHO/EPR.

— —. 2002. Informe sobre la salud en el mundo. Reducir los riesgos y promover una vida sana. Wilches-Chaux, Gustavo. 1993. La Vulnerabilidad Global. In Maskrey, Andrew (Ed.) *Los Desastres no San Naturales.* Bogota, Colombia: La Red.

— —. 1998. Auge, Caida y Levantada de Felipe Pinillo, Mecanico y Soldador o Yo Voy a Correr el Riesgo: Guia de La Red para la Gestion Local de Riesgos. Quito, Ecuador: La Red.

Winchester, P. 1992. *Power, Choice and Vulnerability: A Case Study in Disaster Mismanagement in South India.* London: James and James Science Publishers.

Wisner, B. 1993. Disaster Vulnerability: Scale, Power and Daily Life. *Geojournal* 30 (2): 127-40.

— —. 2000. The Political Economy of Hazards: More Limits to Growth? *Environmental Hazards* 20: 59-61.

— —. 2001. Risk and the Neoliberal State: Why Post-Mitch Lessons Didn't Reduce El Salvador's Earthquake Losses. *Disasters* 25 (3): 251-68.

— —. 2003. Changes in Capitalism and Global Shifts in the Distribution of Hazard and Vulnerability. In Pelling, M. (Ed.) *Natural Disasters and Development in a Globalizing World.* London: Routledge.

— — and Blaikie, P., Cannon, T. and Davis, I. 2003. *At Risk Natural Hazards, People's Vulnerability and Disasters, 2nd Edition.* London: Routledge.

Woolcock, M. 1998. Social Capital and Economic Development: Toward a Theoretical Synthesis and Policy Framework. *Theory and Society* 27 (2): 151-208.

Work towards the consistent implementation of *General Assembly resolution* 57/150.

World Bank. 1999. *Turkey: Marmara Earthquake Assessment.* Turkey Country Office.Washington, DC: World Bank.

— —. 2000. A Review of the Safer Housing Activities in Antigua/

Barbuda, St Kitts/Nevis and St Lucia at www.oas.org/pgdm/document/houserev.doc

——. 2001. *World Development Indicators 2001.*Washington DC: World Bank.

——. 2002. *Poverty and Climate Change: Reducing the Vulnerability of the Poor.* A joint publication with the African Development Bank; Asian Development Bank; Department for International Development, U.K.; Directorate General for Development, European Commission; Federal Ministry for Economic Cooperation and Development, Germany; Ministry of Foreign Affairs, Development Cooperation, the Netherlands; OECD, UNDP and UNEP.Washington, DC: World Bank. www.worldbank.org/povcc

World Bank. 2003a. Urban Development, www.worldbank.org/html/fpd/

——. 2003b. Poverty Net, http://worldbank.int/poverty/wbactivities/erl/index.htm

World Water Day 2003, www.worldwaterday.org/2001/thematic/floods.html www.dartmouth.edu/artsci/geog/floods/index.html.

Zevallos, Othon. 1996. In Fernandez Maria Augusta, *Cities at Risk: Environmental Degradation, Urban Risk and Disaster.* Lima: La Red.

Index